KV-354-6

Talbot Samba Owners Workshop Manual

Peter G Strasman

Models covered
Talbot Samba LE, LS, GL, S, GLS, Cabriolet, Rallye, Roller, Trio and Style with 954 cc, 1124 cc and 1360 cc engines

Covers 4- and 5-speed transmissions

ISBN 1 85010 198 1

© Haynes Publishing Group 1984, 1986

Printed in England *(823–2M1)*

ABCDE
FGHIJ
KLMNO
PQR

THE BOOK

Haynes Publishing Group
Sparkford Nr Yeovil
Somerset BA22 7JJ England

Haynes Publications, Inc
861 Lawrence Drive
Newbury Park
California 91320 USA

British Library Cataloguing in Publication Data
Strasman, Peter G.
Talbot Samba owners workshop manual.–2nd ed.
–(Owners Workshop Manuals/Haynes)
1. Talbot Samba automobile
I. Title   II. Series
629.28'722   TL215.T24
ISBN 1–85010–198–1

Acknowledgements

Thanks are due to the Talbot Motor Company for the provision of technical information and certain illustrations. The Champion Sparking Plug Company supplied the illustrations showing the various spark plug conditions. Sykes-Pickavant provided some of the workshop tools. Thanks are also due to all those people at Sparkford who helped in the production of this manual.

About this manual

Its aim

The aim of this manual is to help you get the best value from your vehicle. It can do so in several ways. It can help you decide what work must be done (even should you choose to get it done by a garage), provide information on routine maintenance and servicing, and give a logical course of action and diagnosis when random faults occur. However, it is hoped that you will use the manual by tackling the work yourself. On simpler jobs it may even be quicker than booking the car into a garage and going there twice, to leave and collect it. Perhaps most important, a lot of money can be saved by avoiding the costs a garage must charge to cover its labour and overheads.

The manual has drawings and descriptions to show the function of the various components so that their layout can be understood. Then the tasks are described and photographed in a step-by-step sequence so that even a novice can do the work.

Its arrangement

The manual is divided into thirteen Chapters, each covering a logical sub-division of the vehicle. The Chapters are each divided into Sections, numbered with single figures, eg 5; and the Sections into paragraphs (or sub-sections), with decimal numbers following on from the Section they are in, eg 5.1, 5.2, 5.3 etc.

It is freely illustrated, especially in those parts where there is a detailed sequence of operations to be carried out. There are two forms of illustration: figures and photographs. The figures are numbered in sequence with decimal numbers, according to their position in the Chapter – eg Fig. 6.4 is the fourth drawing/illustration in Chapter 6. Photographs carry the same number (either individually or in related groups) as the Section or sub-section to which they relate.

There is an alphabetical index at the back of the manual as well as a contents list at the front. Each Chapter is also preceded by its own individual contents list.

References to the 'left' or 'right' of the vehicle are in the sense of a person in the driver's seat facing forwards.

Unless otherwise stated, nuts and bolts are removed by turning anti-clockwise, and tightened by turning clockwise.

Vehicle manufacturers continually make changes to specifications and recommendations, and these, when notified, are incorporated into our manuals at the earliest opportunity.

Whilst every care is taken to ensure that the information in this manual is correct, no liability can be accepted by the authors or publishers for loss, damage or injury caused by any errors in, or omissions from, the information given.

Introduction to the Talbot Samba

The Samba was introduced into Great Britain in February 1982.

The basic body style is of three-door Hatchback type, but in early 1983 a Cabriolet (convertible) became available and various special editions have been launched.

The Samba bears a strong similarity to the Peugeot 104, upon which it is based, and has inherited some characteristics which make life for the home mechanic difficult especially in respect of engine operations. However, servicing and maintenance operations may be carried out quite easily with good accessibility.

Any engine dismantling work during major overhauls can be combined into one session with the engine removed from the car.

The car is generally well built, finished and economical. The wide range of models and options available should meet the needs of most purchasers looking for a practical car in this section of the market.

Contents

Talbot Samba LS

Talbot Samba Cabriolet

General dimensions, weights and capacities

Dimensions
Overall length	3505 mm (138 in)
Overall width	1592 mm (60.2 in)
Overall height	1361 mm (53.6 in)
Ground clearance	119 mm (4.7 in)

Weights
954 and 1124 cc models	740 kg (1632 lb)
1360 cc models	
Except S and Cabriolet	790 kg (1742 lb)
S	800 kg (1764 lb)
Cabriolet	850 kg (1874 lb)
Maximum trailer load:	
With brakes	
954 and 1124 cc models	750 kg (1654 lb)
1360 cc models	800 kg (1764 lb)
Without brakes	
954 and 1124 cc models	370 kg (816 lb)
1360 cc models	390 kg (860 lb)
Roof rack load	75 kg (165 lb)

Capacities
Engine transmission:	
954 cc	4.0 litre (7.0 pint)
1124, 1360 cc	
Four-speed	4.5 litre (7.9 pint)
Five-speed	5.0 litre (8.8 pint)
Cooling system	5.6 litre (10.56 pint)
Fuel tank	40.0 litre (8.8 gal)

Buying spare parts
and vehicle identification numbers

Buying spare parts

Spare parts are available from many sources, for example: Peugeot Talbot garages, other garages and accessory shops, and motor factors. Out advice regarding spare part sources is as follows:

Officially appointed Peugeot Talbot garage – This is the best source of parts which are peculiar to your car and are otherwise not generally available (eg complete cylinder heads, internal gearbox components, badges, interior trim etc). It is also the only place at which you should buy parts if your car is still under warranty – non-Peugeot Talbot components may invalidate the warranty. To be sure of obtaining the correct parts it will always be necessary to give the storeman your car's engine and chassis number, and if possible, to take the old part along for positive identification. Remember that many parts are available on a factory exchange scheme – any parts returned should always be clean. It obviously makes good sense to go straight to the specialists on your car for this type of part for they are best equipped to supply you.

Other garages and accessory shops – These are often very good places to buy material and components needed for the maintenance of your car (eg oil filters, spark plugs, bulbs, fanbelts, oils and grease, touch-up paint, filler paste etc). They also sell general accessories, usually have convenient opening hours, charge lower prices and can often be found not far from home.

Motor factors – Good factors will stock all of the more important components which wear out relatively quickly (eg clutch components, pistons, valves, exhaust systems, brake cylinders/pipes/hoses/shoes and pads etc). Motor factors will often provide new or reconditioned components on a part exchange basis – this can save a considerable amount of money.

Vehicle identification numbers

Modifications are a continuing and unpublicised process in vehicle manufacture, quite apart from major model changes. Spare parts manuals and lists are compiled upon a numerical basis, the individual vehicle numbers being essential for correct identification of the component required.

Although many individual parts, and in some cases, sub-assemblies, fit a number of different models it is dangerous to assume that, just because they look the same, they are the same. Differences are not always easy to detect except by serial, part or identity numbers. Make sure, therefore, that the appropriate numerical details for the model or sub-assembly are known and quoted when a spare part is ordered.

Vehicle identification plate – This is located adjacent to the front suspension strut top mounting within the engine compartment.

Body serial number – This is stamped onto the inner wing valance (photo).

Engine number – This is riveted on the engine block at the flywheel housing flange joint. Always quote this number in connection with transmission components as well.

Paint code – This is shown in the form of a sticker located just forward of the right-hand suspension strut turret.

Vehicle identification number

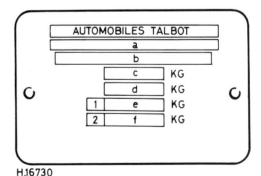

H.16730

Vehicle identification plate

a   Type approval number
b   Identification number
c   Gross vehicle weight
d   Gross train weight
e   Maximum front axle loading
f   Maximum rear axle loading

Tools and working facilities

Introduction

A selection of good tools is a fundamental requirement for anyone contemplating the maintenance and repair of a motor vehicle. For the owner who does not possess any, their purchase will prove a considerable expense, offsetting some of the savings made by doing-it-yourself. However, provided that the tools purchased are of good quality, they will last for many years and prove an extremely worthwhile investment.

To help the average owner to decide which tools are needed to carry out the various tasks detailed in this manual, we have compiled three lists of tools under the following headings: *Maintenance and minor repair, Repair and overhaul,* and *Special.* The newcomer to practical mechanics should start off with the *Maintenance and minor repair* tool kit and confine himself to the simpler jobs around the vehicle. Then, as his confidence and experience grow, he can undertake more difficult tasks, buying extra tools as, and when, they are needed. In this way, a *Maintenance and minor repair* tool kit can be built-up into a *Repair and overhaul* tool kit over a considerable period of time without any major cash outlays. The experienced do-it-yourselfer will have a tool kit good enough for most repair and overhaul procedures and will add tools from the *Special* category when he feels the expense is justified by the amount of use to which these tools will be put.

It is obviously not possible to cover the subject of tools fully here. For those who wish to learn more about tools and their use there is a book entitled *How to Choose and Use Car Tools* available from the publishers of this manual.

Maintenance and minor repair tool kit

The tools given in this list should be considered as a minimum requirement if routine maintenance, servicing and minor repair operations are to be undertaken. We recommend the purchase of combination spanners (ring one end, open-ended the other); although more expensive than open-ended ones, they do give the advantages of both types of spanner.

Combination spanners - 10, 11, 12, 13, 14 & 17 mm
Adjustable spanner - 9 inch
Engine sump/drain plug key
Spark plug spanner (with rubber insert)
Set of feeler gauges
Brake bleed nipple spanner
Screwdriver - 4 in long x $\frac{1}{4}$ in dia (flat blade)
Screwdriver - 4 in long x $\frac{1}{4}$ in dia (cross blade)
Combination pliers - 6 inch
Hacksaw (junior)
Tyre pump
Tyre pressure gauge
Oil can
Fine emery cloth (1 sheet)
Wire brush (small)
Funnel (medium size)

Repair and overhaul tool kit

These tools are virtually essential for anyone undertaking any major repairs to a motor vehicle, and are additional to those given in the *Maintenance and minor repair* list. Included in this list is a comprehensive set of sockets. Although these are expensive they will be found invaluable as they are so versatile - particularly if various drives are included in the set. We recommend the $\frac{1}{2}$ in square-drive type, as this can be used with most proprietary torque wrenches. If you cannot afford a socket set, even bought piecemeal, then inexpensive tubular box spanners are a useful alternative.

The tools in this list will occasionally need to be supplemented by tools from the *Special* list.

Sockets (or box spanners) to cover range in previous list
Reversible ratchet drive (for use with sockets)
Extension piece, 10 inch (for use with sockets)
Universal joint (for use with sockets)
Torque wrench (for use with sockets)
'Mole' wrench - 8 inch
Ball pein hammer
Soft-faced hammer, plastic or rubber
Screwdriver - 6 in long x $\frac{5}{16}$ in dia (flat blade)
Screwdriver - 2 in long x $\frac{5}{16}$ in square (flat blade)
Screwdriver - 1$\frac{1}{2}$ in long x $\frac{1}{4}$ in dia (cross blade)
Screwdriver - 3 in long x $\frac{1}{8}$ in dia (electricians)
Pliers - electricians side cutters
Pliers - needle nosed
Pliers - circlip (internal and external)
Cold chisel - $\frac{1}{2}$ inch
Scriber
Scraper
Centre punch
Pin punch
Hacksaw
Valve grinding tool
Steel rule/straight-edge
Allen keys
Selection of files
Wire brush (large)
Axle-stands
Jack (strong scissor or hydraulic type)

Special tools

The tools in this list are those which are not used regularly, are expensive to buy, or which need to be used in accordance with their manufacturers' instructions. Unless relatively difficult mechanical jobs are undertaken frequently, it will not be economic to buy many of these tools. Where this is the case, you could consider clubbing together with friends (or joining a motorists' club) to make a joint purchase, or borrowing the tools against a deposit from a local garage or tool hire specialist.

The following list contains only those tools and instruments freely available to the public, and not those special tools produced by the vehicle manufacturer specifically for its dealer network. You will find occasional references to these manufacturers' special tools in the text of this manual. Generally, an alternative method of doing the job without the vehicle manufacturers' special tool is given. However, sometimes, there is no alternative to using them. Where this is the case and the relevant tool cannot be bought or borrowed, you will have to entrust the work to a franchised garage.

Valve spring compressor
Piston ring compressor
Balljoint separator
Universal hub/bearing puller
Impact screwdriver
Micrometer and/or vernier gauge
Dial gauge
Stroboscopic timing light
Dwell angle meter/tachometer
Universal electrical multi-meter
Cylinder compression gauge
Trolley jack
Light with extension lead

Buying tools

For practically all tools, a tool factor is the best source since he will have a very comprehensive range compared with the average garage or accessory shop. Having said that, accessory shops often offer excellent quality tools at discount prices, so it pays to shop around.

Remember, you don't have to buy the most expensive items on the shelf, but it is always advisable to steer clear of the very cheap tools. There are plenty of good tools around at reasonable prices, so ask the proprietor or manager of the shop for advice before making a purchase.

Care and maintenance of tools

Having purchased a reasonable tool kit, it is necessary to keep the tools in a clean serviceable condition. After use, always wipe off any dirt, grease and metal particles using a clean, dry cloth, before putting the tools away. Never leave them lying around after they have been used. A simple tool rack on the garage or workshop wall, for items such as screwdrivers and pliers is a good idea. Store all normal wrenches and sockets in a metal box. Any measuring instruments, gauges, meters, etc, must be carefully stored where they cannot be damaged or become rusty.

Take a little care when tools are used. Hammer heads inevitably become marked and screwdrivers lose the keen edge on their blades from time to time. A little timely attention with emery cloth or a file will soon restore items like this to a good serviceable finish.

Working facilities

Not to be forgotten when discussing tools, is the workshop itself. If anything more than routine maintenance is to be carried out, some form of suitable working area becomes essential.

It is appreciated that many an owner mechanic is forced by circumstances to remove an engine or similar item, without the benefit of a garage or workshop. Having done this, any repairs should always be done under the cover of a roof.

Wherever possible, any dismantling should be done on a clean, flat workbench or table at a suitable working height.

Any workbench needs a vice: one with a jaw opening of 4 in (100 mm) is suitable for most jobs. As mentioned previously, some clean dry storage space is also required for tools, as well as for lubricants, cleaning fluids, touch-up paints and so on, which become necessary.

Another item which may be required, and which has a much more general usage, is an electric drill with a chuck capacity of at least $\frac{5}{16}$ in (8 mm). This, together with a good range of twist drills, is virtually essential for fitting accessories such as mirrors and reversing lights.

Last, but not least, always keep a supply of old newspapers and clean, lint-free rags available, and try to keep any working area as clean as possible.

Spanner jaw gap comparison table

Jaw gap (in)	Spanner size
0.250	$\frac{1}{4}$ in AF
0.276	7 mm
0.313	$\frac{5}{16}$ in AF
0.315	8 mm
0.344	$\frac{11}{32}$ in AF; $\frac{1}{8}$ in Whitworth
0.354	9 mm
0.375	$\frac{3}{8}$ in AF
0.394	10 mm
0.433	11 mm
0.438	$\frac{7}{16}$ in AF
0.445	$\frac{3}{16}$ in Whitworth; $\frac{1}{4}$ in BSF
0.472	12 mm
0.500	$\frac{1}{2}$ in AF
0.512	13 mm
0.525	$\frac{1}{4}$ in Whitworth; $\frac{5}{16}$ in BSF
0.551	14 mm
0.563	$\frac{9}{16}$ in AF
0.591	15 mm
0.600	$\frac{5}{16}$ in Whitworth; $\frac{3}{8}$ in BSF
0.625	$\frac{5}{8}$ in AF
0.630	16 mm
0.669	17 mm
0.686	$\frac{11}{16}$ in AF
0.709	18 mm
0.710	$\frac{3}{8}$ in Whitworth; $\frac{7}{16}$ in BSF
0.748	19 mm
0.750	$\frac{3}{4}$ in AF
0.813	$\frac{13}{16}$ in AF
0.820	$\frac{7}{16}$ in Whitworth; $\frac{1}{2}$ in BSF
0.866	22 mm
0.875	$\frac{7}{8}$ in AF
0.920	$\frac{1}{2}$ in Whitworth; $\frac{9}{16}$ in BSF
0.938	$\frac{15}{16}$ in AF
0.945	24 mm
1.000	1 in AF
1.010	$\frac{9}{16}$ in Whitworth; $\frac{5}{8}$ in BSF
1.024	26 mm
1.063	$1\frac{1}{16}$ in AF; 27 mm
1.100	$\frac{5}{8}$ in Whitworth; $\frac{11}{16}$ in BSF
1.125	$1\frac{1}{8}$ in AF
1.181	30 mm
1.200	$\frac{11}{16}$ in Whitworth; $\frac{3}{4}$ in BSF
1.250	$1\frac{1}{4}$ in AF
1.260	32 mm
1.300	$\frac{3}{4}$ in Whitworth; $\frac{7}{8}$ in BSF
1.313	$1\frac{5}{16}$ in AF
1.390	$\frac{13}{16}$ in Whitworth; $\frac{15}{16}$ in BSF
1.417	36 mm
1.438	$1\frac{7}{16}$ in AF
1.480	$\frac{7}{8}$ in Whitworth; 1 in BSF
1.500	$1\frac{1}{2}$ in AF
1.575	40 mm; $\frac{15}{16}$ in Whitworth
1.614	41 mm
1.625	$1\frac{5}{8}$ in AF
1.670	1 in Whitworth; $1\frac{1}{8}$ in BSF
1.688	$1\frac{11}{16}$ in AF
1.811	46 mm
1.813	$1\frac{13}{16}$ in AF
1.860	$1\frac{1}{8}$ in Whitworth; $1\frac{1}{4}$ in BSF
1.875	$1\frac{7}{8}$ in AF
1.969	50 mm
2.000	2 in AF
2.050	$1\frac{1}{4}$ in Whitworth; $1\frac{3}{8}$ in BSF
2.165	55 mm
2.362	60 mm

General repair procedures

Whenever servicing, repair or overhaul work is carried out on the car or its components, it is necessary to observe the following procedures and instructions. This will assist in carrying out the operation efficiently and to a professional standard of workmanship.

Joint mating faces and gaskets

Where a gasket is used between the mating faces of two components, ensure that it is renewed on reassembly, and fit it dry unless otherwise stated in the repair procedure. Make sure that the mating faces are clean and dry with all traces of old gasket removed. When cleaning a joint face, use a tool which is not likely to score or damage the face, and remove any burrs or nicks with an oilstone or fine file.

Make sure that tapped holes are cleaned with a pipe cleaner, and keep them free of jointing compound if this is being used unless specifically instructed otherwise.

Ensure that all orifices, channels or pipes are clear and blow through them, preferably using compressed air.

Oil seals

Whenever an oil seal is removed from its working location, either individually or as part of an assembly, it should be renewed.

The very fine sealing lip of the seal is easily damaged and will not seal if the surface it contacts is not completely clean and free from scratches, nicks or grooves. If the original sealing surface of the component cannot be restored, the component should be renewed.

Protect the lips of the seal from any surface which may damage them in the course of fitting. Use tape or a conical sleeve where possible. Lubricate the seal lips with oil before fitting and, on dual lipped seals, fill the space between the lips with grease.

Unless otherwise stated, oil seals must be fitted with their sealing lips toward the lubricant to be sealed.

Use a tubular drift or block of wood of the appropriate size to install the seal and, if the seal housing is shouldered, drive the seal down to the shoulder. If the seal housing is unshouldered, the seal should be fitted with its face flush with the housing top face.

Screw threads and fastenings

Always ensure that a blind tapped hole is completely free from oil, grease, water or other fluid before installing the bolt or stud. Failure to do this could cause the housing to crack due to the hydraulic action of the bolt or stud as it is screwed in.

When tightening a castellated nut to accept a split pin, tighten the nut to the specified torque, where applicable, and then tighten further to the next split pin hole. Never slacken the nut to align a split pin hole unless stated in the repair procedure.

When checking or retightening a nut or bolt to a specified torque setting, slacken the nut or bolt by a quarter of a turn, and then retighten to the specified setting.

Locknuts, locktabs and washers

Any fastening which will rotate against a component or housing in the course of tightening should always have a washer between it and the relevant component or housing.

Spring or split washers should always be renewed when they are used to lock a critical component such as a big-end bearing retaining nut or bolt.

Locktabs which are folded over to retain a nut or bolt should always be renewed.

Self-locking nuts can be reused in non-critical areas, providing resistance can be felt when the locking portion passes over the bolt or stud thread.

Split pins must always be replaced with new ones of the correct size for the hole.

Special tools

Some repair procedures in this manual entail the use of special tools such as a press, two or three-legged pullers, spring compressors etc. Wherever possible, suitable readily available alternatives to the manufacturer's special tools are described, and are shown in use. In some instances, where no alternative is possible, it has been necessary to resort to the use of a manufacturer's tool and this has been done for reasons of safety as well as the efficient completion of the repair operation. Unless you are highly skilled and have a thorough understanding of the procedure described, never attempt to bypass the use of any special tool when the procedure described specifies its use. Not only is there a very great risk of personal injury, but expensive damage could be caused to the components involved.

Jacking and towing

Jacking

The jack supplied with the car is designed for use only when changing a wheel. The jack engages in one of the two holes provided below each sill on either side of the car (photos).

If you are going to carry out work under the car it is preferable to position the car over an inspection pit. If this is not available use a workshop trolley jack or substantial screw or bottle type hydraulic jack.

Always supplement a jack with axle stands

The sill jacking points or their adjacent re-inforced areas should be used as jacking points for raising the car. A beam may be placed under the front subframe and the front end jacked up under that. The side members of the front subframe should be used as axle stand support points. The rear side members may be used in a similar way.

Jacking point

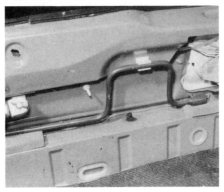
Jack handle/wheelbrace stowed

Jack stowed

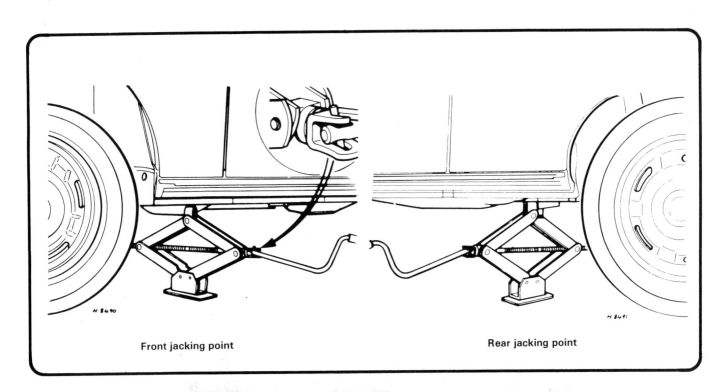
Front jacking point   Rear jacking point

Towing and being towed

Front and rear anchorage points are provided for securing the car during transportation on a car transporter, boat, train and so on. These points can also be used for towing the car or for towing another in an emergency. For permanent towing requirements a tow-bar is necessary, properly attached to the vehicle.

If your car is being towed with the front wheels on the ground *caution is necessary* due to the transmission lubrication problem. The gearbox and final drive are pressure lubricated by the engine oil system and *if the engine is not running, no oil will be fed to the transmission.* Arrange for a front suspended tow, if possible, to prevent damage to the final drive. In exceptional circumstances the car may be towed with the front wheels on the ground provided that a speed of 30 mph (50 kph) and a distance of 18 miles (30 km) are not exceeded.

Towing hook (front)

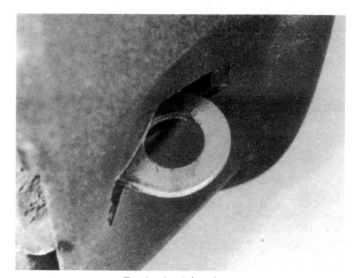

Towing hook (rear)

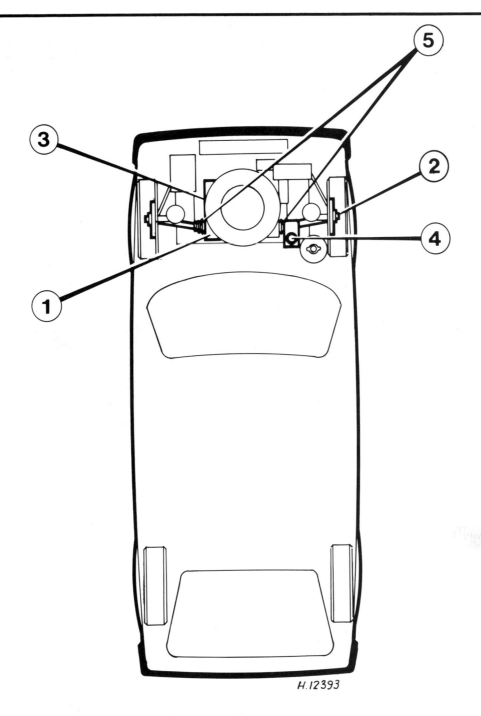

H.12393

Recommended lubricants and fluids

Component or system	Lubricant type or specificaion
Engine/transmission (1)	Multigrade engine oil/SAE 15W/40
Wheel bearings (2)	Multi-purpose grease
Steering rack (3)	Molybdenum disulphide grease
Brake hydraulic fluid (4)	To SAE J 1703 or DOT 3
Driveshaft joints (5)	Special lubricant supplied in repair kit

With regard to lubrication the above are general recommendations. Lubrication requirements vary from territory to territory and also with vehicle usage – consult the operator's handbook supplied with your car.

Safety first!

Professional motor mechanics are trained in safe working procedures. However enthusiastic you may be about getting on with the job in hand, do take the time to ensure that your safety is not put at risk. A moment's lack of attention can result in an accident, as can failure to observe certain elementary precautions.

There will always be new ways of having accidents, and the following points do not pretend to be a comprehensive list of all dangers; they are intended rather to make you aware of the risks and to encourage a safety-conscious approach to all work you carry out on your vehicle.

Essential DOs and DON'Ts

DON'T rely on a single jack when working underneath the vehicle. Always use reliable additional means of support, such as axle stands, securely placed under a part of the vehicle that you know will not give way.

DON'T attempt to loosen or tighten high-torque nuts (e.g. wheel hub nuts) while the vehicle is on a jack; it may be pulled off.

DON'T start the engine without first ascertaining that the transmission is in neutral (or 'Park' where applicable) and the parking brake applied.

DON'T suddenly remove the filler cap from a hot cooling system – cover it with a cloth and release the pressure gradually first, or you may get scalded by escaping coolant.

DON'T attempt to drain oil until you are sure it has cooled sufficiently to avoid scalding you.

DON'T grasp any part of the engine, exhaust or catalytic converter without first ascertaining that it is sufficiently cool to avoid burning you.

DON'T allow brake fluid or antifreeze to contact vehicle paintwork.

DON'T syphon toxic liquids such as fuel, brake fluid or antifreeze by mouth, or allow them to remain on your skin.

DON'T inhale dust – it may be injurious to health (see *Asbestos* below).

DON'T allow any spilt oil or grease to remain on the floor – wipe it up straight away, before someone slips on it.

DON'T use ill-fitting spanners or other tools which may slip and cause injury.

DON'T attempt to lift a heavy component which may be beyond your capability – get assistance.

DON'T rush to finish a job, or take unverified short cuts.

DON'T allow children or animals in or around an unattended vehicle.

DO wear eye protection when using power tools such as drill, sander, bench grinder etc, and when working under the vehicle.

DO use a barrier cream on your hands prior to undertaking dirty jobs – it will protect your skin from infection as well as making the dirt easier to remove afterwards; but make sure your hands aren't left slippery.

DO keep loose clothing (cuffs, tie etc) and long hair well out of the way of moving mechanical parts.

DO remove rings, wristwatch etc, before working on the vehicle – especially the electrical system.

DO ensure that any lifting tackle used has a safe working load rating adequate for the job.

DO keep your work area tidy – it is only too easy to fall over articles left lying around.

DO get someone to check periodically that all is well, when working alone on the vehicle.

DO carry out work in a logical sequence and check that everything is correctly assembled and tightened afterwards.

DO remember that your vehicle's safety affects that of yourself and others. If in doubt on any point, get specialist advice.

IF, in spite of following these precautions, you are unfortunate enough to injure yourself, seek medical attention as soon as possible.

Asbestos

Certain friction, insulating, sealing, and other products – such as brake linings, brake bands, clutch linings, torque converters, gaskets, etc – contain asbestos. *Extreme care must be taken to avoid inhalation of dust from such products since it is hazardous to health.* If in doubt, assume that they *do* contain asbestos.

Fire

Remember at all times that petrol (gasoline) is highly flammable. Never smoke, or have any kind of naked flame around, when working on the vehicle. But the risk does not end there – a spark caused by an electrical short-circuit, by two metal surfaces contacting each other, by careless use of tools, or even by static electricity built up in your body under certain conditions, can ignite petrol vapour, which in a confined space is highly explosive.

Always disconnect the battery earth (ground) terminal before working on any part of the fuel or electrical system, and never risk spilling fuel on to a hot engine or exhaust.

It is recommended that a fire extinguisher of a type suitable for fuel and electrical fires is kept handy in the garage or workplace at all times. Never try to extinguish a fuel or electrical fire with water.

Fumes

Certain fumes are highly toxic and can quickly cause unconsciousness and even death if inhaled to any extent. Petrol (gasoline) vapour comes into this category, as do the vapours from certain solvents such as trichloroethylene. Any draining or pouring of such volatile fluids should be done in a well ventilated area.

When using cleaning fluids and solvents, read the instructions carefully. Never use materials from unmarked containers – they may give off poisonous vapours.

Never run the engine of a motor vehicle in an enclosed space such as a garage. Exhaust fumes contain carbon monoxide which is extremely poisonous; if you need to run the engine, always do so in the open air or at least have the rear of the vehicle outside the workplace.

If you are fortunate enough to have the use of an inspection pit, never drain or pour petrol, and never run the engine, while the vehicle is standing over it; the fumes, being heavier than air, will concentrate in the pit with possibly lethal results.

The battery

Never cause a spark, or allow a naked light, near the vehicle's battery. It will normally be giving off a certain amount of hydrogen gas, which is highly explosive.

Always disconnect the battery earth (ground) terminal before working on the fuel or electrical systems.

If possible, loosen the filler plugs or cover when charging the battery from an external source. Do not charge at an excessive rate or the battery may burst.

Take care when topping up and when carrying the battery. The acid electrolyte, even when diluted, is very corrosive and should not be allowed to contact the eyes or skin.

If you ever need to prepare electrolyte yourself, always add the acid slowly to the water, and never the other way round. Protect against splashes by wearing rubber gloves and goggles.

When jump starting a car using a booster battery, for negative earth (ground) vehicles, connect the jump leads in the following sequence: First connect one jump lead between the positive (+) terminals of the two batteries. Then connect the other jump lead first to the negative (–) terminal of the booster battery, and then to a good earthing (ground) point on the vehicle to be started, at least 18 in (45 cm) from the battery if possible. Ensure that hands and jump leads are clear of any moving parts, and that the two vehicles do not touch. Disconnect the leads in the reverse order.

Mains electricity

When using an electric power tool, inspection light etc, which works from the mains, always ensure that the appliance is correctly connected to its plug and that, where necessary, it is properly earthed (grounded). Do not use such appliances in damp conditions and, again, beware of creating a spark or applying excessive heat in the vicinity of fuel or fuel vapour.

Ignition HT voltage

A severe electric shock can result from touching certain parts of the ignition system, such as the HT leads, when the engine is running or being cranked, particularly if components are damp or the insulation is defective. Where an electronic ignition system is fitted, the HT voltage is much higher and could prove fatal.

Routine maintenance

For modifications, and information applicable to later models, see Supplement at end of manual

Maintenance is essential for ensuring safety and is desirable for the purpose of getting the best in terms of performance and economy from the car. Over the years the need for periodic lubrication – oiling and greasing – has been drastically reduced if not totally eliminated. This has unfortunately tended to lead some owners to think that because no such action is required the components either no longer exist or will last for ever. This is a serious delusion. If anything, there are now more places, particularly in the steering and suspension, where joints and pivots are fitted. Although you do not grease them any more you still have to look at them – and look at them just as often as you may previously have had to grease them. It follows therefore that the largest initial element of maintenance is visual examination. This may lead to repairs or renewal (photos).

Engine compartment viewed from above with carburettor air duct removed for clarity

1	Spark plug tool	6	Spare wheel carrier	11	Coolant pump	16	Radiator fan motor
2	Identification plate	7	Oil filler/breather cap	12	Air cleaner	17	Diagnostic socket*
3	Suspension strut turret	8	Coolant expansion tank	13	Oil filter	18	Battery
4	Brake master cylinder	9	Horn	14	Radiator	19	Washer pump
5	Air cleaner heated air hose	10	Carburettor	15	Cooling system bleed screw	20	Washer fluid reservoir

*See Chapter 4, Section 1.

16

Front end viewed from underneath

1 Anti-roll bar
2 Track control arm
3 Tie-rod
4 Sump cover
5 Drain plug
6 Towing hook
7 Exhaust pipe
8 Scuttle drain hose
9 Gearchange stabiliser rod
10 Gearchange rod

Rear end viewed from underneath

1 Suspension arm   2 Handbrake cable   3 Exhaust silencer   4 Fuel tank   5 Brake pressure regulator

At weekly intervals

Check brake hydraulic fluid level (photo)
Check coolant level (photo)
Check washer fluid level
Check engine oil level (photo)
Check battery electrolyte level (photo)
Check the tyre pressures (photo)
Check the operation of all lights, wipers, washers and the horn

At the first 1600 km (1000 miles) – new cars

Renew the engine oil
Check the drivebelt tension
Check the tightness of the manifold bolts
Check the idle speed and mixture adjustment
Check all hoses and pipes for leakage
Check driveshaft gaiters for oil leakage

Every 8000 km (5000 miles)

Renew engine oil and filter
Clean and re-gap spark plugs
Check driveshaft gaiters for splits
Check tyres for tread wear or carcass damage
Check disc pads for wear

Every 16 000 km (10 000 miles)

Move position of roadwheels to even out wear
Check tightness of roadwheel nuts

Check and adjust drivebelt tension
Check and adjust clutch
Renew contact points (mechanical breaker)
Check dwell angle
Check ignition timing
Renew spark plugs
Lubricate hinges, locks and controls
Check suspension and steering for wear in balljoints and bushes
Check suspension struts for fluid leakage
Check front wheel alignment

Every 32 000 km (20 000 miles)

Check rear brake shoe linings for wear
Renew air filter element
Clean fuel pump

Every 48 000 km (30 000 miles)

Check and adjust the rear hub bearings

Annually

Inspect the protective coating under the wings and underside of the body. Clean and make good or re-coat as necessary.

Every two years

Renew coolant
Renew brake hydraulic fluid by bleeding

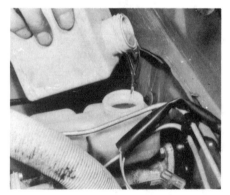
Topping up brake master cylinder

Topping up expansion tank

Topping up engine oil

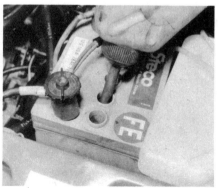
Topping up battery

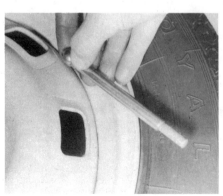
Checking tyre pressure

Fault diagnosis

Introduction

The vehicle owner who does his or her own maintenance according to the recommended schedules should not have to use this section of the manual very often. Modern component reliability is such that, provided those items subject to wear or deterioration are inspected or renewed at the specified intervals, sudden failure is comparatively rare. Faults do not usually just happen as a result of sudden failure, but develop over a period of time. Major mechanical failures in particular are usually preceded by characteristic symptoms over hundreds or even thousands of miles. Those components which do occasionally fail without warning are often small and easily carried in the vehicle.

With any fault finding, the first step is to decide where to begin investigations. Sometimes this is obvious, but on other occasions a little detective work will be necessary. The owner who makes half a dozen haphazard adjustments or replacements may be successful in curing a fault (or its symptoms), but he will be none the wiser if the fault recurs and he may well have spent more time and money than was necessary. A calm and logical approach will be found to be more satisfactory in the long run. Always take into account any warning signs or abnormalities that may have been noticed in the period preceding the fault – power loss, high or low gauge readings, unusual noises or smells, etc – and remember that failure of components such as fuses or spark plugs may only be pointers to some underlying fault.

The pages which follow here are intended to help in cases of failure to start or breakdown on the road. There is also a Fault Diagnosis Section at the end of each Chapter which should be consulted if the preliminary checks prove unfruitful. Whatever the fault, certain basic principles apply. These are as follows:

Verify the fault. This is simply a matter of being sure that you know what the symptoms are before starting work. This is particularly important if you are investigating a fault for someone else who may not have described it very accurately.

Don't overlook the obvious. For example, if the vehicle won't start, is there petrol in the tank? (Don't take anyone else's word on this particular point, and don't trust the fuel gauge either!) If an electrical fault is indicated, look for loose or broken wires before digging out the test gear.

Cure the disease, not the symptom. Substituting a flat battery with a fully charged one will get you off the hard shoulder, but if the underlying cause is not attended to, the new battery will go the same way. Similarly, changing oil-fouled spark plugs for a new set will get you moving again, but remember that the reason for the fouling (if it wasn't simply an incorrect grade of plug) will have to be established and corrected.

Don't take anything for granted. Particularly, don't forget that a 'new' component may itself be defective (especially if it's been rattling round in the boot for months), and don't leave components out of a fault diagnosis sequence just because they are new or recently fitted. When you do finally diagnose a difficult fault, you'll probably realise that all the evidence was there from the start.

Electrical faults

Electrical faults can be more puzzling than straightforward mechanical failures, but they are no less susceptible to logical analysis if the basic principles of operation are understood. Vehicle electrical wiring exists in extremely unfavourable conditions – heat, vibration and chemical attack – and the first things to look for are loose or corroded connections and broken or chafed wires, especially where the wires pass through holes in the bodywork or are subject to vibration.

All metal-bodied vehicles in current production have one pole of the battery 'earthed', ie connected to the vehicle bodywork, and in nearly all modern vehicles it is the negative (–) terminal. The various electrical components – motors, bulb holders etc – are also connected to earth, either by means of a lead or directly by their mountings. Electric current flows through the component and then back to the battery via the bodywork. If the component mounting is loose or corroded, or if a good path back to the battery is not available, the circuit will be incomplete and malfunction will result. The engine and/or gearbox are also earthed by means of flexible metal straps to the body or subframe; if these straps are loose or missing, starter motor, generator and ignition trouble may result.

Assuming the earth return to be satisfactory, electrical faults will be due either to component malfunction or to defects in the current supply. Individual components are dealt with in Chapter 10. If supply wires are broken or cracked internally this results in an open-circuit, and the easiest way to check for this is to bypass the suspect wire temporarily with a length of wire having a crocodile clip or suitable connector at each end. Alternatively, a 12V test lamp can be used to verify the presence of supply voltage at various points along the wire and the break can be thus isolated.

If a bare portion of a live wire touches the bodywork or other earthed metal part, the electricity will take the low-resistance path thus formed back to the battery: this is known as a short-circuit. Hopefully a short-circuit will blow a fuse, but otherwise it may cause burning of the insulation (and possibly further short-circuits) or even a fire. This is why it is inadvisable to bypass persistently blowing fuses with silver foil or wire.

Spares and tool kit

Most vehicles are supplied only with sufficient tools for wheel changing; the *Maintenance and minor repair* tool kit detailed in *Tools and working facilities*, with the addition of a hammer, is probably sufficient for those repairs that most motorists would consider attempting at the roadside. In addition a few items which can be fitted without too much trouble in the event of a breakdown should be carried. Experience and available space will modify the list below, but the following may save having to call on professional assistance:

Spark plugs, clean and correctly gapped
HT lead and plug cap – long enough to reach the plug furthest from the distributor
Distributor rotor, condenser and contact breaker points
Drivebelt(s) – emergency type may suffice
Spare fuses
Set of principal light bulbs
Tin of radiator sealer and hose bandage

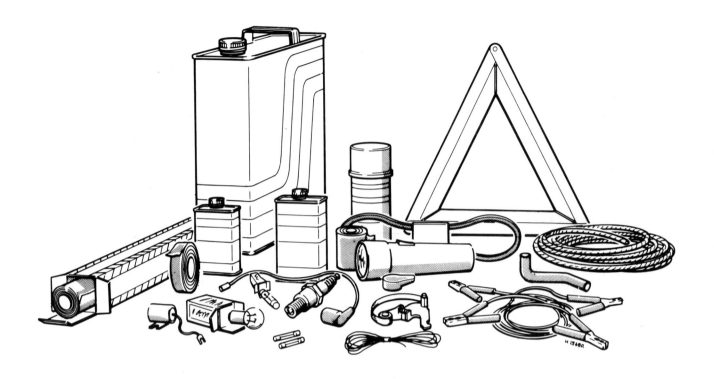

Carrying a few spares can save you a long walk!

Exhaust bandage
Roll of insulating tape
Length of soft iron wire
Length of electrical flex
Torch or inspection lamp (can double as test lamp)
Battery jump leads
Tow-rope
Ignition waterproofing aerosol
Litre of engine oil
Sealed can of hydraulic fluid
Emergency windscreen
Worm drive clips
Tube of filler paste

If spare fuel is carried, a can designed for the purpose should be used to minimise risks of leakage and collision damage. A first aid kit and a warning triangle, whilst not at present compulsory in the UK, are obviously sensible items to carry in addition to the above.

When touring abroad it may be advisable to carry additional spares which, even if you cannot fit them yourself, could save having to wait while parts are obtained. The items below may be worth considering:

Clutch and throttle cables
Cylinder head gasket
Alternator brushes
Fuel pump repair kit
Tyre valve core

One of the motoring organisations will be able to advise on availability of fuel etc in foreign countries.

Engine will not start

Engine fails to turn when starter operated
Flat battery (recharge, use jump leads, or push start)
Battery terminals loose or corroded
Battery earth to body defective
Engine earth strap loose or broken
Starter motor (or solenoid) wiring loose or broken
Ignition/starter switch faulty

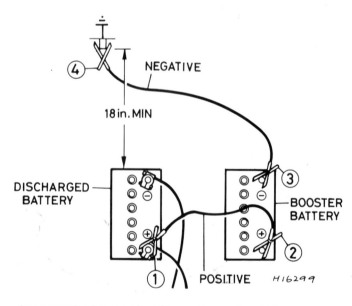

Jump start lead connections for negative earth vehicles – connect leads in order shown

Major mechanical failure (seizure)
Starter or solenoid internal fault (see Chapter 10)

Starter motor turns engine slowly
Partially discharged battery (recharge, use jump leads, or push start)
Battery terminals loose or corroded
Battery earth to body defective
Engine earth strap loose
Starter motor (or solenoid) wiring loose
Starter motor internal fault (see Chapter 10)

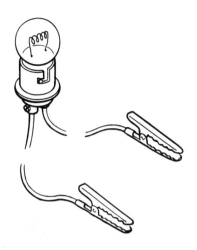

A simple test lamp is useful for tracing electrical faults

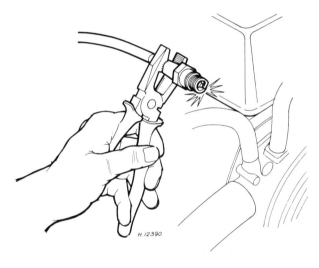

Crank engine and check for spark. Note use of insulated tool to hold plug lead

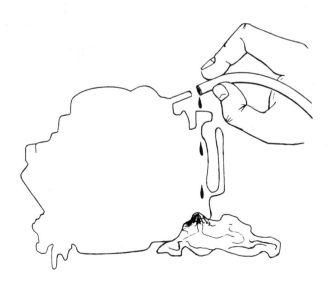

Remove pipe from carburettor and check for fuel delivery

Starter motor spins without turning engine
Flat battery
Starter motor pinion sticking on sleeve
Flywheel gear teeth damaged or worn
Starter motor mounting bolts loose

Engine turns normally but fails to start
Damp or dirty HT leads and distributor cap (crank engine and check for spark)
Dirty or incorrectly gapped distributor points (if applicable)
No fuel in tank (check for delivery at carburettor)
Excessive choke (hot engine) or insufficient choke (cold engine)
Fouled or incorrectly gapped spark plugs (remove, clean and regap)
Other ignition system fault (see Chapter 4)
Other fuel system fault (see Chapter 3)
Poor compression (see Chapter 1)
Major mechanical failure (eg camshaft drive)

Engine fires but will not run
Insufficient choke (cold engine)
Air leaks at carburettor or inlet manifold
Fuel starvation (see Chapter 3)
Ignition fault (see Chapter 4)

Engine cuts out and will not restart

Engine cuts out suddenly – ignition fault
Loose or disconnected LT wires
Wet HT leads or distributor cap (after traversing water splash)
Coil or condenser failure (check for spark)
Other ignition fault (see Chapter 4)

Engine misfires before cutting out – fuel fault
Fuel tank empty
Fuel pump defective or filter blocked (check for delivery)
Fuel tank filler vent blocked (suction will be evident on releasing cap)
Carburettor needle valve sticking
Carburettor jets blocked (fuel contaminated)
Other fuel system fault (see Chapter 3)

Engine cuts out – other causes
Serious overheating
Major mechanical failure (eg camshaft drive)

Engine overheats

Ignition (no-charge) warning light illuminated
Slack or broken drivebelt – retension or renew (Chapter 2)

Ignition warning light not illuminated
Coolant loss due to internal or external leakage (see Chapter 2)
Thermostat defective
Low oil level
Brakes binding
Radiator clogged externally or internally
Electric cooling fan not operating correctly
Engine waterways clogged
Ignition timing incorrect or automatic advance malfunctioning
Mixture too weak

Note: *Do not add cold water to an overheated engine or damage may result*

Low engine oil pressure

Gauge reads low or warning light illuminated with engine running
Oil level low or incorrect grade
Defective gauge or sender unit

Wire to sender unit earthed
Engine overheating
Oil filter clogged or bypass valve defective
Oil pressure relief valve defective
Oil pick-up strainer clogged
Oil pump worn or mountings loose
Worn main or big-end bearings

Note: *Low oil pressure in a high-mileage engine at tickover is not necessarily a cause for concern. Sudden pressure loss at speed is far more significant. In any event, check the gauge or warning light sender before condemning the engine.*

Engine noises

Pre-ignition (pinking) on acceleration
Incorrect grade of fuel
Ignition timing incorrect
Distributor faulty or worn
Worn or maladjusted carburettor
Excessive carbon build-up in engine

Whistling or wheezing noises
Leaking vacuum hose
Leaking carburettor or manifold gasket
Blowing head gasket

Tapping or rattling
Incorrect valve clearances
Worn valve gear
Worn timing chain or belt
Broken piston ring (ticking noise)

Knocking or thumping
Unintentional mechanical contact (eg fan blades)
Worn fanbelt
Peripheral component fault (generator, water pump etc)
Worn big-end bearings (regular heavy knocking, perhaps less under load)
Worn main bearings (rumbling and knocking, perhaps worsening under load)
Piston slap (most noticeable when cold)

Chapter 1 Engine

For modifications, and information applicable to later models, see Supplement at end of manual

Contents

Specifications

Type	Four cylinder in-line overhead camshaft. All alloy with wet cylinder liners. Mounted transversely with transmission and inclined to rear at 72° from vertical.

Identification codes and displacement

108.3 (XV5) 5C1	954 cc (58.2 cu in)
108.C (XV8)	954 cc (58.2 cu in)
109.3 (XW7) 5A1	1124 cc (68.5 cu in)
150.3 (XY6B) 5K2	1360 cc (82.9 cu in)
150.B (XY8) 5K3	1360 cc (82.9 cu in)

Bore

954 cc	70.0 mm
1124 cc	72.0 mm
1360 cc	75.0 mm

Stroke

954 cc	62.0 mm
1124 cc	69.0 mm
1360 cc	77.0 mm

Compression ratio

954 cc	8.8:1. 1983 on, 9.3:1
1124 cc	9.7:1
1360 cc	9.3:1

Maximum power (DIN)

954 cc	44.5 bhp at 6000 rev/min
1124 cc	49.0 bhp at 6000 rev/min
1360 cc	71.0 bhp at 6000 rev/min
1360 cc S model (XY8)	79.0 bhp at 5800 rev/min

Maximum torque (DIN)

954 cc	47 lbf ft at 3000 rev/min
1124 cc	63 lbf ft at 2800 rev/min
1360 cc	79 lbf ft at 3000 rev/min
1360 cc S model (XY8)	81 lbf ft at 2800 rev/min

Firing order ....   1 – 3 – 4 – 2 (No 1 at flywheel end)

Crankshaft

Number of main bearings	5
Journal diameter	49.965 to 49.981 mm
Re-grind undersize	0.30 mm
Crankpin diameter	44.975 to 44.991 mm
Re-grind undersize	0.30 mm
Endfloat	0.07 to 0.27 mm
Thrust washer thicknesses	2.30; 2.40; 2.45; 2.50 mm

Cylinder liners

Type ....   Cast-iron, wet type

Grades:

Piston	**Liner**
A	One file mark
B	Two file marks
C	Three file marks

Paper type gasket seals:

Identification	**Thickness**
Blue	0.087 mm
White	0.102 mm
Red	0.122 mm
Yellow	0.147 mm

Cylinder liner projection above block:

With paper gasket	0.13 to 0.18 mm
With O-ring	0.10 to 0.17 mm

Pistons

Type ....   Aluminium alloy, bulged skirt and oval cross-section. Two compression rings and one oil control ring. Gudgeon pin free in piston, interference fit in connecting rod

Running clearance ....   0.07 to 0.09 mm

Valve and valve gear

Clearance (cold):

Inlet	0.10 mm
Exhaust	0.25 mm

Seat angle (inclusive):

Inlet	120°
Exhaust	90°

Stem diameter ....   8.0 mm

Head diameter:

Inlet	34.8 mm
Exhaust	27.8 mm

Oil capacity (engine/transmission)

954 cc engine ....   4.0 litre, 7.0 pint

1124 cc and 1360 cc engines:

4-speed	4.5 litre, 8.0 pint
5-speed	5.0 litre, 8.8 pint

Oil pump

Maximum endfloat	0.02 and 0.10 mm
Maximum lobe to body clearance	0.064 mm

Torque wrench settings

	Nm	lbf ft
Engine mounting nuts	34	25
Main bearing bolts:		
Stage 1	36	27
Stage 2	51	38
Big-end cap nuts	36	27
Oil pump screws	7	5
Cylinder head bolts (cold):		
Stage 1	49	36
Stage 2	74	55
Chain tensioner bolts	7	5
Camshaft sprocket bolt	73	54
Oil pick-up strainer bolts	10	7
Sump plate bolts	12	9
Engine/transmission connecting bolts	9	7
Timing cover bolts	7	5
Crankshaft pulley nut	88	65
Coolant pump bolts	13	10
Carburettor nuts	17	13

Torque wrench settings (continued)

	Nm	lbf ft
Clutch cover bolts	9	7
Transfer gear plate bolts	9	7
Starter mounting nuts	12	9
Starter motor mounting bolts	16	12
Flywheel bolts	66	49
Rocker cover bolts	7	5
Alternator pivot bolt	45	33
Alternator adjuster link bolt	17	13
Oil drain plug	27	20
Flywheel housing bolts	11	8

1 General description

One of three different capacity engines may be fitted, the difference in displacement being achieved by increasing the bore and stroke. The engine, which has four cylinders and an overhead camshaft, is mounted transversely driving the front wheels and it is inclined to the rear at an angle of 72° from vertical.

The manual gearbox is also mounted transversely in line with the engine, and the final drive to the roadwheels is via the differential unit which is integral with the gearbox. Drive from the engine to the transmission is by means of transfer gears which are separately encased in the clutch housing.

The crankcase, cylinder head, gearcase and clutch housing are all manufactured from aluminium alloy. Removable wet cylinder liners are fitted; the aluminium pistons each have two compression rings and one oil control ring. The valves are operated by the single overhead camshaft and rocker arms. The camshaft drives the distributor at the flywheel end, and the timing sprocket, located at the other end of the camshaft, incorporates a separate eccentric lobe which actuates the fuel pump. The timing chain is driven from the crankshaft sprocket. Next to the timing chain sprocket is the gear wheel which drives the oil pump. This is mounted low down against the crankcase face and is enclosed in the timing chain cover.

The crankshaft runs in five shell main bearings and the endfloat is adjustable via a pair of semi-circular thrust washers. Somewhat inconveniently, the lower half crankcase interconnects the engine with the transmission unit. The engine and transmission units share the same mountings. A forced feed lubrication system is employed and is shown in Fig. 1.1. The oil pump is attached to the crankcase in the

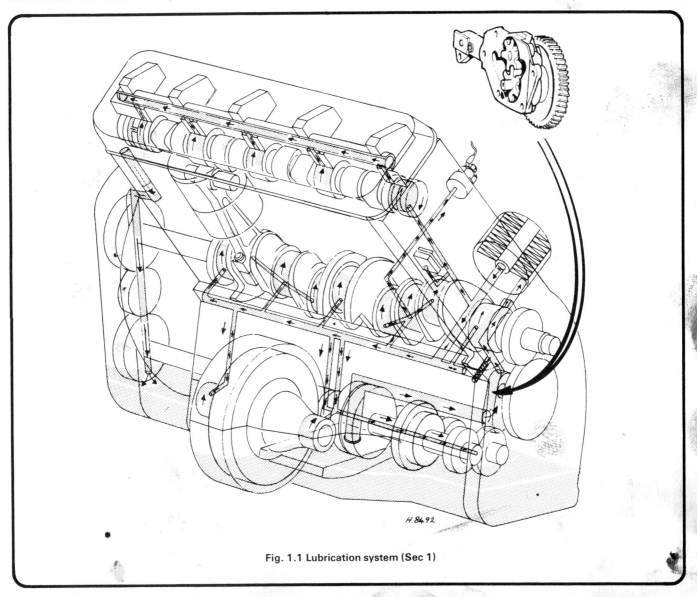

H.8492

Fig. 1.1 Lubrication system (Sec 1)

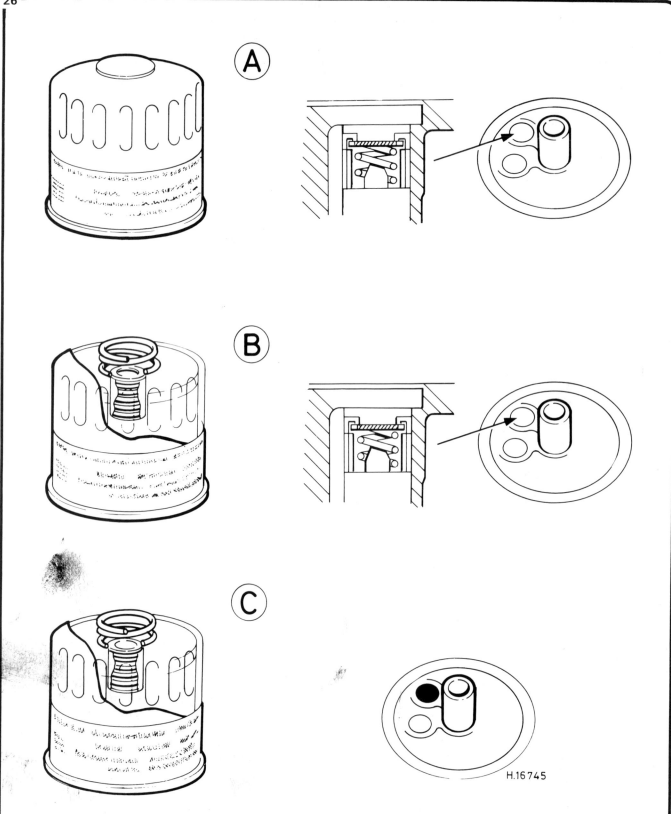

Fig. 1.2 Oil filter cartridge to block fitting arrangements (Sec 2)

A   Oil filter without bypass valve can be fitted to cylinder block with bypass valve
B   Oil filter with bypass valve can be fitted to cylinder block with bypass valve
C   Oil filter with bypass valve can be fitted to cylinder block without bypass valve

Note: Under no circumstances must an oil filter without a bypass valve be fitted to a cylinder block with the bypass valve blanked off

lower section of the timing chest and it incorporates the pressure relief valve. The pump is driven by gears from the crankshaft.

Oil from the pump passes via an oilway to the oil filter, and thence to the crankshaft main bearings, connecting rod bearings and transmission components. Another oilway from the filter delivers oil to the overhead camshaft and rocker components. Oil from the cylinder head passes to the transfer gear housing and then back to the sump contained within the transmission housing.

Apart from the standard replaceable canister filter located on the outside of the crankcase there is a gauze filter incorporated in the oil pump suction intake within the transmission casing.

2 Engine oil and filter

1   The oil level should be checked preferably when the engine is cold.
2   Withdraw the dipstick, wipe it clean, re-insert it and then withdraw it for the second time. The oil level should be between the high and low marks. If it is too low, top up through the filler/breather cap on the rocker cover.
3   The quantity of oil required to raise the oil level from the low to the high mark is 1.0 litre (1.75 pints).
4   At the specified intervals, drain the oil preferably when it is hot. Unscrew the socket-headed plug in the sump plate, remove the filler cap and allow the oil to drain into a suitable container (photo).
5   The oil filter is of the disposable cartridge type, very conveniently located on the top surface of the engine. To remove the filter, unscrew it with an oil filter wrench.
6   If one is not available, a large worm drive hose clip can be fitted to the filter and the screw used as a gripping point. If all else fails, a screwdriver can be driven right through the cartridge and this used as a lever to unscrew it.
7   It is very important to purchase and fit the correct type of filter as some engines have a bypass valve incorporated in the filter mounting base of the crankcase whilst others have the valve incorporated in the filter cartridge.
8   To ensure a satisfactory engine oil circulation in the event of a blockage in the oil filter cartridge, three different arrangements are listed. These are shown in Fig. 1.2 and must be adhered to at all times.
9   Clean the filter mounting ring on the crankcase and apply engine oil to the rubber seal on the cartridge. Do not use grease as it may make the filter difficult to unscrew (photo).
10 Check that the threaded sleeve is tight on the crankcase, offer up the new filter and screw it on using hand pressure only.
11 Refit the oil drain plug, having wiped its magnetic pod free from metal swarf.

12 Fill the engine with the specified quantity and grade of oil.
13 Start the engine. There will be a short delay before the oil warning lamp goes out. This is normal and is caused by the new filter having to fill with oil.
14 Switch off the engine, wait ten minutes and check the oil level and top up if necessary.

3 Crankcase ventilation system – description and maintenance

1   The system is designed to extract oil, fuel and exhaust gas from the engine crankcase. The latter having passed the piston rings (blow-by gas) particularly when the rings have worn.
2   The system consists of an intake for fresh air in the oil filler cap with connecting hoses to the carburettor air intake.
3   The crankcase gases are drawn up into the rocker cover, out through the filler cap hoses and into the manifold where they are burned during the normal engine combustion process.
4   At the intervals specified in Routine Maintenance, remove the cap and hoses and clean them out in paraffin (Fig. 1.3).
5   The appearance of a cream coloured sludge on the inside of the oil filler cap or crankcase ventilation hoses in cold weather indicates that the engine is running cool or is not fully warming up during short journeys. Make sure that the air cleaner control lever is set to the winter position. If the condition persists, a hotter thermostat or partial blanking of the radiator grille may cure the problem.

4 Operations possible without removing the engine from the car

1   Due to the inclination of the engine and transmission, there are very few jobs which can be carried out without removing the power unit from the car. Those possible include:

  1   Valve clearances – adjustment
  2   Timing chain – removal and refitting
  3   Cylinder head – removal and refitting
  4   Engine flexible mountings – renewal

2   It must be emphasised that operations two and three are very involved when attempted with the engine in the car and if suitable lifting gear is readily available, it would probably be better to remove the engine, certainly in respect of the cylinder head.
3   If the cylinder head is being removed with the engine in the car it may be found that the head to bulkhead clearance has been reduced due to softening of the engine flexible mountings. In this case, raise the engine on a jack and tilt slightly to increase the clearance.

2.4 Sump drain plug

Fig. 1.3 Oil filler cap and filter mesh (Sec 3)

5 Valve clearances – adjustment

1   Open the bonnet, remove the spare wheel and obstructing hoses so that the rocker cover can be unbolted.

2   The engine can be turned by using a spanner on the crankshaft pulley bolt – rotation is made easier if the spark plugs are removed.

3   Remove the rocker cover and then turn the engine until the valves on no 1 cylinder are rocking (ie inlet valve opening and exhaust valve closing). The rocker arm clearances of both valves of No 4 cylinder can now be checked and if necessary adjusted. Remember that No 1 cylinder is at the flywheel end of the engine.

4   The feeler gauge of the correct thickness is inserted between the valve stem and rocker arm. When the clearance is correctly set the feeler gauge should be a smooth stiff sliding fit between the valve stem and rocker arm.

5   If the feeler gauge is a tight or loose fit then the clearance must be adjusted. To do this, loosen the locknut of the adjustment stud and screw the adjuster stud in or out until the feeler gauge blade can be felt to drag slightly when drawn from the gap.

6   Hold the adjuster firmly in this position and tighten the locknut. Recheck the gap on completion to ensure that it has not altered when locking the nut and stud (photo).

5.6 Adjusting a valve clearance

7   Check each valve clearance in turn in the following sequence remembering that the clearances for inlet and exhaust valves are different. The valves are numbered from the flywheel end of the engine.

Valves rocking	Valves to adjust
1 In 2 Ex	7 In 8 Ex
5 In 6 Ex	3 In 4 Ex
7 In 8 Ex	1 In 2 Ex
3 In 4 Ex	5 In 6 Ex

8   Fit the rocker cover using a new gasket.

6 Timing chain – removal and refitting

1   Support the engine/transmission on a trolley jack with a block of wood as an insulator.

2   Release the nuts on the right-hand flexible engine mounting at the base of the timing chain cover.

3   Raise the engine just enough to clear the side-member and anti-roll bar.

4   Release the drivebelt tension, remove the belt.

5   Unscrew and remove the crankshaft pulley nut. To do this the crankshaft must be held against rotation by jamming the starter ring

gear. Remove the starter as described in Chapter 10. Alternatively if an assistant is available, have him apply the brakes fully with a gear engaged.

6   Unbolt and remove the rocker cover.

7   Unscrew and remove the timing chain cover bolts. Take off the cover and extract the fuel pump operating rod.

8   Turn the crankshaft either by temporarily refitting the pulley nut or by engaging a gear and turning a front wheel (raised) until the timing marks are located in the following positions. Camshaft sprocket mark between two bright links on chain. Crankshaft sprocket mark opposite centre of single bright link.

9   Remove the crankshaft oil pump drivegear and its Woodruff key.

10   Unbolt the oil pump. Some socket-headed screws are accessible through the holes in the driven gear.

11   Jam the camshaft sprocket and unscrew the sprocket retaining bolt. Take off the fuel pump operating eccentric.

12   Turn the lock on the chain tensioner anti-clockwise to lock it in its retracted state.

13   Remove the camshaft sprocket with timing chain.

14   Commence reassembly by engaging the chain around the crankshaft sprocket so that the timing mark on the sprocket is in the centre of the single bright link on the chain.

15   Now engage the upper loop of the chain over the camshaft sprocket so that the timing mark is between the two bright links on the chain.

16   Now offer the camshaft sprocket to the shaft. Adjust the position of the camshaft so that the sprocket keyway aligns with the key.

17   Push the camshaft sprocket into position. Insert and tighten its retaining bolt with the fuel pump eccentric correctly located.

18   Using a very thin screwdriver blade, turn the lock on the chain tensioner fully clockwise to release the slipper.

19   Refit the oil pump with its spacer plate.

20   Fit the oil pump drivegear to the crankshaft.

21   Bolt on the timing chain cover using a new gasket. The bolt

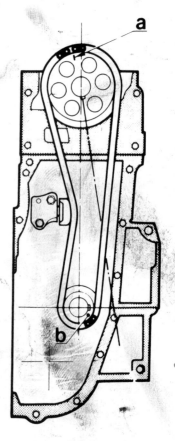

Fig. 1.4 Timing marks (Sec 6)

a   Camshaft sprocket   b   Crankshaft sprocket

Fig. 1.5 Removing crankshaft oil pump drivegear (Sec 6)

4 Drivegear   7 Crankshaft
6 Woodruff key

Fig. 1.7 Camshaft sprocket and fuel pump eccentric retaining bolt (Sec 6)

1 Bolt   2 Fuel pump eccentric

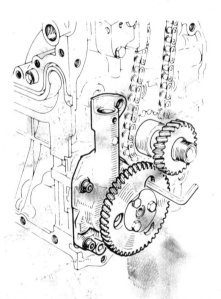

Fig. 1.6 Removing oil pump screw with Allen key (Sec 6)

Fig. 1.8 Timing chain tensioner lock (2) (Sec 6)

Turn lock in direction of arrow to release slipper

nearest the coolant pump pulley must be located in the cover before offering it up, otherwise the pulley will prevent the bolt entering its cover hole. Do not tighten the cover bolts until the crankshaft pulley has been pushed into place to centralise the cover. Fit the coolant hose safety rod under its cover bolts. This rod prevents the coolant hose being cut by the rim of the coolant pump pulley should the hose sag.
22 Fit the fuel pump operating rod.
23 Tighten the timing chain cover bolts to the specified torque and then trim the upper ends of the gasket flush. Fit the rocker cover using a new gasket. Do not overtighten the securing bolts.
24 Tighten the crankshaft pulley nut to the specified torque, again jamming the flywheel to prevent the crankshaft rotating.
25 Refit the starter, if removed.
26 Refit and tension the drivebelt.
27 Lower the engine, reconnect the mounting.

7 Cylinder head – removal and refitting

1 If the engine is in the car, drain the cooling system, disconnect the cylinder head hoses.
2 Remove the spare wheel and support cradle.
3 Remove the rocker cover.
4 Remove the following items:

Distributor – Chapter 4
Carburettor – Chapter 3
Coolant pump – Chapter 2

5 Disconnect the leads from the coolant temperature switch and the spark plugs.
6 Disconnect the exhaust downpipe from the manifold.

7   Remove the timing cover and chain as described in the preceding Section.

8   Progressively unscrew the cylinder head bolts in the sequence shown (Fig. 1.9).

9   Withdraw the through-bolts and recover the nuts from their channels in the crankcase. Remove the rocker shaft assembly.

10 Before removing the cylinder head the following must be noted. The cylinder head is positioned during assembly by means of two dowels, located as shown in Fig. 1.10. When removing the cylinder head it is most important not to lift it directly from the cylinder block; it must be twisted slightly. This action prevents the cylinder liners from sticking to the cylinder head face and being lifted with it, thus breaking their bottom seals.

11 Before the cylinder head can be twisted, the dowel at the flywheel end must be tapped down flush with the top of the cylinder block, using a drift as shown in Fig. 1.11.

12 When the dowel is flush with the top of the cylinder block, twist the cylinder head by tapping it with a plastic-faced mallet.

13 When the seal between the top of the liners and the cylinder head face has been broken lift the head clear and remove the gasket.

14 Do not rotate the crankshaft or the cylinder liners will be displaced and their base seals broken. If there is any fear of this happening, fit

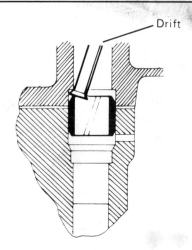

Fig. 1.11 Driving cylinder head dowel down flush with block (Sec 7)

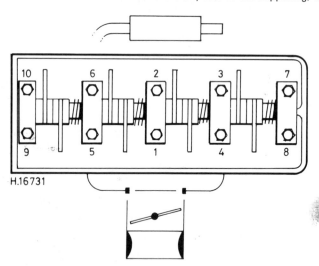

Fig. 1.9 Sequence for tightening or loosening cylinder head bolts (Sec 7)

7.14 One method of clamping cylinder liners

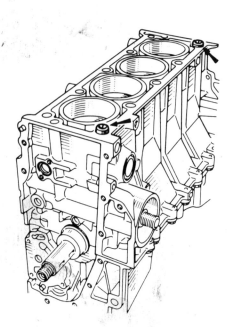

Fig. 1.10 Cylinder head locating dowels (Sec 7)

liner clamps using washers and bolts as shown. Refer to Section 16 for details of decarbonising and overhaul of the cylinder head (photo).

15 Commence reassembly by checking that the crankshaft is still as originally set just prior to timing chain removal with the Woodruff key aligned with the casing flange joint (Fig. 1.12) also the camshaft key (Fig. 1.13).

16 Raise the cylinder block dowel, previously punched flush, by tapping a pin into the hole provided (photo).

17 Locate a new cylinder head gasket on the cylinder block. Make sure that all the holes align (photo).

18 The difficult job is to locate the lower row of cylinder head nuts in their channels whilst the bolts are screwed in. The help of an assistant can solve the problem or the nuts can be retained in their channels using thick grease or a tacky adhesive product (photo).

19 Offer the cylinder head with camshaft, rocker gear and bolts located in their holes onto the block. Screw in the bolts finger tight, having lightly oiled their threads (photo).

20 Tighten the bolts in the following way, and in the sequence shown in Fig. 1.9.

Stage 1 – Tighten to 49 Nm (36 lbf ft)
Stage 2 – Tighten to 74 Nm (55 lbf ft)

21 Refit the timing chain and cover as described in Section 6.

22 Adjust the valve clearances as described in Section 5.

23 Refit the rocker cover (photo).

24 Refit the carburettor, distributor and coolant pump by reference to the appropriate Chapters.

25 Reconnect the exhaust pipe.

26 Refill and bleed the cooling system as described in Chapter 2.

27 After the engine has been started and run to full operating temperature, it should be switched off and allowed to cool for at least two hours. Remove the rocker cover.

28 Unscrew the first cylinder head bolt one half a turn and then retighten it to a torque of 74 Nm (55 lbf ft). Repeat the operation on the remaining bolts, one at a time in the sequence specified (Fig. 1.9).

29 Check the valve clearances and readjust if necessary.

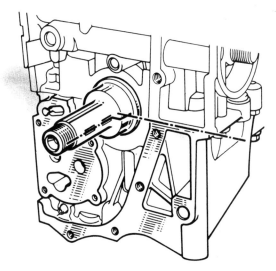

Fig. 1.12 Crankshaft Woodruff key aligned with flange joint (Sec 7)

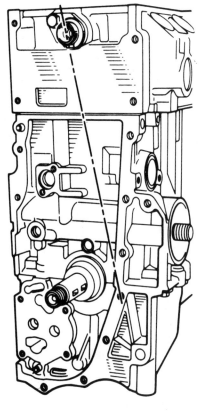

Fig. 1.13 Camshaft Woodruff key alignment (Sec 7)

7.16 Raising cylinder block dowel

7.17 Cylinder head gasket

7.18 Cylinder head nut

7.19 Cylinder head on block

7.20 Tightening cylinder head bolt

7.23 Fitting rocker cover

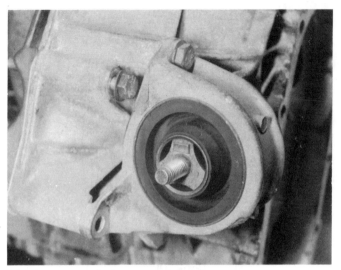
8.1A Transmission flexible mounting (front)

8.1B Transmission flexible mounting (rear)

8 Engine flexible mountings – renewal

1   The engine/transmission is supported on one mounting at the timing chain cover, and one on each side of the transmission (photos).
2   It is recommended that one mounting is renewed at a time after

the weight of the engine and transmission has been taken on a jack with a block of wood as an insulator.
3   Unscrew the nuts which hold the mounting studs to the brackets and unbolt the clamp type holders from the left-hand mountings.
4   Remove the old and refit the new parts, tightening nuts and bolts to the specified torque.

9 Engine – methods of removal

1   The engine is removed together with the transmission and separated after removal.
2   Removal may be upwards using a hoist or downwards using a hoist or trolley jacks. If the latter method is used, the subframe is unbolted from the body sidemembers.

10 Engine/transmission – removal upwards

1   Remove the bonnet as described in Chapter 12.
2   Remove the spare wheel and its support cradle. The cradle nuts need only be released, not removed, as the cradle tubes have slotted ends (photo).
3   Disconnect and remove the battery and its support extension piece (photo).
4   Remove the air cleaner and ducting.
5   Disconnect the leads from the radiator fan and thermostatic switch. Unbolt and remove the radiator with fan (Chapter 2).
6   Move the cooling system expansion tank to the side of the engine compartment.
7   Drain the cooling system.
8   Disconnect the coolant and heater hoses from the engine.
9   Disconnect the fuel hose from the fuel pump. Disconnect all earth connections (photo).
10 Disconnect leads from the alternator, the starter motor, the coolant temperature switch, the oil pressure switch and the reverse lamp switch.
11 Disconnect the coil HT and LT leads on cars with mechanical breaker ignition or the plug from the control unit on cars with electronic ignition.
12 On cars with four-speed transmission, remove the distributor cap and rotor. On cars with five-speed transmission, remove the complete distributor.
13 On cars equipped with a brake vacuum servo unit, unbolt the master cylinder from its front face so that the master cylinder may be carefully moved as the engine is withdrawn. There should be no need to disconnect the hydraulic pipes.
14 Drain the engine/transmission oil.
15 Raise the front of the car so that the roadwheels hang free.
16 On cars with five-speed transmission, the driveshafts will not disengage from the final drive as the engine is hoisted upwards. So remove the roadwheels, the brake hose clips, disconnect the tie-rod end balljoints from the steering arms and the suspension strut base clamps. Pull the hub carriers outwards until the driveshafts are disengaged from the transmission. Support the shafts.
17 Disconnect the exhaust downpipe from the manifold.
18 Disconnect the speedometer cable and clutch cable from transmission.
19 Drive out the roll pin and disconnect the remote control

10.2 Spare wheel support cradle

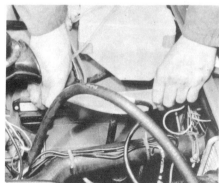
10.3 Battery tray extension piece

10.9 Earth connection

10.19A Disconnecting rod balljoint

10.19B Balljoint stud nut

10.21 Hoisting engine/transmission from engine compartment

gearchange rod. Disconnect the gearchange stabiliser rod balljoint by prising with an open-ended spanner (photos).
20 Take the weight of the engine/transmission with the hoist and lifting tackle and then unscrew the nuts from the engine and transmission flexible mountings. The mountings are slotted so there is no need to remove the nuts.
21 Carefully hoist the engine/transmission out of the engine compartment. On cars with four-speed transmission, prepare for the driveshafts to drop out of engagement with the final drive as the engine/transmission is raised (photo).

11 Engine/transmission – removal downwards

1 Carry out the operations described in paragraphs 1 to 14 in the preceding Section.
2 Disconnect the remote control gearchange rods by driving out the roll pin from one balljoint socket and prising the other balljoint with an open-ended spanner.
3 Disconnect the exhaust downpipe from the manifold (photo).
4 Disconnect the exhaust system flexible mountings and remove the safety cable then lower the complete exhaust system to the floor.
5 Unscrew the steering rack bolts.
6 Disconnect the speedometer drive cable from the transmission by unscrewing the pinch-bolt and nut. Disconnect the clutch cable.
7 Unscrew the upper coupling pinch-bolt on the steering shaft, pull the rack downwards to disengage the coupling control rod pivot bolt.
8 Unscrew the gearchange.
9 Raise the front of the car and support it securely under the sill jacking points. The clearance between the lower edge of the front air dam and the floor must not be less than 838.0 mm (33.0 in) in order that the power unit can be pulled out on the trolley jack.

10 Remove the front roadwheels.
11 Remove the disc pads, unbolt the calipers and tie them up out of the way.
12 Unscrew the pinch-bolts from the clamps at the base of the struts.
13 Pull the hub carriers outwards and disengage the driveshafts from the final drive.
14 Support the subframe on a trolley jack and block of wood and unscrew and remove the six subframe retaining bolts (photos).

11.14A Removing subframe bolt

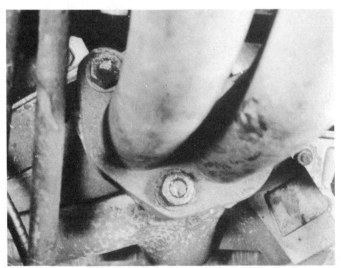

11.3 Exhaust downpipe flange

11.14B Subframe bolt captive nuts

11.15 Lowering subframe

11.16 Subframe with engine/transmission removed

15 Lower the subframe and withdraw it from under the car. The subframe will come out complete with power unit steering gear, driveshafts, hub carriers and anti-roll bar (photo).
16 Support the engine/transmission and release the mounting nuts and detach the subframe (photo).

12 Engine/transmission – separation

1   With the power unit out of the car, clean away external dirt using paraffin and a stiff brush or a water soluble solvent.
2   Unscrew and remove the flywheel housing-to-engine connecting bolts and nuts (photo).
3   There are thirteen bolts and two nuts altogether. Note that an engine lifting lug and earth strap are fitted under some of the bolts.
4   Refer to Chapter 5 and remove the clutch assembly.
5   Unbolt and remove the flywheel.
6   Unscrew and remove the two bolts and the nut close to the crankshaft oil seal.
7   Unscrew the engine to transmission flange connecting bolts. Unbolt the engine mountings.

Fig. 1.15 Engine/transmission flange connecting bolts (3) (Sec 12)

12.2 Flywheel housing upper bolts

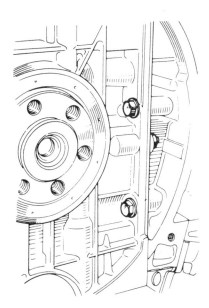

Fig. 1.14 Flange connecting bolts and nuts adjacent to crankshaft oil seal (Sec 12)

Fig. 1.16 Engine/transmission connecting bolts near driveshaft oil seal (Sec 12)

1 Nut   3 Bolt
2 Bolt

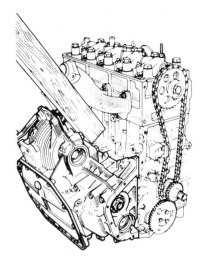

Fig. 1.17 Separating transmission from engine (Sec 12)

8   Unscrew and remove the crankshaft pulley nut. In order to hold the crankshaft against rotation, temporarily screw in two bolts into the holes in the flywheel mounting flange and place a long lever between them.
9   Remove the crankshaft pulley.
10   Remove the rocker cover.
11   Remove the timing chain cover and extract the fuel pump operating plunger.
12   Unscrew and remove the remaining connecting bolts and nuts which are located on the final drive casing side near the driveshaft oil seals.
13   Using a length of wood, prise the engine and transmission apart.

13 Engine – dismantling general

1   As the engine is stripped, clean each part in a bath of paraffin.
2   Never immerse parts with oilways in paraffin (eg crankshaft and rocker shaft). To clean these parts, wipe down carefully with a petrol dampened rag. Oilways can be cleaned out with wire. If an air-line is available, all parts can be blown dry and the oilways blown through as an added precaution.
3   Re-use of old gaskets or oil seals is false economy. To avoid the possibility of trouble after the engine has been reassembled always use new items throughout.
4   Do not throw away the old gaskets, for sometimes it happens that an immediate replacement cannot be found and the old gasket is then very useful as a template. Hang up the gaskets as they are removed.
5   If this is the first time that you have dismantled your engine/transmission unit then special attention should be given to the location of the various components and sub-assemblies. This is especially necessary due to the slightly unconventional layout of the model.
6   Many of the component casings are manufactured in aluminium alloy and special care must therefore be taken not to knock, drop or put any unnecessary pressure on these components.
7   Whenever possible, refit nuts, bolts and washers from where they were removed in order not to mix them up. If they cannot be reinstalled lay them out in such a way that it is clear where they came from.
8   Do not remove or disturb the timing plate on the clutch housing, if this can be avoided. To reset, refer to Chapter 4.

14 Engine – complete dismantling

1   Support the engine on the bench or strong table. If such facilities

are not available then it will have to be dismantled on the floor, but at least cover the floor with a sheet of hardboard.
2   Unbolt and remove the exhaust manifold (three bolts and two nuts) with hot air box.
3   Unbolt the spring-loaded throttle reel from the cylinder head and the thermostat housing. Remove the carburettor(s).
4   Unscrew the oil pressure switch from the crankcase. Unscrew and discard the oil filter.
5   Unbolt and remove the alternator adjuster link and the coolant pump (Chapter 2).
6   Remove the spark plugs using the special spanner supplied with the car. Remove the distributor.
7   Retract the chain tensioner by turning the lock in an anti-clockwise direction. Unbolt the tensioner and remove it.
8   Unscrew the camshaft sprocket bolt which is of socket-headed type. The crankshaft must be held against rotation for this operation. Do this by screwing two bolts into the flange and passing a long lever between them.
9   Remove the fuel pump eccentric cam.
10   Remove the oil pump socket-headed screws. Some of these are accessible through the holes in the oil pump driven gear.
11   Remove the oil pump and backplate.
12   Remove the camshaft sprocket with the timing chain.
13   Remove the Woodruff key and take off the crankshaft oil pump gear.
14   Remove the second Woodruff key and take off the crankshaft timing chain sprocket.
15   Remove the cylinder head bolts by unscrewing them in the order shown in Fig. 1.9.
16   Lift off the rocker assembly.
17   Drive down the cylinder head positioning dowel as described in Section 7 so that the cylinder head can be swivelled rather than lifted from the block. This is to prevent breaking the cylinder liner base seals. If the liners are to be removed then obviously this precaution is not necessary, neither is the need to fit cylinder liner clamps to hold the liners down once the cylinder head has been removed.
18   Dismantling the cylinder head and removal of the camshaft is covered in Section 16.
19   Unscrew and remove the bolts which hold the crankcase half sections together. Split the crankcase and keep the main bearing shells with their crankcase web recesses if the shells are to be used again.
20   Remove the crankshaft oil seal.
21   Mark the rim of the cylinder liners in respect of position in the block and orientation.
22   Mark the big-end caps and the connecting rods so that they can be refitted in their original sequence and the correct way round. A centre punch or hacksaw blade is useful for this purpose.
23   Unscrew the big-end nuts, remove the caps. If the bearing shells are to be used again, keep them taped to their respective cap or connecting rod.
24   Lift the crankshaft half section, keep the shell bearings in their original web recesses if they are to be used again and retrieve the semi-circular thrust washers from either side of Number 2 web.
25   Remove each liner/piston/connecting rod as an assembly from the crankcase. Use a plastic-faced or wooden mallet to tap the liners out if necessary. Make sure that the liners and their respective piston rod assemblies are marked as to position in the block and orientation. A spirit marker is useful for this purpose.
26   Discard the liner base seals which may be of paper or rubber O-ring type.

15 Engine components – examination and renovation – general

1   With the engine dismantled, all components must be thoroughly cleaned and examined for wear as described in the following Sections.
2   If a high mileage has been covered since new or the last engine rebuild, and general wear is evident, consideration should be given to renewing the engine with a reconditioned one.
3   If a single component has malfunctioned and the rest of the engine is in good condition endeavour to find out the cause of its failure if not readily apparent. For example, if a bearing has failed, check that the adjoining oilways are clear; the new bearing will not last long if it is not being lubricated!
4   If uncertain about the condition of any components, seek a second

opinion, preferably from a Peugeot Talbot dealer/mechanic who will obviously have an expert knowledge of your model and be able to advise on the best course of action.

5   Check on the availability of replacement parts before discarding the old ones. Check the new part against the old to ensure that you have the correct replacement.

6   Some of the measurements required will need the use of feeler blades or a micrometer, but in many instances wear will be visually evident or the old component can be compared with a new one.

16   Cylinder head – dismantling, decarbonising and reassembly

1   Having removed the cylinder head, place it onto a clean workbench where it can be dismantled and examined. Unbolt the retaining plate and withdraw the camshaft (photos).

2   Remove each valve and spring assembly using a valve spring compressor. Extract the split collets from between the spring retaining cup washer and valve stem (photo).

3   Progressively release the tension of the compressor until it can be removed, the spring and retainer withdrawn, and the valve extracted from the guide (photos).

4   As the valves are removed, keep them in order by inserting them in a card having suitable holes punched in it, numbered from 1 to 8. Discard the valve stem oil seals.

5   Wash the cylinder head clean and carefully scrape away the carbon build-up in the combustion chambers and exhaust ports, using a scraper which will not damage the surfaces to be cleaned. If a rotary wire brush and drill is available this may be used for removing the carbon. Take care to prevent foreign matter entering the inlet manifold, since it is cast into the cylinder head, cleaning is difficult.

6   The valves may also be scraped and wire-brushed clean in a similar manner.

7   With the cylinder head cleaned and dry, examine it for cracks or damage. In particular inspect the valve seat areas for signs of hairline cracks, pitting or burning. Check the head mating surfaces for

distortion, the maximum permissible amount being 0.002 in (0.05 mm).

8   Minor surface wear and pitting of the valve seats can probably be removed when the valves are reground. More serious wear or damage should be shown to your Peugeot Talbot dealer or a competent automotive engineer who will advise you on the action necessary.

9   Carefully inspect the valves, in particular the exhaust valves. Check the stems for distortion and signs of wear. The valve seat faces must be in reasonable condition and if they have covered a high mileage they will probably need to be refaced on a valve grinding machine; again, this is a job for your Peugeot Talbot dealer or local garage/automotive machine shop.

10   Insert each valve into its respective guide and check for excessive side play. Worn valve guides allow oil to be drained past the inlet valve stem causing a smoky exhaust, while exhaust leakage through the exhaust valve guide can overheat the valve guide and cause sticking valves.

11   If the valve guides are to be renewed this is a job best left to your Peugeot Talbot agent who will have the required specialist equipment.

12   Assuming the valves and seats are in reasonable condition they should be reseated by grinding them using valve grinding carborundum paste. The grinding process must also be carried out when new valves are fitted.

13   The carborundum paste used for this job is normally supplied in a double-ended tin with coarse paste at one end and fine at the other. In addition, a suction tool for holding the valve head so that it may be rotated is also required. To grind in a valve, first smear a trace of the coarse paste onto the seat face and fit the suction grinder to the valve head. Then with a semi-rotary motion grind the valve head into its seat, lifting the valve occasionally to redistribute the grinding paste. When a dull matt continuous line is produced on both the valve seat and the valve then the paste can be wiped off. Apply a little fine paste and finish off the grinding process, then remove all traces of the paste. If a light spring is placed over the valve stem behind the head this can often be of assistance in raising the valve from time to time against the pressure of the grinding tool so as to redistribute the paste evenly round the job. The width of the line which is produced after grinding

16.1A Camshaft retaining plate

16.1B Removing camshaft

16.2 Compressing a valve spring

16.3A Valve spring cup retainer

16.3B Removing a valve spring

16.3C Removing a valve

16.14 Valve stem oil seal

16.15 Valve spring seating washer

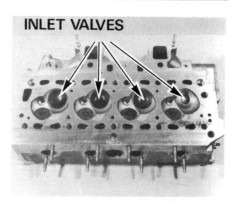

16.16 Cylinder head cleaned and reassembled

indicates the seat width, and this width should not exceed about 0.08 in (2 mm). If, after a moderate amount of grinding, it is apparent that the seating line is too wide, it probably means that the seat has already been cut back one or more times previously, or else the valve has been ground several times. Here again, specialist advice is best sought.

14 Examine all the valve springs to make sure that they are in good condition and not distorted. If the engine has covered 48 000 km (30 000 miles) then fit new springs at reassembly. Renew the valve stem oil seals. Earlier models are fitted with seals on the inlet valves only, later models have seals on all valves (photo).

15 At the same time renew the valve spring seating washers which sit directly on the cylinder head. These wear reasonably quickly (photo).

16 Before reassembling the valve and springs to the cylinder head make a final check that everything is thoroughly clean and free from grit, then lightly smear all the valve stems with engine oil prior to reassembly. The camshaft can now be refitted in the cylinder head and located with the retaining plate. This is then secured with its bolt and a new shakeproof washer (photo).

17 Examination and renovation of dismantled components

Crankshaft and main bearings

1　Carefully examine the crankpin and main journal surfaces for signs of scoring or scratches, and check the ovality and taper of each journal in turn. Use a dial gauge and V-blocks and check the main bearing journals for ovality. If any journals are found to be more than 0.001 in (0.02 mm) out of round they they will have to be reground. If the crankpins are scored or scratched, don't bother measuring them as they will have to be reground.

2　If a bearing has failed after a short period of operation look for the cause and rectify before reassembly.

3　If the crankshaft is to be reground this will have to be done by your Peugeot Talbot dealer or a competent automotive engineer. The regrinder will also be able to supply the new shell bearings to suit the undersize requirement. New thrust washers to control endfloat will also be supplied.

Big-end bearings

4　The main bearing shells themselves are normally a matt grey in colour all over and should have no signs of pitting or ridging or discolouration as this usually indicates that the surface bearing metal has worn away and the backing material is showing through. It is worthwhile renewing the main bearing shells anyway if you have gone to the trouble of removing the crankshaft, but they must, of course, be renewed if there is any sign of damage to them or if the crankshaft has been reground.

5　If the crankshaft is not being reground, yet bearing shells are being renewed, make sure that you check whether or not the crankshaft has been reground before. This will be indicated by looking at the back of the bearing shell and this will indicate whether it is undersize or not. The same type of shell bearing must be used when they are renewed.

6　The big-end bearings are subject to wear at a greater rate than the crankshaft journals. A sign that one or more big-end bearings are

getting badly worn is a pronounced knocking noise from the engine, accompanied by a significant drop in oil pressure due to the increased clearance between the bearing and the journal permitting oil to flow more freely through the resultantly larger space. If this should happen quite suddenly and action is taken immediately, and by immediately is meant within a few miles, then it is possible that the bearing shell may be renewed without any further work needing to be done.

7　If this happens in an engine which has been neglected, and oil changes and oil filter changes have not been carried out as they should have been, it is most likely that the rest of the engine is in a pretty terrible state anyway. If it occurs in an engine which has been recently overhauled, then it is almost certainly due to a piece of grit or swarf which has got into the oil circulation system and finally come to rest in the bearing shell and scored it. In these instances renewal of the shell alone accompanied by a thorough flush through of the lubrication system may be all that is required.

Cylinder liners

8　The liner bores may be examined for wear either in or out of the engine block; the cylinder head must, of course, be removed in each case.

9　First of all examine the top of the cylinder about a quarter of an inch below the top of the liner and with the finger feel if there is any ridge running round the circumference of the bore. In a worn cylinder bore a ridge will develop at the point where the top ring on the piston comes to the uppermost limit of its stroke. An excessive ridge indicates that the bore below the ridge is worn. If there is no ridge, it is reasonable to assume that the cylinder is not badly worn. Measurement of the diameter of the cylinder both in line and with the piston gudgeon pin and at right angles to it, at the top and bottom of the cylinder, is another check to be made. A cylinder is expected to wear at the sides where the thrust of the piston presses against it. In time this causes the cylinder to assume an oval shape. Furthermore, the top of the cylinder is likely to wear more than the bottom of the cylinder. It will be necessary to use a proper bore measuring instrument in order to measure the differences in bore diameter across the cylinder, and variations between the top and bottom ends of the cylinder. As a general guide it may be assumed that any variation more than 0.010 inch (0.25 mm) indicates that the liners should be renewed. Provided all variations are less than 0.010 inch (0.25 mm) it is probable that the fitting of new piston rings will cure the problem of piston-to-cylinder bore clearances. Once again it is difficult to give a firm ruling on this as so much depends on the amount of time, effort and money which the individual owner is prepared, or wishes to spend, on the task. Certainly if the cylinder bores are obviously deeply grooved or scored, the liners must be renewed, regardless of any measurement differences in the cylinder diameter.

10 If new liners are to be fitted, new pistons will be required also, as they are supplied as matched sets.

11 Examine the piston surface and look for signs of any hairline cracks especially round the gudgeon pin area. Check that the oil drain holes below the oil control ring groove are clear, and, if not, carefully clean them out using a suitable size drill, but don't mark the piston.

12 If any of the pistons are obviously badly worn or defective they must be renewed. A badly worn top ring land may be machined to

accept a wider, stepped ring, the step on the outer face of this type of ring being necessary to avoid fouling the unworn ridge at the top of the cylinder bore.

13 Providing the engine has not seized up or suffered any other severe damage, the connecting rods should not require any attention other than cleaning. If damage has occurred or the piston/s show signs of irregular wear it is advisable to have the connecting rod alignment checked. This requires the use of specialised tools and should therefore be entrusted to a Peugeot Talbot agent or a competent automotive engineer, who will be able to check and realign any defective rods.

14 New Peugeot Talbot rings are supplied with their gaps already preset, but if you intend to use other makes the gaps should be checked and adjusted if necessary. Before fitting the new rings on the pistons, each should be inserted approximately 3 in (75 mm) down the cylinder bore and the gap measured with a feeler gauge. This should be between 0.015 in (0.38 mm) and 0.038 in (0.97 mm). It is essential that the gap should be measured at the bottom of the ring travel, as if it is measured at the top of a worn bore and gives a perfect fit, it could easily seize at the bottom. If the ring gap is too small, rub down the ends of the ring with a very fine file until the gap, when fitted, is correct. To keep the rings square in the bore for measurement, line each up in turn by inserting an old piston in the bore upside down, and use the piston to push the ring down. Remove the piston and measure the piston ring gap.

Gudgeon pins

15 The gudgeon pins float in the piston and are an interference fit in the connecting rods. This interference fit between gudgeon pin and connecting rod means that heat is required (230 – 260°C/450 – 500°F) before a pin can be satisfactorily fitted in the connecting rod. If it is necessary to renew either the piston or connecting rod, we strongly recommend that the separation and assembly of the two be entrusted to someone with experience. Misapplied heat can ruin one, or all, of the components very easily.

16 Never re-use a piston if the original gudgeon pin has been removed from it.

Connecting rod/piston

17 With the pistons removed from the liners, carefully clean them and remove the old rings, keeping them in order and the correct way up. The ring grooves will have to be cleaned out, especially the top, which will contain a burnt carbon coating that may prevent the ring from seating correctly. A broken piston ring will assist in groove cleaning. Take care not to scratch the ring lands or piston surface in any way.

18 The top ring groove is likely to have worn the most. After the groove has been cleaned out, refit the top ring and any excessive wear will be obvious by a sloppy fit. The degree of wear may be checked by using a feeler gauge (photo).

Timing chain, sprocket and tensioner

19 Examine the teeth of both sprockets for wear. Each tooth on a sprocket is an inverted V-shape and wear is apparent when one side of the tooth becomes more concave in shape than the other. When badly worn, the teeth become hook-shaped and the sprockets must be renewed.

20 If the sprockets need to be renewed then the chain will have worn also and should also be renewed. If the sprockets are satisfactory, examine the chain and look for play between the links. When the chain is held out horizontally, it should not bend appreciably. Remember, a chain is only as strong as its weakest link, and being a relatively cheap item it is worthwhile fitting a replacement anyway.

21 Check the condition of the tensioner slipper. If it is worn, renew it.

22 Inspect the oil pump drive gears for wear or damage and renew if necessary. Always fit a new timing cover oil seal (photo).

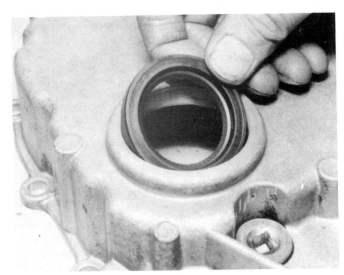

17.22 Timing chain cover oil seal

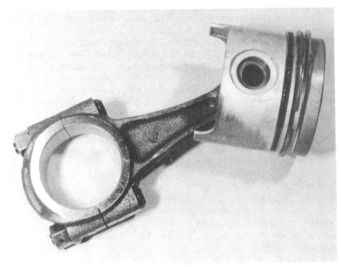

17.18 Piston/connecting rod assembly

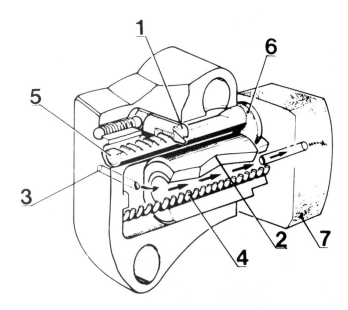

Fig. 1.18 Cutaway view of timing chain tensioner (Sec 17)

1	Ratchet screw	5	Rack
2	Piston	6	Washer
3	Oil supply	7	Slipper
4	Spring		

Transfer gears (refer also to Chapter 5)

23 The condition of the transfer gears, their bearings and the input and output shafts, is obviously critical as they transmit the power of the engine to the transmission unit, and are liable to be a source of noise if worn.

24 Clean the input and output shaft ball bearings and check them for excessive play and/or signs of damage. Inspect the intermediate shaft needle roller bearings. Renew any suspect or worn bearings. If a bearing has collapsed due to general wear and fatigue, then the chances are that the other bearings are close to failure and it is therefore advisable to renew all the bearings.

25 Carefully inspect the transfer gears. If excessive transmission noise has been experienced it may be reduced by changing the transfer gears. If the teeth are worn or damaged, then the gears should be renewed. Renew the gear set rather than a single gear; it is not good practice to mesh new gears with old as the wear rate of both is increased and they will be noisy in operation.

26 Check the input and output shafts, and inspect their splines for wear or damage. Renew them if necessary.

Camshaft and rocker gear

27 The camshaft lobes should be examined for signs of flats or scoring or any other form of wear and damage. At the same time the rocker arms should also be examined, particularly on the faces where they bear against the camshaft, for signs of wear. Very slight wear may be removed by rubbing with an oilstone but maintain the original contour.

28 The camshaft bearing journals should be in good condition and show no signs of pitting or scoring as they are relatively free from stress.

29 If the bearing surfaces are scored or discoloured it is possible that the shaft is not running true, and in this case it will have to be renewed. For an accurate check get your Peugeot Talbot agent to inspect both the camshaft and cylinder head.

30 Worn camshaft bearings in the cylinder head can only be rectified by renewal of the head, an expensive business, as the bearings are machined directly in the head.

31 The rocker arm assembly can be dismantled on removing the circlip from the end of the rocker shaft (photos).

32 When removing the various rocker components from the shaft take careful note of the sequence in which they are removed. In particular note that the No 2 and 4 rocker bearings are identical, keep the components in order as they are removed from the shaft for inspection.

33 Check the rocker shaft for signs of wear. Check it for straightness by rolling it on a flat surface. It is unlikely to be bent but if this is the case it must either be straightened or renewed. The shaft surface should be free of wear ridges caused by the rocker arms. Check the oil feed holes and clear them out if blocked or sludged-up.

34 Check each rocker arm for wear on an unworn part of the shaft. Check the end of the adjuster screw and the face of the rocker arm where it bears on the camshaft. Any signs of cracks or serious wear will necessitate renewal of the rocker arm.

17.31A Rocker shaft retaining circlip

17.31B Rocker arms and spring

Flywheel and starter ring gear

35 There are two areas in which the flywheel may have been worn or damaged. The first is on the driving face where the clutch friction plate bears against it. Should the clutch plate have been permitted to wear down beyond the level of the rivets, it is possible that the flywheel will have been scored. If this scoring is severe it may be necessary to have it refaced or even renewed.

36 Evidence of tiny cracks on the flywheel driving face will indicate that overheating has occurred.

37 The other part to examine is the teeth of the starter ring gear around the periphery of the flywheel. If several of the teeth are broken or missing, or the front edges of all teeth are obviously very badly chewed up, then it would be advisable to fit a new ring gear.

38 The old ring gear can be removed by cutting a slot with a hacksaw down between two of the teeth as far as possible, without cutting into the flywheel itself. Once the cut is made a chisel will split the ring gear which can then be drawn off. To fit a new ring gear requires it to be heated first to a temperature of 220°C (435°F), no more. This is best done in a bath of oil or an oven, but not, preferably, with a naked flame. It is much more difficult to heat evenly and to the required temperature with a naked flame. Once the ring gear has attained the correct temperature it can be placed onto the flywheel making sure that it beds down properly onto the register. It should then be allowed to cool down naturally. If by mischance, the ring gear is overheated, it should not be used. The temper will have been lost, therefore softening it, and it will wear out in a very short space of time.

39 Although not actually fitted into the flywheel itself, there is a bush in the centre of the crankshaft flange onto which the flywheel fits. Whilst more associated with gearbox and clutch it should always be inspected when the clutch is removed. The main bearing oil seal is revealed when the flywheel is removed. This can be prised out with a screwdriver but must always be renewed once removed. The spigot bush is best removed using a suitable extractor. Another method is to fill the recess with grease and then drive in a piece of close fitting steel bar. This should force the bush out. A new bush may be pressed in, together with a new seal. Make sure that the chamfered end of the bush abuts the seal. The bush is self-lubricating.

Oil pump

40 The oil pump gears are exposed once the spacer plate is removed.

41 Slide movement of the gear spindles will indicate wear in the bushes and the pump should be renewed complete.

42 Worn or chipped gear teeth must be rectified by renewal of the gear.

43 Check the endfloat of the gears using a straight edge and feeler blades (photo).

44 Check the clearance between the tip of the gear lobes and the oil pump body (photo).

17.43 Checking oil pump gear endfloat

17.44 Checking oil pump lobe tip clearance

17.46 Oil pump relief valve components

45 If any of these clearances exceed the specified limit, renew the pump.

46 Remove the retaining pin from the relief valve housing and withdraw the cup, spring, guide and piston. Renew any worn components (photo).

18 Engine reassembly – general

1 It is during the process of engine reassembly that the job is either made a success or a failure. From the word go there are certain basic rules which it is folly to ignore, namely:

(a) *Absolute cleanliness. The working area, the components of the engine and the hands of those working on the engine must be completely free of grime and grit. One small piece of carborundum dust or swarf can ruin a big-end in no time, and nullify all the time and effort you have spent.*

(b) *Always, no matter what the circumstances may be, use new gaskets, locking tabs, seats, nyloc nuts and any other parts mentioned in the Sections in this Chapter. It is pointless to dismantle an engine, spend considerable money and time on it and then to waste all this for the sake of something as small as a failed oil seal. Delay the rebuilding if necessary.*

(c) *Don't rush it. The most skilled and experienced mechanic can easily make a mistake if he is rushed*

(d) *Check that all nuts and bolts are clean and in good condition and ideally renew all spring washers, lockwashers and tab washers as a matter of course. A supply of clean engine oil and clean cloths (to wipe excess oil off your hands only!) and a torque spanner are the only things which should be required in addition to all the tools used in dismantling the engine*

(e) *The torque wrench is an essential requirement when reassembling the engine (and transmission) components. This is because the various housings are manufactured from aluminium alloy and whilst this gives the advantage of less weight, it also means that the various fastenings must be accurately tightened as specified to avoid distortion and/or damage to the components.*

19 Engine – preparation for reassembly

1 Assuming that the engine has been completely stripped for reconditioning and that the block is now bare, before any reassembly takes place it must be thoroughly cleaned both inside and out.

2 Clean out the oilways using a bottle brush wire or other suitable implement, and blow through with compressed air. Squirt some clean engine oil through to check that the oilways are clear.

3 If the core plugs are defective and show signs of weeping, they must be renewed at this stage. To remove, carefully drive a punch through the centre of the plug and use the punch to lever the plug out. Clean the aperture thoroughly and prior to fitting the new plug, smear the orifice with sealant. Use a small-headed hammer and carefully drive the new core plug into position with the convex side outwards. Check that it is correctly seated on completion.

4 As the components are assembled, lubricate them with clean engine oil and use a suitable sealant as and where applicable.

5 Make sure that all blind tapped holes are clean, with any oil mopped out of them. This is because it is possible for a casting to fracture when a bolt is screwed in owing to hydraulic pressure.

20 Cylinder liners – checking projection

Paper type gasket seals

1 If the cylinder liners had paper type base seals, the first thing to do is to check the liner projection and select new paper seals.

20.1 Liner with paper gasket

2 If rubber O-rings are used, no checking or measurement of liner projection is required, simply renew the O-rings.

3 Paper gaskets are available in four different thicknesses:

Blue 0.087 mm
White 0.102 mm
Red 0.122 mm
Yellow 0.147 mm

4 The correct projection for each liner above the surface of the cylinder block is between 0.13 and 0.18 mm, preferably nearer to the greater projection.

5 Fit the liners without gaskets into their original locations. If new liners are being fitted, they of course can be fitted in any order.

6 Using a dial indicator or feeler gauges and a straight edge, measure the projection of each liner.

7   It is now a simple matter to select a paper gasket which, when its thickness is added to the recorded projection, will equal the specified projection.

8   Make sure that the difference in projection between adjacent liners does not exceed 0.04 mm. If it does, reduce the gasket thickness on the greater projecting liner.

9   If new liners are being fitted, the projection differences can be eliminated by changing the position of the liner in the block or by twisting it on its base.

10 Once selected, mark the liner position in the block, remove them and place them with their paper gaskets ready for final assembly.

O-ring type seals

11 If the original liners are being refitted then the projection should be correct once new O-ring seals have been fitted.

12 If new liners are being fitted, then measure the projection of each liner without its seal. This should be between 0.10 and 0.17 mm, with a maximum difference between liners of 0.05 mm (photo).

13 If the difference between adjacent liners exceeds 0.05 mm, rotate the liners through half a turn or interchange the liner position in the block.

14 Once correctly located, mark their sequence in the block and withdraw them so that their piston/rods can be fitted.

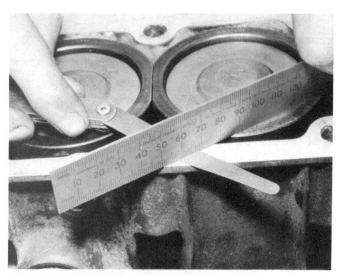

20.12 Measuring cylinder liner projection

Fig. 1.19 Cylinder liner and block match marks (a) (Sec 20)

21 Engine – complete reassembly

1   Fit the piston rings to the pistons. Always fit the rings from the piston crown end. Use three old feeler blades equally spaced behind the ring so that it will slide down to the lower grooves without dropping into the higher ones (photo).

2   Make sure that the rings are correctly located and the right way up. If genuine Peugeot Talbot piston rings are being used, refer to Fig. 1.20. If special proprietary rings are being fitted, follow the manufacturers instructions.

3   Twist the piston rings so that the gap in the oil control ring expander aligns with the gudgeon pin and the gaps in the rails are offset from the gudgeon pin by between 20.0 and 50.0 mm (0.79 and 1.97 in). The caps in the top two compression rings should be equally

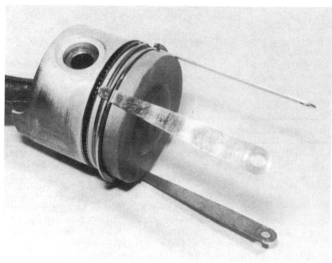

21.1 Method of fitting piston rings

Fig. 1.20 Piston ring identification (Séc 21)

1	Oil control ring	b Oil control expander gap
2	Compression ring (tapered)	c Oil control rail gaps
3	Compression ring	

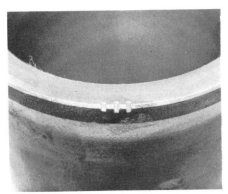
21.4 Piston/liner grading mark

21.6 Piston crown showing directional arrow

21.7 Piston ring clamp fitted

21.10 Cylinder liner O-ring seal

21.12 Installing piston/liner assembly

21.14 Shell bearings in position

spaced (120°) from the gap in the oil control expander around the piston.
4 If new piston/liner assemblies have been supplied, the identification marks on the piston and liner should be:

Piston	Liner
A	One file mark on rim
B	Two file marks on rim
C	Three file marks on rim

5 All four pistons should be of the same grading.
6 Fit the liners to the piston/connecting rod assemblies so that when installed in the cylinder block, the rim mark on the liner will be towards the oil gallery side and the arrow on the piston crown facing towards the timing chain cover end of the engine. Piston to rod relationship is not important (photo).
7 Oil the piston rings liberally and fit a compressor to the piston and compress the rings fully (photo).
8 Lubricate the bore of the liner and insert the piston. As this is done, the compressor will be pushed off.
9 Push the piston into the liner until the piston crown is level with the top of the liner.
10 Fit either the selected paper gasket seals so that their tabs are diametrically opposite to the liner rim marks or locate the O-ring seals making sure that they are not twisted (photo).
11 Remove the big-end caps, wipe the recesses in rod and cap absolutely clean and fit the bearing shells. If the original shells are being used again, make sure that they are being returned to their original locations.
12 Push the liner/rod assemblies into the block, without disturbing the seals and aligning the location marks (photo).
13 Fit clamps to hold the liners in the block.
14 Place the block so that it rests on its top face and wipe out the recesses and fit the main bearing shells (photo).
15 Fit the semi-circular thrust washers which control crankshaft

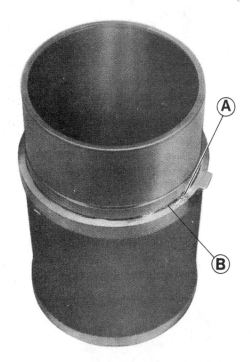
Fig. 1.21 Fit cylinder liner paper gasket inner tab (A) into liner groove (B) (Sec 21)

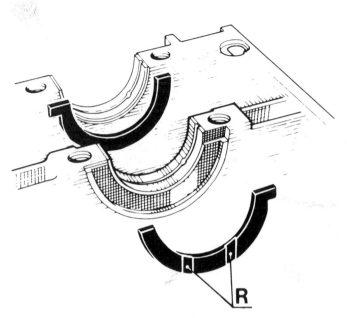

Fig. 1.22 Crankshaft thrust washer (Sec 21)

R   Oil grooves

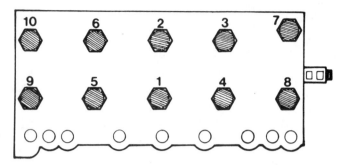

Fig. 1.23 Main bearing bolt loosening and tightening sequence
(Sec 21)

endfloat. The oil grooves of the thrust washers must be against the machined face of the crankshaft (photo).
16 Oil the shell bearings and lower the crankshaft into position (photo).
17 Now check the crankshaft endfloat. Do this by first pushing the crankshaft fully in one direction and then in the other. A dial gauge or feeler blades should be used to measure the endfloat. If the endfloat

is outside the specified tolerance, change the thrust washers for ones of different thickness, from the four thicknesses available (photo).
18 Fit the big-end caps complete with bearing shells, well lubricated. Make sure that the cap/rod matching marks are in alignment. This will ensure that both tongues of the shells are on the same side (photo).
19 Tighten the big-end nuts to the specified torque (photo).
20 Into the crankcase flange fit a new O-ring seal and check that the locating dowels are in position (photo).
21 Apply jointing compound to the flange.
22 Clean the recesses in the remaining crankcase housing section and fit the main bearing shells. Note that the grooved shells are located in positions 2 and 4.
23 Locate the housing taking care not to displace the bearing shells (photo).
24 Screw in the ten main bearing/casing bolts with flat washers noting that the two longer bolts are at the flywheel housing end and the very long one at the crankshaft pulley end on the oil pump side (photo).
25 Tighten the bolts in the sequence given in two stages to the specified torque.

21.15 Crankshaft thrust washers

21.16 Lowering crankshaft into place

21.17 Checking crankshaft endfloat

21.18 Fitting a big-end cap

21.19 Tightening a big-end cap nut

21.20 Crankcase flange O-ring seal

21.23 Fitting crankcase housing

21.24 Tightening main bearing bolts

21.26 Crankcase housing flange bolts

21.27 Fitting crankshaft oil seal

21.29A Chain tensioner filter

21.29B Fitting chain tensioner

26 Now screw in the seven housing flange bolts with their spring washers to the specified torque (photo).

27 Grease the lips of a new crankshaft oil seal and drive it squarely into position (photo).

28 Fit the cylinder head as described in Section 7, paragraphs 15 to 21.

29 Fit the timing chain tensioner oil filter and the crankshaft and camshaft Woodruff keys. Bolt the chain tensioner into position (photos).

30 Rotate the crankshaft by temporarily screwing in two flywheel bolts and placing a bar between them until the key is in alignment with the crankcase joint.

31 Temporarily fit the camshaft sprocket and rotate the camshaft until the keyway is positioned as shown in Fig. 1.13.

32 Fit the crankshaft sprocket (photo).

33 Loop the chain around the crankshaft sprocket so that the bright

Fig. 1.24 Camshaft sprocket, fuel pump eccentric (5) and bolt (6) showing key (a) (Sec 21)

link on the chain is centred on the timing mark on the sprocket (photo).

34 Now loop the chain around the camshaft sprocket so that the two bright links are positioned one on each side of the sprocket timing mark. Push the sprocket with chain onto the camshaft, if necessary move the camshaft a fraction to align the keyway (photo).

35 Screw in the camshaft sprocket bolt with fuel pump eccentric and tighten to the specified torque (photos).

36 Turn the key in the chain tensioner fully clockwise to release the slipper.

37 Check that the locating dowel is in position and fit the oil pump with spacer plate, no gasket is used. If the pump driven sprocket is hard to turn, release the pump mounting bolts and turn the pump slightly on its locating dowel. Re-tighten the bolts (photo).

38 Fit the oil pump drive sprocket and Woodruff key to the crankshaft (photo).

39 Fit the spark plugs. Do not overtighten them.

40 Fit the alternator adjuster link and coolant pump.

41 Screw in the oil pressure switch (photo).

42 Fit a new oil filter.

43 Bolt on the throttle reel with return spring (photo).

44 Bolt on the exhaust manifold using new gaskets. Leave the end nuts loose until the hot air collector has been fitted and then tighten them (photos).

45 Fit the fuel pump and operating rod.

46 Fit the distributor (Chapter 4) on four-speed models only and without cap and rotor.

47 Fit the carburettor with a new gasket.

48 Fit the thermostat and thermostat housing cover using a new gasket.

49 The engine is now ready for connecting to the transmission as described in the next Section.

21.32 Crankshaft sprocket

21.33 Timing chain bright link (arrowed) at crankshaft sprocket

21.34 Timing chain bright links (arrowed) at camshaft sprocket

21.35A Fuel pump eccentric

21.35B Tightening camshaft sprocket bolt

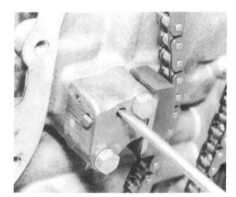
21.36 Releasing timing chain tensioner. Turn lock in clockwise direction

21.37 Fitting oil pump with spacer plate

21.38 Oil pump drive sprocket

21.41 Oil pressure switch

21.43 Throttle cable reel

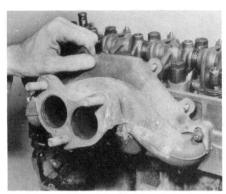

21.44A Exhaust manifold with hot air box back plate

21.44B Exhaust manifold with hot air box

22 Engine/transmission – reconnection

1 Check that the oil pick-up strainer is in position within the transmission casing.
2 Fit the sump cover using a new gasket.
3 Tighten the fixing bolts and drain plug to the specified torque.
4 Fit the cover plate.
5 Apply jointing compound to the mating surfaces on the engine and transmission.
6 On the transmission locate a new O-ring seal and check that the locating dowels and the studs are in position (photo).
7 Offer the transmission to the engine, screw in the connecting bolts and nuts and tighten to the specified torque (photo).
8 Locate a new timing chain cover gasket and fit the cover.

9 Before offering the cover to the engine, put the bolt nearest the coolant pump pulley into its cover hole otherwise the pulley will prevent it being fitted later. Do not tighten the cover bolts yet (photo).
10 Fit the coolant hose safety rod under its cover bolts (photo).
11 Use the crankshaft pulley to centralise the timing chain cover and then tighten the cover bolts.
12 Cut off the upper ends of the cover gasket flush.
13 Apply grease to the crankshaft pulley oil seal contact surface and push it onto its key. Fit a new lockplate, tighten the nut to the specified torque and then bend up the lockplate (photo).
14 Fit the flywheel. Apply thread locking fluid to clean threads and screw in the flywheel bolts to the specified torque.
15 The flywheel holes are offset so it will only go onto the crankshaft flange in one position (photos).

22.6 O-ring seal on transmission casing

22.7 Offering transmission to engine

22.9A Fitting timing chain cover and gasket

22.9B Timing cover bolt nearest coolant pump pulley

22.10 Coolant hose safety support rod

22.13 Tightening crankshaft pulley nut

22.15A Inserting flywheel bolts

22.15B Tightening flywheel bolts

22.17 Offering up flywheel housing

16 Fit the clutch and centralise the driven plate as described in Chapter 5.

17 Fit a new gasket and the flywheel housing (Chapter 5, Section 5) complete with transfer gears. Make sure that the engine lifting lug and earth strap are correctly located under their respective bolts (photo).

18 If they were removed, bolt the engine mountings to the flywheel housing.

19 Fit the starter motor. Tighten the bolts and nuts in the following order:

   1   Starter drive end flange to flywheel housing
   2   Brush end bracket to engine crankcase
   3   Brush end bracket to starter motor

20 Adjust the valve clearances. Use a new gasket and fit the rocker cover.

21 Fit the alternator.

22 The engine/transmission is now ready for refitting to the car.

23 Engine/transmission – refitting

1   Refitting the engine is a reversal of removal whichever method was employed.

2   If the power unit was lowered complete with subframe then the engine/transmission must be located on its subframe under the car ready for jacking or hoisting into the engine compartment.

3   The mountings will already have been connected so it is just a matter of screwing in the subframe fixing bolts and reconnecting the steering system.

4   If the power unit was removed upwards, then it must be lowered into position until the flexible mounting studs engage in the slots in the brackets. Remember that if a four-speed transmission is fitted then the inboard ends of the driveshafts should be engaged in the transmission as soon as possible as the power unit is lowered (photos).

5   With the five-speed models, the driveshafts can only be engaged after the power unit has been fully lowered onto its mountings.

6   Fit the flexible mounting stud nuts and tighten to the specified torque.

7   On five-speed models, reconnect the driveshafts with the transmission and then reconnect the suspension strut base clamps, the tie-rod balljoints and the brake flexible hose clips. Refit the disc calipers (photo).

8   Connect the exhaust pipe to the manifold or refit the complete exhaust system dependent upon method of removal.

9   Reconnect the gearchange rod.

10 Reconnect the speedometer drive cable. Reconnect the clutch cable and adjust (Chapter 5).

11 Refit the distributor (five-speed) or cap and rotor (four-speed).

12 Reconnect the ignition and spark plug leads and all the earth connections (engine/transmission to body).

13 Reconnect the starter motor leads.

14 Reconnect the alternator leads.

15 Reconnect the leads to the oil pressure switch, the coolant temperature switch and the reverse lamp switch (photos).

16 Reconnect the fuel pump hose.

17 Reconnect the coolant and heater hoses to the engine.

18 Position the cooling system expansion tank in its original location.

19 Refit the radiator/fan.

20 Reconnect the radiator coolant hoses.

21 Reconnect the leads to the fan, then the thermostatic switch and the low coolant level switch (later models) which are screwed into the radiator.

22 Refit the air cleaner and ducting.

23 Refit the battery and connect the leads.

24 Refit the spare wheel cradle.

25 Refit the bonnet and the roadwheels.

26 Fill and bleed the cooling system.

27 Fill the engine/transmission with oil.

23.4A Rear right-hand mounting in bracket slot

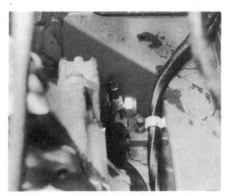
23.4B Front left-hand mounting in bracket slot

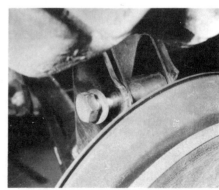
23.7 Front suspension strut base clamp bolt

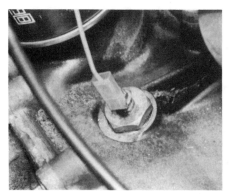

23.15A Oil pressure switch lead

23.15B Coolant temperature switch lead

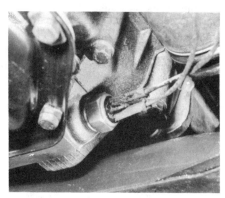

23.15C Reverse lamp switch leads

24 Engine – initial start up after overhaul

1   Make sure that the battery is fully charged and that all lubricants, coolant and fuel are replenished.

2   It will require several revolutions of the engine on the starter motor to pump the petrol up to the carburettor.

3   As soon as the engine fires and runs, keep it going at a fast tickover only (no faster), and bring it up to the normal working temperature.

4   As the engine warms up there will be odd smells and some smoke from parts getting hot and burning off oil deposits. The signs to look for are leaks of water or oil which will be obvious if serious. Check also the exhaust pipe and manifold connections, as these do not always 'find' their exact gas tight position until the warmth and vibration have acted on them, and it is almost certain that they will need tightening further. This should be done of course, with the engine stopped.

5   When normal running temperature has been reached adjust the engine idling speed, as described in Chapter 3. Run the engine until the fan cuts in and then switch off. Check that no oil or coolant is leaking with the engine stationary.

6   Allow at least two hours for the engine to cool down and then retighten the cylinder head bolts after removing the rocker cover. Follow the bolt tightening sequence and, starting with the first, slacken the bolt and retighten it to the specified final tightening torque before loosening the second bolt. Repeat until all bolts have been retightened.

7   Check and adjust the valve clearances.

8   Check the ignition timing.

9   Road test the car to check that the timing is correct and that the engine is giving the necessary smoothness and power. Do not race the engine – if new bearings and/or pistons have been fitted it should be treated as a new engine and run in at a reduced speed.

10 Change the engine oil at 1600 km (1000 miles) if many of the engine internal components have been renewed. At the same mileage, check the tension of the drivebelt.

Fault diagnosis appears overleaf

25 Fault diagnosis – engine

Symptom	Reason(s)
Engine will not turn over when starter switch is operated	Flat battery Bad battery conditions Bad connections at solenoid switch and/or starter motor Starter motor jammed Defective solenoid Starter motor defective
Engine turns over normally but fails to fire and run	No sparks at plugs No fuel reaching engine Too much fuel reaching engine (flooding)
Engine starts but runs unevenly and misfires	Ignition and/or fuel system faults Incorrect valve clearance Burnt out valves Blown cylinder head gasket, dropped liners Worn out piston rings Worn cylinder bores
Lack of power	Ignition and/or fuel system faults Incorrect valve clearance Burnt out valves Blown cylinder head gasket Worn out piston rings Worn cylinder bores
Excessive oil consumption	Oil leaks from crankshaft oil seal, timing cover gasket and oil seal, rocker cover gasket, crankcase or gearbox joint Worn piston rings or cylinder bores resulting in oil being burnt by engine (smoky exhaust is an indication) Worn valve guides and/or defective valve stem
Excessive mechanical noise from engine	Wrong valve to rocker clearance Worn crankshaft bearings Worn cylinders (piston slap) Slack or worn timing chain and sprockets Worn transfer gears and/or bearings

Chapter 2
Cooling, heating and ventilation systems

For modifications, and information applicable to later models, see Supplement at end of manual

Contents

Specifications

System type	Pressurised with expansion tank and front mounted radiator, belt-driven coolant pump and thermostat. Electric cooling fan.
Electric fan cut-in temperature	90°C (194°F)
Thermostat	
Starts to open	82°C (180°F)
Fully open	94°C (201°F)
Drivebelt tension	12.5 mm (0.5 in)
Coolant capacity	5.6 litres, 10.0 Imp pts

Torque wrench settings	Nm	lbf ft
Coolant pump mounting bolts	13	10
Alternator mounting bolts	45	33
Alternator adjuster link bolts	17	13

1 General description

The cooling system is of pressurized type incorporating a remotely sited expansion tank (photo).

Main components of the system include a crossflow type radiator, a belt-driven pump and a thermostatically controlled electric cooling fan.

A thermostat is incorporated in the cylinder head to prevent coolant circulation during warm up.

The car interior heater is supplied with coolant from the engine cooling system.

A drain plug is fitted to the cylinder block and on some models, a drain plug is located at the base of the radiator on the left-hand side.

The cooling system functions in the following way. At cold start with the thermostat valve closed the coolant is virtually motionless. As the result of combustion temperatures the coolant in the cylinder head and block heats up rapidly and causes the temperature sensitive capsule in the thermostat to open the valve.

Coolant now flows across the radiator, impelled by the coolant pump, where it is cooled by the inrush of air due to the forward motion of the car.

Should the coolant temperature reach a pre-determined level or if

1.1 Expansion tank

1.9A Carburettor throttle block coolant hose and coolant temperature switch (arrowed)

1.9B Inlet manifold coolant hose

the car is stationary for an extended period, the electric cooling fan will operate in order to draw air through the radiator.

The carburettor throttle valve block is coolant-heated as a means of warming the fuel/air mixture as it is drawn into the manifold which is also coolant-heated (photos).

2   Maintenance

1   At the intervals specified in Routine Maintenance, carry out the following.
2   Visually check the coolant level in the expansion tank. This should be between the MIN and MAX marks when the engine is cold.
3   Where necessary, top up using a coolant mixture made up in similar proportions to the original antifreeze solution. Add the coolant to the expansion tank. The need for topping up should arise only very infrequently. If regular topping up is needed, check for a leaking hose or gasket.
4   Check the security and condition of the system hoses regularly.
5   Renew the coolant every two years. **Warning:** *Do not remove the expansion tank cap if the engine is hot or escaping steam may scald.*

3   Cooling system – draining, flushing and refilling

1   Set the heater temperature control to HOT and remove the cap from the expansion tank.
2   Remove the drain plug from the radiator or if one is not fitted, disconnect the radiator lower hose (photo).
3   Remove the cylinder block drain plug (photo). The plug is located

3.2 Radiator drain plug

3.3 Cylinder block drain plug (arrowed)

on the rear of the cylinder block and can be reached from under the car on the driver's side. If it is necessary to jack up the car to gain access to this plug, observe all safety precautions described in *Safety first!* on page 14.
4   If the reason for draining is for other than renewal of the coolant, catch the coolant in a suitable container so that it can be used again.
5   Provided the coolant has been renewed at the specified intervals, there should be no need to flush the system, but simply refill with fresh mixture.
6   If the system has been neglected however, disconnect the radiator top hose and insert a cold water hose into the radiator pipe stub and let the water flow until it runs clear from the radiator and cylinder block outlets.
7   In severe cases, remove the radiator and reverse flush. If this fails, use a chemical cleaner, but strictly in accordance with the manufacturers instructions.
8   Once the system is clean, refit the drain plugs or reconnect the hoses.

3.11 Bleed screw

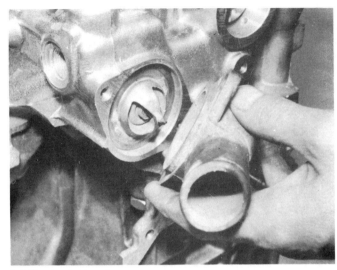
5.4 Thermostat housing cover

9   Open the bleed screw.
10 Release and then raise the expansion tank as high as possible and support it in this position with the help of an assistant or by tying it to the bonnet.
11 Fill the system slowly with coolant until it is ejected from the bleed screw, then close the bleed screw (photo).
12 Fit the cap to the expansion tank and then re-locate the tank.
13 Start and run the engine until the electric cooling fan operates. Open the bleed screw to release trapped air and close it as soon as coolant is ejected. Switch off the engine.
14 Allow the engine to cool and top up the expansion tank.

4   Coolant mixtures

1   Plain water should never be used in the cooling system.Apart from giving protection against freezing, an anti-freeze mixture protects the engine internal surfaces and components against corrosion. This is very important in an alloy engine.
2   Always use a top quality glycol-based antifreeze which is recommended for alloy engines.
3   Ideally a 50% mixture of antifreeze and soft or demineralised water should be used to maintain maximum protection against freezing and corrosion. On no account use less than 25% antifreeze.
4   Renew the coolant at the specified intervals as the inhibitors contained in the antifreeze gradually lose their effectiveness.
5   Even when operating in climates where antifreeze is not required, never use plain water, but add a corrosion inhibitor to it.

5   Thermostat – removal, testing and refitting

1   The thermostat housing is located on the cylinder head adjacent to the distributor.
2   Drain the cooling system as previously described.
3   Disconnect the radiator top hose from the thermostat housing.
4   Unscrew and remove the two thermostat housing cover bolts and remove the cover. This may need a little persuasion with a wooden or plastic-faced hammer (photo).
5   Remove the thermostat. If it is stuck, do not lever it out under its bridge piece, but cut around its edge with a sharp knife.
6   Clean off all the old gasket from the housing and cover faces, extract the rubber rings.
7   If the thermostat is suspected of being faulty, suspend it in a container of water which is being heated. Using a thermometer, check that the thermostat starts to open at the specified temperature and is fully open also at the specified temperature.

5.9 Thermostat

8   Remove the thermostat from the water and allow it to cool. The valve plate should close smoothly.
9   If the unit fails to operate as described or is stuck open or shut, renew it with one of similar temperature rating (photo).
10 Fit the thermostat using a new rubber ring on each side of it. Bolt on the cover using a new gasket.
11 Reconnect the coolant hose and refill and bleed the system as described in Section 3.

6   Radiator – removal, repair and refitting

1   Drain the cooling system as described in Section 3.
2   Release but do not remove, the fixing bolts for the spare wheel cradle. Withdraw the cradle from its grommets.
3   Disconnect the coolant hoses from the radiator.
4   Disconnect the radiator top mounting and earth straps, also the cooling fan and radiator thermostatic switch leads.
5   Lift the radiator complete with cooling fan and remove it from the engine compartment. There is very little room to manoeuvre so take care not to damage the radiator core. The base of the radiator

6.5 Removing radiator

incorporates locating spigots which are held in rubber grommets (photo).

6   If the radiator is leaking, a temporary cure will probably already have been tried by pouring a proprietary product into the system.

7   The radiator is of aluminium construction with plastic side tanks. Any repair must be left to specialists or a new or rebuilt radiator obtained.

8   Refitting is a reversal of removal, fill and bleed the system as described in Section 3.

7   Cooling fan and switch – removal and refitting

1   The electric cooling fan may be removed together with the radiator as described in the preceding Section and then separated. Alternatively it may be unbolted from the radiator and removed from the engine compartment independently.

2   The thermostatically controlled switch for the cooling fan is screwed into the radiator. Before this can be removed, the system must be drained and the switch leads disconnected (photo).

3   When refitting the switch, use a new sealing ring.

7.2 Fan switch in radiator

8   Coolant temperature switch and gauge, and coolant level switch

1   The coolant temperature switch is screwed into the cylinder head adjacent to the thermostat housing (photo).

2   It is difficult to test a temperature switch without special equipment and the best method to use if a fault develops is to substitute a new switch, but only after the wiring to the gauge has been thoroughly checked.

3   When refitting the switch, make sure that the seal is in good condition and do not overtighten it.

4   If the switch is changed and the gauge still does not register, then the gauge should be checked by a competent auto. electrician. Access to the gauge is obtained after removing the instrument panel as described in Chapter 10.

5   On later models, the radiator side tank incorporates a low level switch which actuates a warning lamp in the event of low coolant level in the system. The switch is float-operated.

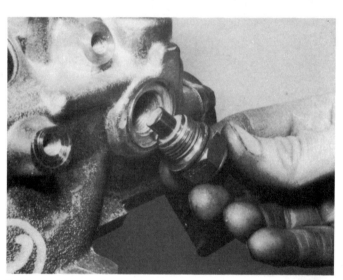

8.1 Coolant temperature switch

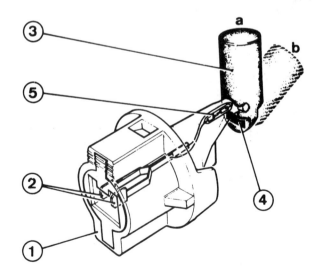

Fig. 2.1 Low coolant level switch (Sec 8)

1	Body	4	Magnet
2	Terminal	5	Reed contact
3	Float		

9 Drivebelt – tensioning, removal and refitting

1 The tension of the drivebelt should be maintained so that when it is depressed at the centre point of its longest run there is a deflection of 12.5 mm (0.5 in).
2 To adjust the tension, release the mounting and adjuster link bolts and prise the alternator away from the engine.
3 Tighten the adjuster link bolt and check the tension. Tighten the mounting bolts.
4 If the belt shows signs of fraying then it must be renewed immediately.
5 Release the adjuster link and mounting bolts and push the alternator in towards the engine. Slip the belt off the pulleys. If there is any difficulty in removing or refitting a belt over the pulley rim, turn the crankshaft pulley bolt with a spanner whilst pressing the belt over the pulley rim.
6 Tension the belt as described earlier.
7 When a new belt is fitted, check its tension again after ten minutes of engine running and re-adjust if necessary.

10 Coolant pump – removal and refitting

1 Drain the coolant as described in Section 3.
2 Remove the drivebelt as described in the preceding Section.
3 Disconnect the coolant hoses from the pump (photo).
4 Unscrew the three pump mounting bolts and remove the pump.
5 Any wear in the pump or leakage of coolant at the shaft gland will mean renewal of the pump, as repair is not possible.
6 Always renew the O-ring seal before fitting the pump to the cylinder block (photos).
7 Tighten the pump bolts to the specified torque.

11 Heating and ventilation system – description

1 The heater is located centrally under the facia and it supplies warm air for interior heating or windscreen demisting. Hot coolant is piped from the engine through a heater matrix and back to the engine when a manually operated valve mounted on the left side of the matrix

10.3 Coolant pump hoses

10.6A Coolant pump O-ring seal

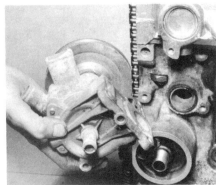
10.6B Fitting coolant pump

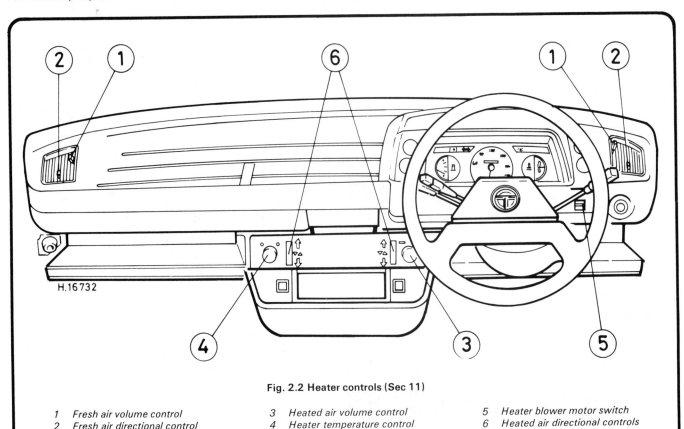

H.16732

Fig. 2.2 Heater controls (Sec 11)

1 Fresh air volume control
2 Fresh air directional control
3 Heated air volume control
4 Heater temperature control
5 Heater blower motor switch
6 Heated air directional controls

is opened. The valve is controlled by the left-hand knob on the heater control panel – blue spot, cold, and red spot, hot. With the car in motion, air is forced through the system when the right-hand knob on the control panel is turned clockwise. When the car is stopped, or when additional hot air is required, an electrically driven fan, located under the facia on the right-hand side, can be switched on to high or low speed.

2   Stale air from the car interior is exhausted through slots in the tailgate closure recess.

3   Normally the heater components give very little trouble and require negligible maintenance. An occasional check of the hoses and connections for condition and leaks is all that is usually required.

4   Fresh air inlets are located at the ends of the facia.

12 Heater – removal and refitting

1   Drain the cooling system as described in Section 3.

2   Disconnect the heater hoses at the engine compartment rear bulkhead.

3   Working inside the car, remove the cowl which surrounds the radio panel. This is held by four self-tapping screws and two nuts and bolts. Remove the heater control panel (photos).

4   Extract the self-tapping screws and remove the heater under cover (photo).

5   Reach up on either side of the heater and unscrew the mounting nuts.

6   Unscrew the nut which is located between the heater and the bulkhead.

7   Lower the heater carefully to the floor, taking care to prevent spilled coolant staining the carpet. Note the duct which runs between the heater casing and the blower motor under the facia (photo).

8   The coolant control valve is now accessible (photo). If the heater is to be dismantled for access to the matrix, prise off the clips and remove the screws which hold the casing sections together.

9   If the matrix is blocked, try reverse flushing it with a cold water hose. If this fails or if the matrix is leaking, renew it.

10   Reassembly and refitting are reversals of removal and dismantling, but when offering up the control panel make sure that the control rods for the coolant valve and air flap engage correctly (photo).

11   On completion, refill the cooling system.

12.3A Radio panel cowl bolt. Heater blower resistor (arrowed)

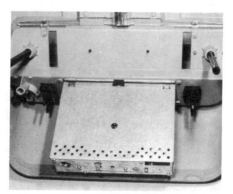

12.3B Reverse side of radio/heater control panel

12.4 Heater undercover removed

12.7 Heater blower motor location

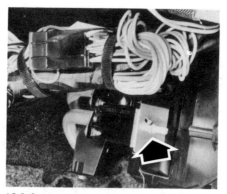

12.8 Coolant control valve for heater (arrowed)

12.10 Heater air direction control (arrowed)

13 Fault diagnosis – cooling system

Symptom	Reason(s)
Loss of coolant	Loose clips on hoses Hoses perished or leaking Radiator leaking Filler/pressure cap spring weak or seal ineffective Blown cylinder head gasket Cracked cylinder block or head
Overheating	Insufficient coolant in system Pump ineffective due to slack drivebelt Radiator blocked either internally or externally Kinked or collapsed hose causing coolant flow restriction Thermostat not working properly Engine out of tune Cylinder head gasket blown Engine not yet run-in Exhaust system partially blocked Engine oil level too low
Engine running too cool	Faulty, incorrect or missing thermostat

Chapter 3 Fuel system

For modifications, and information applicable to later models, see Supplement at end of manual

Contents

Specifications

System type .... Rear mounted fuel tank, mechanical fuel pump, single or twin venturi carburettor

Fuel tank capacity .... 40.0 litres, 8.8 gallons

Fuel octane rating (RON)
954 cc engine (up to Aug 83) .... 92 (2 star)
954 cc (Sept 83 on), 1124 and 1360 cc engines .... 98 (4 star)

Carburettor
Type .... Fixed jet, downdraught
Application:
    954 cc engine (XV5) .... Solex 32 PBISA-11 manual choke
    954 cc engine (XV8) .... Solex 32 PBISA-12 manual choke
    1124 cc engine (XW7) .... Solex 32 PBISA-12 manual choke
    1360 cc engine (XY6B) .... Solex 32.35 TACIV automatic choke
    1360 cc engine (XY8) .... Twin Solex 35 PBISA 8

Calibrations and settings

	32 PBISA-11 (XV5)	32 PBISA-12 (XW7)	32.35 TACIC Primary	32.35 TACIC Secondary	35 PBISA-8
Choke	24	25	24	24	28
Main jet	120/125	120/130	115/125	122.5/127.5	135/155
Air correction jet	175/195	165/195	165/185	170/190	165/185
Fuel enrichment	–	45/75	–	–	
Econostat	55/75	–	–	–	
Fuel idle jet	35/45	37/47	33/43	45/55	41/52
Idle air jet	–	165/195	–	–	
Progression	–	0.6 x 4.5	–	–	
Accelerator pump jet	35/45	30/40	40/50	35/45	30/50
Accelerator pump stroke (valve plate gap)	3.0 mm	2.4 mm	–	–	
Fuel inlet needle valve	1.5 mm	1.6 mm	1.5 mm	1.5 mm	1.5 mm
Float weight	5.7 g	5.7 g	–	–	5.7 g
Float setting	36.5 mm	18.0 to 22.0 mm	41.0 mm	41.0 mm	non-adjustable
Fast idle gap	1.0 mm	1.0 mm			
Constant CO jet	25/35	–	25/35	–	
Idle speed (rev/min)	900/950	650/750	900/950	–	950/1000
CO percentage in exhaust gas	1.5 to 2.5	1 to 2	1.5 to 2.5	1.5 to 2.5	1.5 to 2.5

Torque wrench settings

	Nm	lbf ft
Exhaust manifold nuts and bolts	20	15
Inlet manifold bolts	18	13
Carburettor nuts	18	13
Fuel pump bolts	18	13
Exhaust downpipe to manifold nuts	20	15

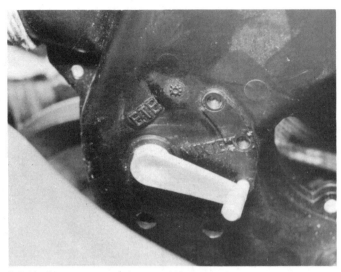
1.4 Air cleaner summer/winter position lever

1 Description and maintenance

1 The fuel system consists of a rear mounted fuel tank, a mechanical fuel pump operated by an eccentric cam on the camshaft and a single or dual venturi carburettor, depending upon vehicle model.
2 The air cleaner is of renewable element type with winter and summer setting positions.
3 Maintenance consists of adjusting the carburettor, cleaning the fuel pump and renewing the air cleaner element at the intervals specified in Routine Maintenance at the front of this Manual.
4 The air cleaner to carburettor duct has a deflector lever and valve with winter and summer positions. In summer, cold air is drawn from a spout under the air cleaner body. In winter warm air is drawn from the heater box which surrounds the exhaust manifold (photo).

2 Air cleaner – element renewal

1 Unscrew the knurled screw on the air cleaner casing end-face.
2 Withdraw the end cover with element (photo).
3 Discard the element and wipe the casing interior clean.
4 Fit the new element and the cover, tighten the knurled screw.

3 Air cleaner – removal and refitting

1 Disconnect the hoses from the air cleaner casing and release the ducting clip (photo).
2 Unscrew and remove the single casing bolt and withdraw the air cleaner casing by pulling its locating spigots from its grommets (photos).
3 Refitting is a reversal of removal.

4 Fuel pump – cleaning

1 The fuel pump may be one of several types. On one type, the filter cover is simply unbolted and removed. On another, the pump cover is removed (two screws), and with some pumps, the fuel outlet hose must be removed in order to be able to withdraw the pump cover. Inspection will determine (photo).
2 With the cover removed, take out the filter screen and wash it in fuel until it is free from fluff and dirt (photo).
3 Mop out the fuel from the pump body and wipe out any sediment.
4 Refit the filter screen and cover making sure that the gasket is in good condition.

2.2 Withdrawing air cleaner element

3.1 Air cleaner ducting clip

3.2A Air cleaner casing bolt

3.2B Removing air cleaner casing

4.1 Fuel pump cover

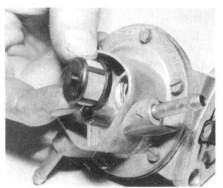
4.2 Fuel pump filter

5 Fuel pump – removal, overhaul and refitting

1   Disconnect the fuel hoses from the pump. Plug the inlet hose.
2   Unscrew the pump mounting bolts and lift the pump away (photo).
3   An insulator block with a gasket in each side is fitted between the pump flange and the cylinder head. New gaskets should be used at refitting.
4   Once the pump is removed, the pushrod may be withdrawn (photo).
5   If the pump is to be dismantled, remove the cover, gasket and filter screen.
6   Scribe a mark across the edges of the upper and lower body flanges and extract the flange screws.
7   Remove the upper body.
8   Drive out the operating arm pivot pin, withdraw the arm and lift out the diaphragm.
9   Obtain a repair kit which will contain a new diaphragm and the necessary gaskets.
10 If the valves are damaged, reassemble the pump and obtain a new one complete.
11 If the valves are in good condition, locate the diaphragm, push the operating arm into position so that its forked end engages with the groove in the end of the diaphragm rod, with the coil springs in position.

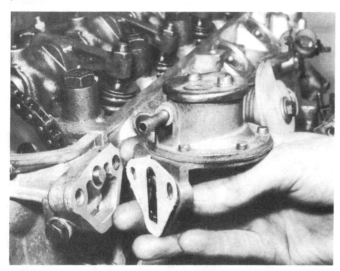

5.2 Fuel pump removed

5.4 Fuel pump pushrod

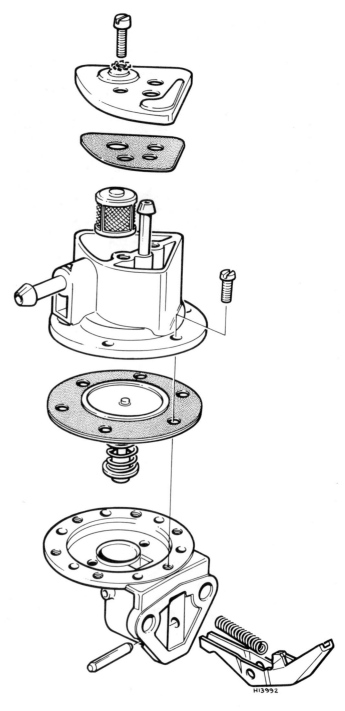

Fig. 3.1A Exploded view of typical fuel pump (Sec 5)

12 Fit the pivot pin and stake around the holes to secure both ends of the pin.
13 Fit the upper body so that the alignment marks are opposite and then fit the screws and tighten evenly.
14 Fit the filter screen and cover with gasket.
15 Refitting to the cylinder head is a reversal of removal.

6 Fuel level transmitter – removal and refitting

1   Disconnect the battery earth lead.
2   Open the tailgate and remove the floor covering from the luggage area.

3   Remove the circular plastic cover to expose the fuel level transmitter.
4   Disconnect the electrical lead.
5   Using a suitable tool unscrew the transmitter mounting plate to release it from the securing tabs.
6   Withdraw the transmitter unit taking care not to damage the float as it passes through the hole in the tank.
7   Refitting is a reversal of removal, but use a new sealing ring if there is any doubt about the condition of the original one.

7   Fuel tank – removal, repair and refitting

1   As a drain plug is not fitted, the tank must be syphoned empty of fuel using a length of plastic or rubber tubing.
2   Disconnect the filler pipe, breather and supply hoses (photo).
3   Remove the bolt from the triangular-shaped support bracket first and then unscrew the remaining flange mounting bolts (photo).
4   Lower the tank and disconnect the leads from the fuel level transmitter unit.
5   If the tank is leaking or badly rusted, leave repair to a specialist. *On no account attempt to solder or weld a fuel tank as it requires a great deal of purging before every trace of explosive vapour is removed.*

6   If the tank contains sediment, pour in some paraffin, remove the fuel level transmitter and shake the tank vigorously. Repeat as necessary and finally rinse out with clean fuel.
7   Refitting is a reversal of removal.

8   Carburettors – description

1   A Solex carburettor is fitted to all models, but the type will differ according to engine capacity. Refer to the Specifications for application details.
2   All carburettors are of fixed jet design with either a manual or automatic choke.

9   Carburettor – idle speed and mixture adjustment

Solex 32 PBISA–11
1   Normally, the only adjustment required is to set the idle speed to the specified level with the engine at normal operating temperature.
2   For accurate results, a tachometer must be connected to the engine.

7.2 Fuel tank filler and breather pipe connections

7.3 Fuel tank support bracket

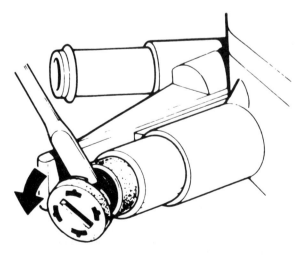

Fig. 3.1B Breaking off plastic cap covering mixture screw (Solex 32 PBISA-11 tamperproof carburettor) (Sec 9)

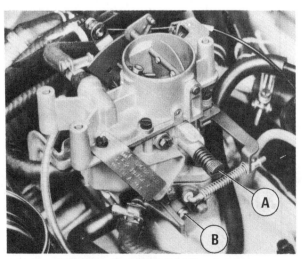

Fig. 3.1C Solex 32 PBISA-11 adjusting screws

A   Volume screw
B   Mixture screw

3   Turn the volume screw (A) as necessary to obtain the specified idle speed (Fig. 3.1C).

4   If the carburettor has been overhauled or the mixture setting no longer provides immediate cold starting or smooth even idling, then the tamperproof cap must be broken off the mixture screw (B).

5   With the engine at normal operating temperature and idling at specified speed, turn the mixture screw out until the maximum idle speed is obtained. Now turn the screw in until the engine speed just starts to fall. Readjust the idle speed to the specified level using the volume screw.

Solex 32 PBISA-12

6   This carburettor does not have a constant CO circuit and in consequence the idle speed is set by turning the throttle speed screw which adjusts the position of the throttle valve plate. Otherwise the procedure is as described in paragraphs 1 to 5 (photos).

9.6A Throttle speed screw (Solex 32 PBISA-12)

9.6B Mixture screw with tamperproof cap (Solex 32 PBISA-12)

Solex 32.35 TACIC

7   The adjustments are carried out in a similar way to those described for the 32 PBISA-11 carburettor.

8   On completion of the adjustment, switch off the engine, remove the tachometer and fit a new tamperproof cap to the mixture screw (Fig. 3.2).

Fig. 3.2 Solex 32.35 TACIC carburettor adjustment screws (Sec 9)

W   Mixture screw   Va   Volume screw

Twin Solex 35 PBISA-8

Synchronising

9   Have the engine at working temperature with the air cleaner removed.

10 Turn the mixture screws (1) and (2) in until they lightly seat and then unscrew them four complete turns (Fig. 3.2A).

11 With the engine running, set the idle speed screw (3) until the speed is 1000 rev/min.

Using a vacuum gauge

12 Disconnect the pipes (4) and (5) and connect the gauge at (a).

13 Turn the screw (3) to obtain a reading on the gauge of 100 mm Hg (150 m bar).

14 Transfer the gauge to (b). If the reading is not as previously recorded, turn the screw (6) in or out until it is.

15 Blip the throttle once or twice and check that both vacuum readings are as previously indicated.

Using a synchroniser

16 These are available at most motor stores and should be used as directed by the manufacturers.

17 These instruments are basically air flow meters and should show identical readings when moved from one venturi to the other. Adjust where necessary by turning screws (3) and (6).

18 Whichever method is used, check and adjust the mixture on completion.

Idle speed and mixture

19 Have the engine at normal operating temperature.

20 Disconnect the twin wiring plug from the rear face of the alternator.

21 Turn the mixture screws (1) and (2) in until they lightly seat and then unscrew them four complete turns.

Without using an exhaust gas analyser

22 Obtain the highest idle speed by turning the mixture screws (1) and (2) by equal amounts.

23 Re-set the idle speed to 1000 rev/min by means of screw (3).

24 Repeat the operations with screws (1) and (2) and then reset once again by using screw (3).

25 With the engine idling, at 1000 rev/min reduce its speed by screwing in screws (1) and (2) equally until the engine speed drops to the specified setting.

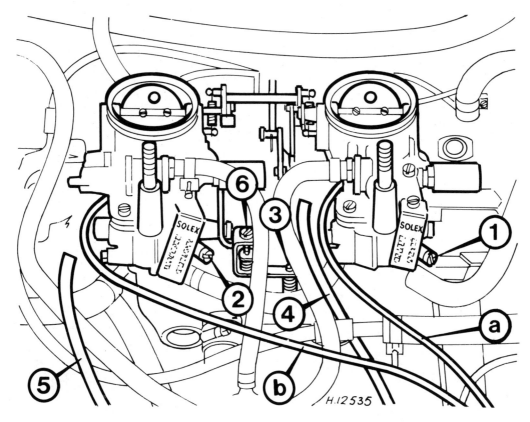

Fig. 3.2A Twin Solex 35 PBISA-8 carburettors (Sec 9)

| 1 | Mixture screw | 3 | Idle speed screw | 5 | Disconnected vacuum pipe | (a) | Vacuum gauge connection |
| 2 | Mixture screw | 4 | Disconnected vacuum pipe | 6 | Synchronising screw | (b) | Vacuum gauge connection |

With an exhaust gas analyser

26 Set the idle speed to 950 rev/min by means of the throttle stop screw (3).

27 Turn the mixture screws (1) and (2) until the CO level is as specified.

28 Re-set the idle speed to specified level using screw (3).

29 Reconnect the alternator wiring plug and where originally fitted, fit new tamperproof caps to screws (1) and (2).

10 Carburettor (Solex 32 PBISA) – in car adjustments

Float level adjustment

1 Remove the spare wheel and carburettor air intake then remove the top cover from the carburettor, hold the cover vertically with the float hanging down, depressing the fuel inlet valve needle under its own weight.

2 Now measure between the carburettor flange and the highest point on the bottom of the float. The gasket should be in position on the flange. Check the dimension against that specified.

3 If adjustment is required, use the method appropriate to the particular carburettor, described in the following paragraphs.

4 On 32 PBISA – 11 carburettors, the level of the fuel in the float chamber is altered by varying the thickness of the aluminium washer under the fuel inlet needle valve.

5 On 32 PBISA-12 units, adjustment is made by bending the tab which bears on the needle valve.

11 Carburettor (Solex 32.35 TACIC) – in car adjustments

Float level

1 Remove the spare wheel and the air intake duct from the top of the carburettor.

2 Extract the screws and carefully lift the top cover from the carburettor body.

3 Invert the top cover. Using a gauge made up to the dimensions shown in Fig. 3.3 check the float height. The gasket should be in position on the flange when the gauge is used.

4 If the float setting is not as specified, bend the float tab which bears against the needle valve.

5 When refitting the top cover make sure that the progression circuit O-ring seal is in position and the cover gasket is in good condition.

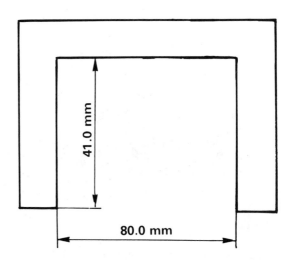

Fig. 3.3 Float setting gauge (Solex 32.35 TACIC) (Sec 11)

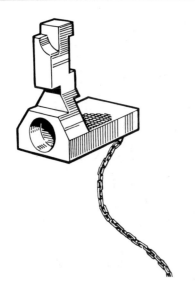

Fig. 3.4 Special automatic choke gauge (8.0143) for Solex 32.35
TACIC carburettor (Sec 11)

Fig. 3.5 Checking choke opening with special tool (Solex 32.35
TACIC carburettor) (Sec 11)

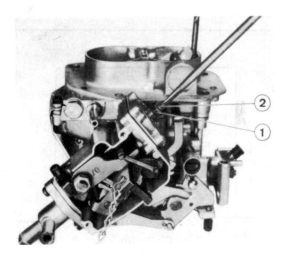

Fig. 3.6 Adjusting choke opening (Solex 32.35 TACIC carburettor)
(Sec 11)

1   Locknut   2   Adjuster screw

Choke opening
6   A special gauge will be required for this (8.0143) obtainable from
your Peugeot Talbot dealer.
7   Run the engine until the radiator fan cuts-in.
8   Remove the air intake duct from the carburettor.
9   Remove the cover from the automatic choke housing.
10 With the engine idling place the hole in the special gauge over the
moving roller within the choke housing.
11 Tilt the gauge to bring it in contact with the carburettor body.
12 Now check that the choke valve plate is open so that a 5.0 mm
diameter rod will pass between the edge of the plate and the wall of
the top cover.
13 Where necessary, adjust by releasing the locknut (1) and turning
the screw (2). Fig. 3.6.

Positive throttle opening
14 Have the engine idling with the air intake duct and automatic
choke housing cover removed.
15 Turn the screw (1) Fig. 3.7 until the clearance (X) is 2.0 mm. If
necessary prevent the nut from turning by placing a blade in its slot.
16 Place the special gauge (8.0143) on the automatic choke housing
(Fig. 3.8).

Fig. 3.7 Adjusting position of automatic choke moving roller
(Solex 32.35 TACIC carburettor) (Sec 11)

1   Screw   X   2.0 mm
2   Slot in nut

Fig. 3.8 Roller entering slot in special gauge (Solex 32.35 TACIC
carburettor) (Sec 11)

17 Tighten the screw (1) (Fig. 3.7) until the roller just enters the slot in the gauge. Now turn the screw in one full turn.

18 Disconnect the spring (3) (Fig. 3.9), push the lever up as far as it will go and observe whether the engine speed increases to between 3250 and 3350 rev/min registered on a tachometer. Adjust if necessary by turning screw (1) in or out. Remove the gauge.

19 Refit the automatic choke housing cover, the air intake duct and spare wheel.

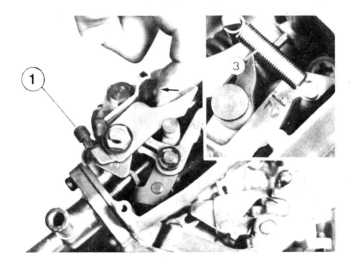

Fig. 3.9 Checking fast idle speed (Solex 32.35 TACIC carburettor) (Sec 11)

1   Adjustment screw   3   Spring

12 Carburettor(s) – removal and refitting

1   Extract the three screws and remove the air intake duct from the top of the carburettor(s) (photo).

2   Remove the short hose which runs between the oil filler cap and the carburettor(s).

3   Disconnect the distributor vacuum hose(s) from the carburettor(s).

4   Disconnect the fuel intake hose from the carburettor(s).

5   Disconnect the balljointed throttle control rod from the carburettor(s) (photo).

6   On cars with a manual choke, disconnect the cable from the carburettor(s).

7   Disconnect the coolant hoses from carburettor(s). Tie them up to avoid coolant loss.

8   Unscrew the fixing nuts and lift the carburettor(s) from the inlet manifold.

9   Refitting is a reversal of removal, but use a new flange gasket(s) and bleed the cooling system as described in Chapter 2.

13 Carburettor(s) – overhaul

1   The need for full carburettor(s) overhaul seldom arises. Normal servicing should be limited to removing the carburettor fuel bowl drain plug(s) (where fitted) and draining any sediment or water. Also disconnect the fuel inlet hose, unscrew the pipe stub, take out the cylindrical filter mesh and clean it. Finally, lubricate the spindles and pivots and other moving parts with light oil (photos). The idle jet on 32 PBISA type carburettors is externally removable for cleaning.

2   Where more extensive servicing is required due to symptoms of blocked jets, extract the screws and remove the top cover (photo).

3   Mop out the sediment from the float chamber and then remove the various jets and bleed screws. Clean them by blowing through them, never probe with wire as this will ruin their calibration.

12.1 Carburettor air intake duct

12.5 Carburettor throttle control rod

13.1A Solex 32 PBISA-12 showing fuel bowl drain plug

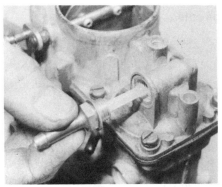

13.1B Fuel inlet filter

13.2 Removing Solex 32 PBISA-12 top cover

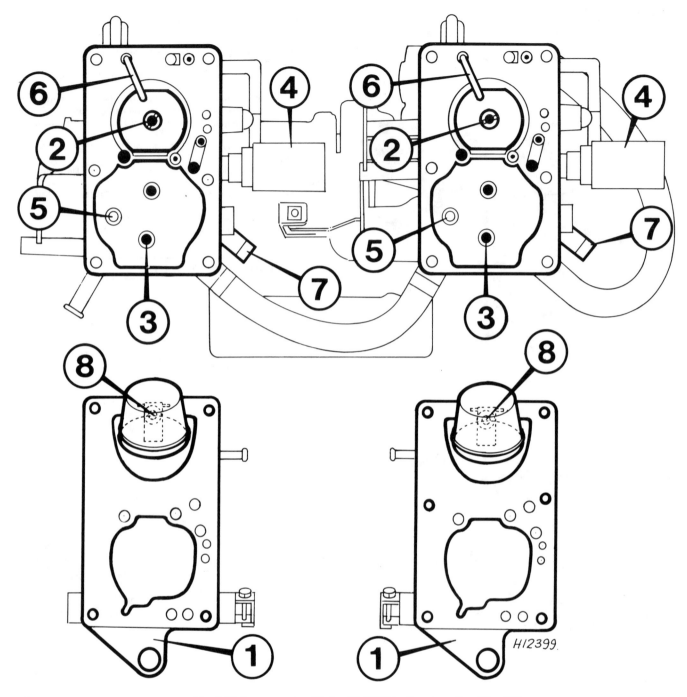

Fig. 3.10 Components of Solex 35 PBISA – 8 carburettors (Sec 13)

1	Top covers	3	Main jets	5 Accelerator pump valves 7 Mixture screws
2	Air correction jets	4	Idle fuel jets	6 Accelerator pump injectors 8 Fuel inlet needle valves

4   The fuel inlet needle valve can be unscrewed once the float pivot pin has been driven out and the float removed.

5   Always obtain the appropriate repair kit for your carburettor. These are usually available in two forms. The basic kit is inexpensive and contains simply new gaskets, seals and small renewable items. The more comprehensive kit is usually very expensive and may contain new jets, needle valve and float, many items not normally being required for a carburettor in reasonable condition.

6   If the carburettor is so worn that the valve plate spindle bushes are worn and other movable components are in need of replacement, then it will be found more economical to obtain a new or factory reconditioned unit rather than attempt to renew individual items.

7   As the carburettor is reassembled, carry out the following checks and adjustments.

Float level – see Sections 10 and 11

Accelerator pump stroke (Solex 32 PBISA)

8   Open the throttle valve plate and insert a twist drill of specified diameter (see Specifications) between the edge of the plate and the venturi wall.

9   Now adjust the position of the nut on the accelerator pump rod so that the nut just makes contact with the lever.

10 Remove the twist drill.

Fast idle gap (Solex 32 PBISA)

11 The small fast idle screw is fitted with a tamperproof clip which must be removed before adjustment can be carried out.
12 With the choke cam plate fully actuated to close the choke valve plate, the throttle valve plate should be open just enough to permit a 1.0 mm diameter twist drill to pass between the edge of the plate and the venturi wall.
13 Adjust if necessary by turning the fast idle screw.

14 Throttle and choke control cables – removal and refitting

1 The throttle cable is connected to a spring-loaded reel which pivots on the face of the cylinder head. The reel then operates the throttle lever on the carburettor through a plastic balljointed control rod (photo).
2 Slacken the outer cable adjuster so that both the inner and outer cables can be detached at the carburettor end.
3 Working inside the car, pull the tubular end fitting sleeve towards you to compress the coil spring inside the sleeve and then slide the sleeve off the cranked end of the accelerator pedal rod (photo).
4 Withdraw the throttle cable through the bulkhead grommet.
5 Fit the new cable by reversing the removal operations, then adjust the cable by means of the threaded end fitting to remove all but the slightest amount of slackness.
6 Check that full throttle can be obtained with the accelerator pedal fully depressed.

Choke cable (32 PBISA)

7 Unscrew the pinch-bolt and slip the outer cable from its clamp bracket at the carburettor (photo).
8 Disconnect the inner cable from its swivel on the choke cam plate.
9 Working inside the car, unscrew and remove the choke control knob (photo).
10 Unscrew the bezel nut, lower the control end fitting and disconnect the warning lamp cable (photo).
11 Withdraw the cable assembly into the car interior.

14.1 Typical carburettor connections

12 Refitting is a reversal of removal, but adjust the cable at the carburettor end so that when the control knob is pushed fully in, the choke valve plate is fully open.

15 Manifolds and exhaust system

1 The inlet and exhaust manifolds are located on opposite sides of the cylinder head.
2 The exhaust manifold is simply bolted into position with separate flange gaskets for each port (photos).

14.3 Throttle cable connection at accelerator pedal

14.7 Choke cable connections at carburettor

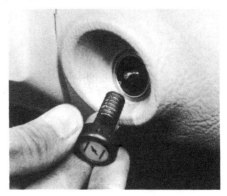
14.9 Removing choke control knob

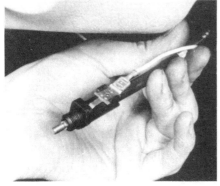
14.10 Choke control showing warning lamp connection

15.2A Exhaust manifold gaskets

15.2B Locating exhaust manifold

3   The inlet manifold has coolant connections and before it can be removed, the cooling system should be at least partially drained to avoid any coolant running into the cylinder bores as the manifold is removed (photos).

4   The exhaust system is in two sections with twin downpipes. The mountings are of flexible type and a safety cable is used to support the system should the forward end fracture (photos).

5   Even if only one section of the system is to be renewed, it is recommended that the complete assembly is removed from under the car.

6   Unscrew the centre connecting sockets and separate the front pipe from the rear sections.

7   When fitting the sections together, do not tighten the socket clamps until the system has been refitted and its alignment checked to ensure that no part of the pipe or silencers are likely to knock against adjacent body or suspension components.

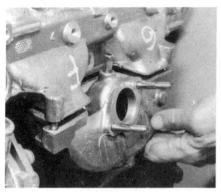
15.3A Fitting inlet manifold

15.3B Inlet manifold coolant connections

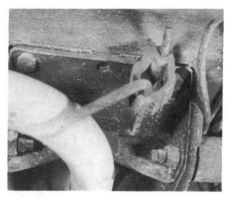
15.4A Exhaust mounting

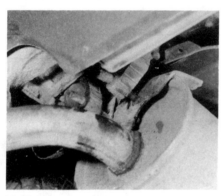
15.4B Silencer mounting

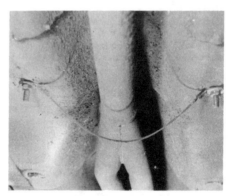
15.4C Exhaust system safety cable

16 Fault diagnosis – fuel system

Unsatisfactory engine performance and excessive fuel consumption are not necessarily the fault of the fuel system or carburettor. In fact they more commonly occur as a result of ignition and timing faults. Before acting on the following it is necessary to check the ignition system first. Even though a fault may lie in the fuel system it will be difficult to trace unless the ignition is correct. The faults below, therefore, assume that this has been attended to first (where appropriate).

Symptom	Reason(s)
Smell of petrol when engine is stopped	Leaking fuel lines or unions Leaking fuel tank
Smell of petrol when engine is idling	Leaking fuel line unions between pump and carburettor(s) Overflow of fuel from fuel chamber due to wrong level setting(s), ineffective needle valve(s)
Excessive fuel consumption for reasons not covered by leaks or float chamber faults	Worn jets Over-rich setting Sticking mechanism Dirty air cleaner element
Difficult starting, uneven running, lack of power, cutting out	One or more jets blocked or restricted Float chamber fuel level(s) too low or needle valve(s) sticking Fuel pump not delivering sufficient fuel Induction leak
Difficult starting when cold	Choke control or automatic choke maladjusted Insufficient use of manual choke Automatic choke not cocked before starting Weak mixture
Difficult starting when hot	Excessive use of manual choke, or automatic choke malfunction Accelerator pedal pumped before starting Vapour lock (especially in hot weather or at high altitude) Over rich mixture
Engine does not respond properly to throttle	Faulty accelerator pump(s) Blocked jet(s) Slack in accelerator cable
Engine idle speed drops when hot	Overheated fuel pump
Engine runs on	Weak mixture Idle speed too high
Engine cuts out at idle speed	Idle jet(s) blocked

Chapter 4 Ignition system

For modifications, and information applicable to later models, see Supplement at end of manual

Contents

Specifications

System type
954 cc (to Aug 1983) .... Mechanical breaker distributor
Later 954 cc and all 1124 cc and 1360 cc .... Electronic (breakerless) system

Distributor
Make .... Ducellier and Bosch
Rotor rotation .... Anti-clockwise
Firing order .... 1 - 3 - 4 - 2 (No. 1 at flywheel end)
Contact points gap (mechanical breaker) .... 0.4 mm (0.016 in)
Dwell angle (mechanical breaker) .... 60–66°

Ignition timing
Engine type

954 cc (XV5) ....
954 cc (XV8) ....
1124 cc (XW7) ....
1360 cc (XY6B) ....
1360 cc (XY8)
  1983 ....
  1984 on ....

Vacuum pipe disconnected and plugged

Distributor curve	Static	Dynamic*
M119	5° BTDC	5° BTDC at 900/950 rev/min
M160E	6° BTDC	6° BTDC at 900/950 rev/min
M146E	6° BTDC	6° BTDC at 650/750 rev/min
M122E	10° BTDC	10° BTDC at 900/950 rev/min
M152E	0° BTDC	0° BTDC at 900/950 rev/min
M159E	7-9° BTDC	7-9° BTDC at 850/900 rev/min

Spark plugs
Type .... Champion BN9Y, AC 42LTS
Electrode gap .... 0.6 mm (0.025 in)

Torque wrench settings

	Nm	lbf ft
Spark plug	15 to 20	11 to 15
Timing plate bolt	7	5
Timing rod plug	27	20

1 General description

The ignition system on the early 954 cc engine is of mechanical contact breaker type, whilst on all other engines an electronic, breakerless system is used.

Mechanical breaker system

In order that the engine may run correctly it is necessary for an electrical spark to ignite the fuel/air mixture in the combustion chamber at exactly the right moment in relation to engine speed and load.

Basically the ignition system functions as follows. Low tension voltage from the battery is fed to the ignition coil, where it is converted into high tension voltage. The high tension voltage is powerful enough to jump the spark plug gap in the cylinder many times a second under high compression pressure, providing that the ignition system is in good working order and that all adjustments are correct.

The ignition system consists of two individual circuits known as the low tension (LT) circuit and high tension (HT) circuit.

The low tension circuit (sometimes known as the primary circuit) comprises the battery, lead to ignition switch, lead to the low tension or primary coil windings and the lead from the low tension coil windings to the contact breaker points and condenser in the distributor.

The high tension circuit (sometimes known as the secondary circuit) consists of the high tension or secondary coil winding, the heavily insulated ignition lead from the centre of the coil to the centre of the distributor cap, the rotor arm, the spark plug leads and the spark plugs.

The complete ignition system operation is as follows. Low tension voltage from the battery is changed within the ignition coil to high tension voltage by the opening and closing of the contact breaker points in the low tension circuit. High tension voltage is then fed, via a contact in the centre of the distributor cap, to the rotor arm of the distributor. The rotor arm revolves inside the distributor cap, and each time it comes in line with one of the four metal segments in the cap, these being connected to the spark plug leads, the high tension voltage jumps the gap from the rotor arm to the appropriate metal segment and so, via the spark plug lead, to the spark plug where it finally jumps the gap between the two spark plug electrodes, one being earthed.

The ignition timing is advanced and retarded automatically to ensure the spark occurs at just the right instant for the particular load and prevailing engine speed.

The ignition advance is controlled both mechanically and by a vacuum operated system. The mechanical governor mechanism consists of two weights which move out under centrifugal force from the central distributor shaft as the engine speed rises. As they move outwards they rotate the cam relative to the distributor shaft, and so advance the spark. The weights are held in position by two light springs, and it is the tension of these springs which is largely responsible for correct spark advancement.

The vacuum control consists of a diaphragm, one side of which is connected, via a small bore tube, to the inlet manifold, and the other side, via a link rod, to the contact breaker baseplate. Depression in the induction manifold and carburettor, which varies with engine speed and throttle opening, causes the diaphragm to move so moving the contact breaker plate and advancing or retarding the spark.

The timing marks on this engine differ from established practice in that they refer to No 2 and No 3 cylinders, not to No 1.

Electronic (breakerless) system

The main difference between this system and a mechanical breaker type is that a magnetic pick-up device is used in the distributor to interrupt the low tension circuit entirely without any mechanical contact. The function of the system is otherwise similar.

Diagnostic socket

The diagnostic socket is only of use to a dealer or service station having suitable monitoring equipment which can be plugged in to assist engine tuning and checking.

2 Maintenance

Mechanical breaker ignition
1   At the intervals specified in Routine Maintenance, check, clean or renew the contact breaker points (Section 3).
2   Also at the specified intervals, clean and re-gap the spark plugs or renew them (Section 12) and check the dwell angle and ignition timing (Sections 5 and 6).

Electronic ignition
3   This system is virtually maintenance-free except for checking the ignition timing and attention to the spark plugs at the specified service intervals.

3 Contact breaker points adjustment using feeler gauges

Checking the contact breaker points for serviceability and the correct gap in situ is extremely difficult, as access to the points is severely restricted. This is due to the distributor being fitted in a horizontal position on the left-hand end of the cylinder head.

However, with dexterity, and the use of a mirror, the task can be undertaken satisfactorily although, ideally, if the points are suspect, they should be removed for closer examination. This can only be done after the distributor has been removed.

Those readers who wish to ease the task of checking the contact breaker points by removing the distributor should follow the sequence given in Section 7, paras 1 to 5, otherwise the procedure is as follows.
1   Release the distributor cap retaining clips and withdraw the cap, at the same time releasing the HT leads from the clip above the distributor (if fitted). Position the cap to one side together with its weatherproof cover (if fitted). Disconnect the HT leads from the spark plugs and coil if necessary.
2   Remove the rotor arm and dust shield.
3   Prise open the points using the tip of a screwdriver and examine the condition of the point faces. If they are burnt, pitted or worn, it will be necessary to remove them for cleaning or renewal (see Section 5). Badly pitted points may be due to a poor earth (battery or engine earth lead), or a faulty condenser.
4   Presuming the points are satisfactory, or that they have been cleaned or renewed, prepare the points gap for measuring by turning the engine over, using a spanner on the crankshaft nut, or by turning the distributor driveshaft, if removed from engine, until the contact breaker arm is on the peak of one of the four cam lobes. Use the mirror mentioned earlier to confirm this if distributor is still fitted.
5   Insert a feeler gauge of the specified thickness between the point faces where the feeler gauge should be a sliding fit. If the points gap requires adjustment, follow the procedure given in the following paragraph for the particular type of distributor fitted.
6   Using a 7 mm open-ended or ring spanner on the adjusting nut (Ducellier), or a 3 mm Allen key inserted through the hole in the plug engaged with the adjuster (Paris-Rhône), adjust the points to achieve the specified gap. Recheck points gap after adjustment.
7   Refit the distributor, if removed, by following the sequence in Section 7, paragraphs 6 to 10.
8   Refit the dust shield, rotor arm and distributor cap, and also ensure that all HT leads are reconnected correctly.
9   This method of adjustment should be regarded as an initial setting only in order that the engine can be started. The dwell angle should now be checked and adjusted as described in the following Section.

4 Contact breaker points adjustment using a dwell meter

1   The adjustment of the contact breaker points gap using feeler gauges should be regarded as an initial setting only. For optimum engine performance the contact breaker points should be checked using a dwell meter.
2   The dwell angle is the number of degrees through which the distributor cam turns during the period the contact breaker points are closed, and can only be checked using a dwell meter with the engine running.
3   The dwell meter should be connected according to the manufacturer's instructions and the contact breaker points adjusted, to obtain the specified dwell angle, following the relevant procedure given in Section 3, paragraph 5 for the type of distributor fitted. If the dwell angle is too large, increase the points gap, or if it is too small, reduce it.
4   The dwell angle should always be checked, or adjusted, before carrying out an ignition timing check.

5 Contact breaker points – renewal

There are two types of mechanical breaker distributor available, both fitted with an external adjustment for the contact breaker points. Because of the difficulty involved in renewing the points in situ it is necessary to remove the distributor to perform this task. Refer to Section 7 and follow the relevant paragraphs for removing the distributor. Where the dismantling procedure differs, due to the different type of distributor fitted, a separate sub-section is given, otherwise the procedures given under the headings All models is to be followed.

All models
1   Withdraw the rotor arm and dust shield.
2   Unscrew and remove the bearing carrier securing screws.
3   Extract the circlip from above the bearing carrier and remove the bearing carrier.

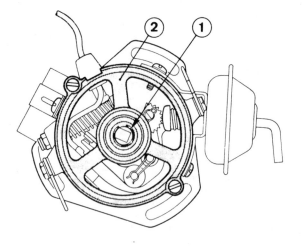

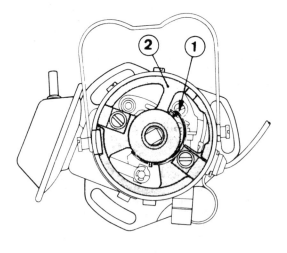

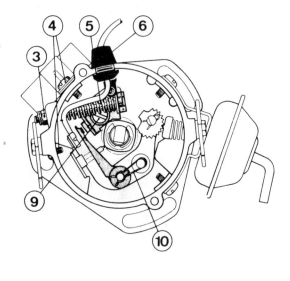

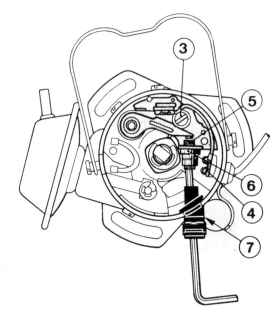

Fig. 4.2 The Paris-Rhône externally adjustable distributor (Sec 5)

1	Anti-vibration clip	5	Adjuster contact
2	Bearing carrier	6	Adjuster support
3	Retaining screw	7	Plug
4	Spring clip		

Ducellier distributor

4   Referring to Fig. 4.1, unscrew and remove the adjustment nut (3) and the two screws (4). Withdraw the adjustment rod (5) and its spring. Slide the grommet (6) from its location in the distributor body flange and remove the blanking plug (7). Remove the retaining clip (8) noting that the hole is fitted uppermost. Undo and remove the fixed contact retaining screw (9) and remove the fixed contact. Remove the long spring clip (10), taking care not to lose it, and withdraw the moving contact.

Note: *the setting of the serrated cam at the end of the vacuum capsule link rod must not be altered, otherwise the advance characteristics of the distributor will be disturbed.*

Paris-Rhône distributor

5   Referring to Fig. 4.2, undo and remove the contact breaker retaining screw (3), disconnect the spring clip (4) and remove the contact breaker assembly. Note the fitted position of the adjuster (5) and its holder (6).

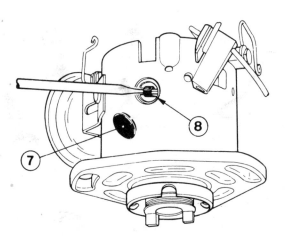

Fig. 4.1 The Ducellier externally adjustable distributor (Sec 5)

1	Driveshaft circlip	6	Cable grommet
2	Bearing carrier	7	Plug
3	Adjusting nut	8	Retaining lug
4	Screws	9	Retaining screw
5	Spring and adjusting rod		

All models

6 Refitting the contact breaker points is a reversal of the relevant removal procedure, noting the following points.

 a) Clean the contact breaker point faces using methylated spirit and lightly grease the pivot post
 b) Apply a smear of grease to the peak of each cam

7 Refit the bearing carrier, bearing carrier circlip and the two retaining screws, tightening securely.

8 Adjust the contact breaker gap, described in Section 3, before refitting the dust shield and rotor arm.

9 Refit the distributor following the procedure given in Section 7.

10 Check the dwell angle as described in Section 4.

6 Ignition timing

Mechanical breaker distributor

1 It will be necessary to time the ignition in instances where the distributor has been removed, or if an adjustment has been made to the dwell angle.

2 It should be established, before the ignition timing is checked, that the spark plug gaps, valve clearances and dwell angle are correctly adjusted according to the specifications.

Initial advance setting

3 To set the initial advance (static timing), first remove the plastic cover from the flywheel cover (see Fig. 4.3) and rotate the engine to align the TDC mark on the rim of the flywheel with the O-mark on the timing plate. Pistons No 2 and 3 are now at TDC. If it is wished to simply check the initial advance setting, it is immaterial whether No 2 or 3 cylinder is on the firing stroke.

4 If, for some reason, it is necessary to establish which cylinder is on its firing stroke, remove the spark plugs and place a cork, attached to the end of a wooden rod or screwdriver, over one of the plug holes. Pressure will be felt against the cork as the piston approaches TDC on its firing stroke.

5 An alternative indication of which cylinder is on its firing stroke is given by the position of the rotor arm, which will be pointing at No 2 or 3 cylinder contact in the distributor cap when the timing marks are aligned.

6 Turn the crankshaft so that the TDC mark on the flywheel is aligned with the specific static ignition timing mark on the timing plate with No 2 or 3 cylinder on its compression stroke. Loosen the distributor retaining bolts and turn the distributor gently anti-clockwise then clockwise until the points are just opening. Tighten the retaining bolts.

7 The accuracy of this operation can be improved by using a test light to indicate when the points open. Connect a 12 volt bulb in parallel with the contact breaker points (one lead to earth and the other to the distributor low tension terminal). Switch on the ignition and turn the distributor body anti-clockwise until the bulb just lights up, indicating that the points have opened. Tighten the distributor retaining bolts. Check the setting by turning the crankshaft back a few degrees and carefully turn it in the normal direction of rotation until the light just lights. Check that the flywheel mark is exactly opposite the timing plate ignition advance mark.

Ignition timing using stroboscopic lamp

8 Connect a stroboscopic lamp by following the maker's directions to No 2 or No 3 cylinder spark plug lead. Disconnect the vacuum advance pipe and fit a temporary plug on the suction side. Mark the TDC line on the flywheel with a little white paint to make it easier to see. Also mark the specified timing plate pointer.

9 Start the engine and allow it to idle at the specified speed.

10 Point the lamp at the timing marks. The one on the flywheel should appear to be stationary and in alignment with the specified pointer on the timing plate. If it is not in alignment, release the distributor and rotate it as necessary to align the marks.

11 Having set the ignition timing correctly, fully tighten the distributor retaining bolts, reconnect the vacuum pipe and refit the plastic cover to the flywheel cover.

Electronic (breakerless) distributor

12 If the distributor has been removed, and no alignment marks were made to assist its refitment (see Section 7, para 4), it will be necessary to set the ignition timing to enable the engine to start.

13 It should be established, before the ignition timing is checked, that the spark plug gaps and valve clearances are correctly adjusted, according to the specifications.

14 Remove the plastic cover from the flywheel cover (see Fig. 4.3) and rotate the engine to align the TDC mark on the flywheel with the specified pointer on the timing plate.

15 Place two marks, on the distributor body, adjacent to Nos 2 and 3 cylinder HT contacts in the distributor cap.

16 Remove distributor cap and then turn the distributor body until the contact end of the rotor arm aligns with one of the marks made on the distributor body.

17 To establish which cylinder is on its firing stroke follow the method described in para 4.

18 Having correctly aligned the rotor arm, the distributor retaining bolts can be finger-tightened, and the ignition timing checked using a stroboscope as described in paras 8 to 11, ignoring the reference to the vacuum advance pipe.

7 Distributor – removal and refitting

1 Disconnect the HT leads from the spark plugs and from their positioning clips.

2 Unclip the distributor cap and place it to one side together with its weatherproof cover.

3 Disconnect the coil HT lead and the LT lead from mechanical breaker distributors. On breakerless distributors, disconnect the wiring harness at the plug. Before the two halves of the plug can be separated, pull out the spring clip (photo).

4 Mark the position of the distributor retaining plate in relation to the cylinder head. Disconnect the vacuum hose.

5 Unscrew the two bolts and one nut (one bolt can only be reached from underneath) and lift the distributor from the engine. Note the HT lead positioning clip held by the distributor upper bolt.

6 The distributor drive is by offset tongue and slot so refitting is simply a matter of aligning the slot and tongue and pushing the distributor into position (photos).

7 Turn the distributor until the retaining plate marks are in their marked position.

8 Tighten the bolts and nut. Connect the vacuum hose.

9 Reconnect the leads and fit the cap.

10 It is recommended that the ignition timing is checked as described in Section 6.

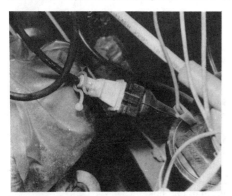

7.3 Distributor LT lead connector

7.6A Distributor offset drive slot

7.6B Refitting distributor (breakerless type)

8 Distributor – overhaul

Mechanical breaker type

1   It has been found from practical experience that overhauling a distributor is not worthwhile even if all parts are available. The usual items needing attention are such parts as the distributor cap, rotor arm, contact breaker points and condenser. These are readily available.

2   After a very high mileage, the shaft bushes or advance mechanism may be worn, in which event it will be cheaper and more satisfactory to purchase a new or factory rebuilt unit.

3   When purchasing a new distribtuor, it is most important to obtain one bearing the same number as the original as this determines the advance characteristics of the particular engine.

4   The vacuum advance unit toothed segment within the distributor should not be altered or the timing characteristics will be changed. It is worthwhile recording in which notch of the segment the tongue on the vacuum link rod engages so that if the setting is altered owing to the dismantling, then the original adjustment can be restored (photo).

8.4 Removing toothed cam retaining clip

Breakerless (electronic type)

5   With this type of distributor, it is more likely that a breakdown in the electronic components might occur rather than wear in mechanical parts. Dismantling is therefore described so that a new component can be fitted.

6   Remove the rotor and take off the plastic cover.

7   Extract the screw and remove the clamp and wiring plug.

8   Extract the three body screws. The lugs are offset so the body sections cannot be misaligned when reassembled. Separate the body sections.

9   Invert the body upper section, pull out the plastic ring and lift out the magnetic coil (photo).

10   From the body upper section, extract the circlip and the thrust washer (photo).

11   Extract the vacuum unit screw and then lift out the baseplate at the same time unhooking the vacuum link.

12   Extract the circlip and shim from the body lower section shaft.

13   Lift out the counterweight assembly.

14   The drive dog is secured to the shaft by a pin.

15   Reassembly is a reversal of dismantling, but note that one baseplate hole is marked for engagement of the vacuum unit link rod (photo).

9 Timing plate – setting

1   The timing plate which is located in the aperture under the plastic cover at the top of the flywheel housing can be moved within the limits of its elongated slot.

2   The plate is set during production and should not be disturbed unless a new flywheel, flywheel housing or other associated components have been fitted.

3   To set the timing plate, carry out the following operations.

4   Remove the plastic cover.

5   Using the crankshaft pulley nut, turn the crankshaft until the mark on the flywheel is at the start of the timing plate.

6   Remove the plug from behind the crankshaft pulley using an Allen key.

7   Insert the special tool 80133 into the plug hole and turn the crankshaft until the tool is felt to drop into the cut-out in the counterbalance weight of the crankshaft.

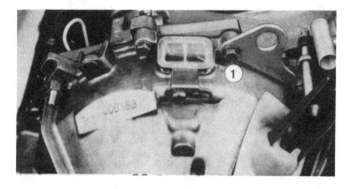

Fig. 4.3 Timing scale plastic cover (1) (Sec 9)

8.9 Removing magnetic coil

8.10 Upper body circlip and thrust washer

8.15 Hole marked for engagement of vacuum unit link

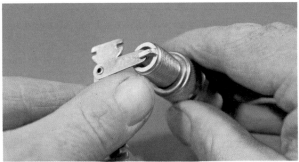

Measuring plug gap. A feeler gauge of the correct size (see ignition system specifications) should have a slight 'drag' when slid between the electrodes. Adjust gap if necessary

Adjusting plug gap. The plug gap is adjusted by bending the earth electrode inwards, or outwards, as necessary until the correct clearance is obtained. Note the use of the correct tool

Normal. Grey-brown deposits, lightly coated core nose. Gap increasing by around 0.001 in (0.025 mm) per 1000 miles (1600 km). Plugs ideally suited to engine, and engine in good condition

Carbon fouling. Dry, black, sooty deposits. Will cause weak spark and eventually misfire. Fault: over-rich fuel mixture. Check: carburettor mixture settings, float level and jet sizes; choke operation and cleanliness of air filter. Plugs can be re-used after cleaning

Oil fouling. Wet, oily deposits. Will cause weak spark and eventually misfire. Fault: worn bores/piston rings or valve guides; sometimes occurs (temporarily) during running-in period. Plugs can be re-used after thorough cleaning

Overheating. Electrodes have glazed appearance, core nose very white – few deposits. Fault: plug overheating. Check: plug value, ignition timing, fuel octane rating (too low) and fuel mixture (too weak). Discard plugs and cure fault immediately

Electrode damage. Electrodes burned away; core nose has burned, glazed appearance. Fault: pre-ignition. Check: as for 'Overheating' but may be more severe. Discard plugs and remedy fault before piston or valve damage occurs

Split core nose (may appear initially as a crack). Damage is self-evident, but cracks will only show after cleaning. Fault: pre-ignition or wrong gap-setting technique. Check: ignition timing, cooling system, fuel octane rating (too low) and fuel mixture (too weak). Discard plugs, rectify fault immediately

Fig. 4.4 Removing plug (2) from behind crankshaft pulley
(Sec 9)

9.8 Substitute rod for setting crankshaft position

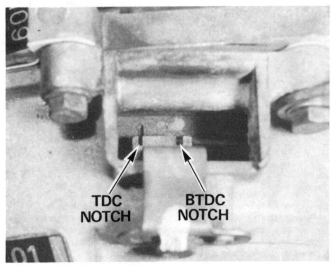

9.10 Timing plate (breakerless distributor)

8 If the special tool is not available, use a rod 8.0 mm diameter x 100.0 mm long (photo).
9 The pistons 2 and 3 are now located at TDC.
10 Release the timing plate bolt and move the plate to align the flywheel and 0 (TDC) mark on the plate. Tighten the bolt to the specified torque (photo).
11 Withdraw the pin, fit a new sealing ring to the plug and tighten to the specified torque.

Fig. 4.5 Using pin (A) to set pistons 2 and 3 at TDC (Sec 9)

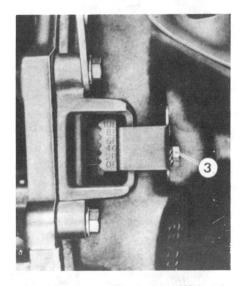

Fig. 4.6 Timing plate and securing bolt (3) (marks at TDC)
(Sec 9)

10 Condenser (mechanical breaker distributor) – testing, removal and refitting

1 The purpose of the condenser (sometimes known as a capacitor) is to ensure that when the contact breaker points open there is no sparking across them which would waste voltage and cause wear.
2 The condenser is fitted in parallel with the contact breaker points.

If it develops a short circuit, it will cause ignition failure, as the points will be prevented from interrupting the low tension circuit. If it develops an open circuit it will also cause malfunction, if not total failure.

3   If the engine becomes very difficult to start, or begins to misfire after several miles running, and the breaker points show signs of excessive burning then the condition of the condenser must be suspect. A further test can be made by separating the points manually (using an insulated screwdriver) with the ignition switched on. If this is accompanied by a strong blue flash it is indicative that the condenser has failed in the open circuit mode.

4   Without special test equipment, the only sure way to diagnose condenser trouble is to replace a suspected unit with a new one, noting if there is any improvement.

5   To remove the condenser from the distributor, first detach the condenser lead from the LT terminal post on the side of the distributor body.

6   Undo and remove the securing screw, or screws depending on model, noting the locations of the washers, and remove the condenser.

7   Refitting of the condenser is simply the reverse of the removal procedure.

11 Ignition coil

1   The maintenance of the coil is minimal and is limited to periodically wiping its surfaces clean and dry and ensuring that the lead connectors are secure. High voltages generated by the coil can easily leak to earth over its surface and prevent the spark plugs from receiving the electrical pulses. Water repellent sprays are now available to prevent dampness causing this type of malfunction (photo).

2   Wipe clean and spray the HT leads and distributor cap also.

3   Special equipment is required to test a coil and is best left to an auto electrician. Substitution of another coil is an alternative method of fault tracing.

4   The coils used in mechanical breaker and electric ignition systems are not interchangeable.

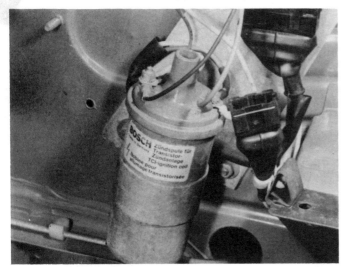

11.1 Coil (breakerless ignition system)

12 Spark plugs and HT leads

1   The correct functioning of the spark plugs is vital for the correct running and efficiency of the engine.

2   At the intervals specified in Routine Maintenance the plugs should be removed, cleaned and re-gapped.

3   To remove the plugs, first open the bonnet and pull the HT leads from them. Grip the rubber end fitting not the lead otherwise the lead connection may be fractured.

4   The spark plugs are deeply recessed in the cylinder head and it is recommended that dirt is removed from the recesses using a vacuum cleaner or compressed air, before removing the plugs, to prevent dirt dropping into the cylinders.

5   Unscrew the plugs using the special box wrench supplied with the car and located on the engine compartment rear bulkhead (photos).

6   Examination of the spark plugs will give a good indication of the condition of the engine.

7   If the insulator nose of the spark plug is clean and white, with no deposits, this is indicative of a weak mixture, or too hot a plug (a hot plug transfers heat away from the electrode slowly, a cold plug transfers heat away quickly).

8   The plugs fitted as standard are specified at the beginning of this Chapter. If the top and insulator nose are covered with hard black-looking deposits, then this is indicative that the mixture is too rich. Should the plug be black and oily, then it is likely that the engine is fairly worn, as well as the mixture being too rich.

9   If the insulator nose is covered with light tan to greyish brown deposits, then the mixture is correct and it is likely that the engine is in good condition.

10   If there are any traces of long brown tapering stains on the outside of the white portion of the plug, then the plug will have to be renewed, as this shows that there is a faulty joint between the plug body and the insulator, and compression is being allowed to leak away.

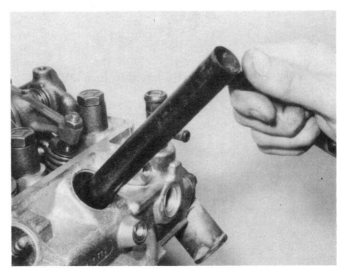

12.5A Special spark plug tool

12.5B Spark plug tool stowage clips

Fig. 4.7 Spark plug with extension (Sec 12)

a Tapered seat

11 Before cleaning a spark plug, wash it in petrol to remove oily deposits.
12 Although a wire brush can be used to clean the electrode end of the spark plug this method can cause metal conductance paths across the nose of the insulator. It is therefore to be preferred that an abrasive powder cleaning machine is used. Such machines are available quite cheaply from motor accessory stores or you may prefer to take the plugs to your dealer who will not only be able to clean them, but also to check the sparking efficiency of each plug under compression.
13 The spark plug gap is of considerable importance as, if it is too large or too small, the size of the spark and its efficiency will be seriously impaired. For the best results the spark plug gap should be set in accordance with the Specifications at the beginning of this Chapter.
14 To set it, measure the gap with a feeler gauge, and then bend open, or close, the outer plug electrode until the correct gap is achieved. The centre electrode should never be bent as this may crack the insulation and cause plug failure if nothing worse.
15 Special spark plug electrode gap adjusting tools are available from most motor accessory stores.

16 Before refitting the spark plugs, wash each one thoroughly again in fuel in order to remove all trace of abrasive powder and then apply a trace of grease to the plug threads.
17 Screw each plug in by hand. This will make sure that there is no chance of cross-threading.
18 Tighten to the specified torque. If a torque wrench is not available, just nip up each plug. It is better to slightly undertighten rather then over do it and strip the threads from the light alloy cylinder head. The spark plugs have tapered seats without sealing washers. Overtightening this type of plug can make them extremely difficult to remove.
19 When reconnecting the spark plug leads, make sure that they are refitted in their correct order, 1 - 3 - 4 -2. No 1 cylinder being at the flywheel end of the engine.
20 The plug leads require no routine attention other than being kept clean and wiped over regularly. At intervals of 6000 miles (10 000 km), however, pull each lead off the plug in turn and remove it from the distributor. Water can seep down into the joints giving rise to a white corrosive deposit which must be carefully removed from the end of each cable.

13 Ignition switch and steering lock

1 Removal and separation of the switch and lock is described in Chapter 8.
2 The switch positions are shown in the illustration.

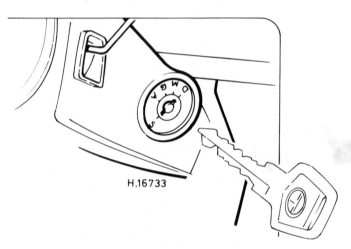

Fig. 4.8 Ignition switch positions (Sec 13)

S Off. Steering locked when key removed
A Ignition off, accessories on
M Ignition on
D Starter motor energised

14 Fault diagnosis — ignition system

Mechanical breaker type

Symptom	Reason(s)
Engine fails to start	Loose battery connections Discharged battery Oil on contact points Disconnected ignition leads Faulty condenser
Engine starts and runs but misfires	Faulty spark plug Cracked distributor cap Cracked rotor arm Worn advance mechanism Incorrect spark plug gap Incorrect contact points gap Faulty condenser Faulty coil Incorrect timing Poor engine/transmission earth connections
Engine overheats, lacks power	Seized distributor weights Perforated vacuum pipe Incorrect ignition timing
Engine 'pinks'	Timing too advanced Advanced mechanism stuck in advanced position Broken distributor weight spring Low fuel octane Upper cylinder oil used in fuel Excessive oil vapour from crankcase ventilation system (worn piston rings)

Electronic (breakerless) type

Symptom	Reason(s)
Starter turns but engine will not start	Faulty or disconnected leads Faulty spark plug Air gap incorrect Fault in ignition coil Fault in pick-up/starter unit
Engine starts but runs erratically	Incorrect timing Fouled spark plug Incorrectly connected HT leads Crack in distributor cap or rotor Poor battery, engine and earth connections

Chapter 5 Clutch

Contents

Specifications

Type .... Single dry plate with diaphragm spring. Cable actuation

Driven plate diameter .... 180.0 mm (7.0 in)

Release bearing .... Sealed ball

Pedal stroke .... 135.0 mm (5.3 in) minimum

Pedal free movement (lifted) .... 10.0 mm (0.39 in) minimum

Torque wrench settings

	Nm	lbf ft
Clutch cover bolts	9	7
Flywheel housing bolts	11	8
Engine mounting nuts	34	25
Starter motor bolts	16	12
Starter motor nuts	12	9
Transfer gear cover plate bolts	9	7

1 General description

The clutch is of diaphragm spring, single dry plate type with cable actuation.

The clutch pedal pivots in a bracket mounted under the facia and operates a cable to the clutch release arm. The release arm operates a thrust bearing (clutch release bearing) which bears on the diaphragm spring of the pressure plate. The diaphragm then releases or engages the clutch driven plate which floats on a splined shaft. This shaft (the engine output shaft) is part of the transfer gear assembly which is mounted on the clutch housing. The drive passes via an intermediate pinion to the gearbox input shaft.

The clutch release mechanism consists of a fork and bearing which are in permanent contact with release fingers on the pressure plate assembly. The fork pushes the release bearing forwards to bear against the release fingers, so moving the centre of the diaphragm spring inwards. The spring is sandwiched between two rings which act as fulcrum points. As the centre of the spring is pushed in, the outside of the spring is pushed out, so moving the pressure plate backwards and disengaging it from the clutch disc.

When the clutch pedal is released, the diaphragm spring forces the pressure plate into contact with the friction linings on the clutch disc and at the same time pushes the clutch disc a fraction of an inch forwards on its splines so engaging the clutch disc with the flywheel. The clutch disc is now firmly sandwiched between the pressure plate and the flywheel, so the drive is taken up.

As wear takes place on the clutch disc the clearance between the release bearing and the diaphragm decreases. This wear can be compensated for by adjusting the screws and locknut on the clutch operating lever.

2 Clutch – adjustment

1 At the intervals specified in Routine Maintenance, check the free movement by lifting the clutch pedal with the fingers. This should not be less than 10.0 mm (0.39 in) with a pedal stroke of 135.0 mm (5.3 in).

2 Where adjustment is required, open the bonnet and release the locknut at the cable end fitting (photo).

3 Turn the end fitting as necessary to adjust the specification. Retighten the locknut.

2.2 Clutch cable adjuster (A) and locknut (B)

3 Clutch cable – removal and refitting

1 The clutch cable connects the clutch pedal to the operating lever/rod assembly. It is a simple item to replace. To remove proceed as follows.
2 Unscrew the clutch lever adjustment screw locknut and slacken the adjustment.
3 Inside the car, unhook the cable from the clutch pedal. Release the other end of the cable from the clutch operating lever.
4 Release the cable conduit positioning clips and withdraw the cable through the grommet in the engine compartment rear bulkhead (photos).
5 Refitting is a direct reversal of the removal procedure. When fitted readjust the operating lever clearance as given in Section 2.

3.4A Clutch cable support at steering rack

3.4B Clutch cable grommet on engine bulkhead (arrowed)

4 Clutch pedal – removal and refitting

1 Slacken the clutch cable right off.
2 Working under the facia panel, disconnect the clutch pedal return spring.
3 Disconnect the clutch cable from the pedal arm.
4 Unscrew and remove the nut from the pedal pivot bolt.

5 Push the pivot bolt until the clutch pedal is free and can be removed from the support bracket. The brake and clutch pedals operate on a common pivot bolt.
6 Refitting is a reversal of removal. Adjust the clutch cable as described in Section 2.

5 Clutch – removal

1 Access to the clutch can only be obtained after having removed the engine/transmission as described in Chapter 1.
2 With the power unit removed and supported securely, detach the return spring from the end of the clutch release lever, remove the pushrod and slip off the plastic protective cover. Remove the starter and left-hand mounting.
3 Unscrew and remove the bolts which hold the clutch/flywheel housing to the engine. One bolt is located under the oil gallery. Note also the locations of the clutch cable bracket and the lifting lug.
4 Remove the clutch/flywheel housing. This will require tapping off with a plastic-faced hammer applied to the casting bosses.
5 Unscrew the clutch fixing bolts, these are of socket-headed type. Jam the teeth of the flywheel ring gear to prevent rotation as the bolts are unscrewed.
6 Lift away the cover and driven plate (photo).

5.6 Clutch pressure plate and driven plate

Fig. 5.1 Clutch cover socket-head bolts (5) (Sec 5)

6 Clutch – inspection and renovation

1   The clutch driven plate should be inspected for wear and for contamination by oil. Wear is gauged by the depth of the rivet heads below the surface of the friction material. If this is less than 0.025 in (0.6 mm) the linings are worn enough to justify renewal.

2   Examine the friction faces of the flywheel and clutch pressure plate. These should be bright and smooth. If the linings have worn too much it is possible that the metal surfaces may have been scored by the rivet heads. Dust and grit can have the same effect. If the scoring is very severe it could mean that even with a new clutch driven plate, slip and juddering and other malfunctions will recur. Deep scoring on the flywheel face is serious because the flywheel will have to be removed and machined by a specialist, or renewed. This can be costly. The same applies to the pressure plate in the cover although this is a less costly affair. If the friction linings seem unworn yet are blackened and shiny then the cause is almost certainly due to oil. Such a condition also requires renewal of the plate. The source of oil must be traced also. It could be due to a leaking seal on the transmission input shaft (photos) or from a leaking crankshaft oil seal (see Chapter 1 for details of renewal).

3   If the reason for removal of the clutch has been because of slip and the slip has been allowed to go on for any length of time, it is possible that the heat generated will have adversely affected the diaphragm spring in the cover with the result that the pressure is now uneven and/or insufficient to prevent slip, even with a new friction plate. It is recommended that under such circumstances a new assembly is fitted.

4   Do not attempt to re-line the driven plate or dismantle the pressure plate cover, but obtain new or factory reconditioned units which are sometimes supplied on an exchange basis.

5   Clean away all old gasket from the housing mating flanges without scratching or scoring the surfaces of the metal. Obtain a new gasket.

7 Clutch – refitting

1   Support the driven plate centrally between the flywheel and the cover. The greater projecting hub of the driven plate should face towards the flywheel.

2   Retain the cover in position on the flywheel with the bolts (hand tight only).

3   It is now necessary to align the centre of the driven plate with that of the flywheel. To do this use a special alignment tool or alternatively use a suitable diameter bar inserted through the driven plate into the flywheel spigot bearing, but take care not to damage the output shaft seal. It is possible to align the driven plate by eye, but difficulty will probably be experienced when refitting the output shaft. If the transfer gears have been separated from the clutch housing the driven plate

7.3 Using transfer gear output shaft to centralise clutch driven plate

can be aligned using the engine output shaft located in its normal running position (photo).

4   With the driven plate centralized the cover bolts should be tightened diagonally and evenly to the specified torque. Ideally new spring washers should be used each time a replacement clutch is fitted. When the bolts are tight remove the centralizing tool.

5   Before fitting the clutch housing, check the condition of the release bearing and operating mechanism, renewing any parts as necessary.

6   Before refitting the housing, check that the mating surfaces are clean and dry. Smear the bearing surface of the withdrawal pad on the diaphragm spring with medium grease.

7   Place a new gasket over the location dowels and then carefully offer the clutch housing/transfer pinion unit to the engine and insert the output and input shafts.

8   To assist the respective shaft splines to engage, rotate the flywheel and gearbox input shaft alternately until they slide home into position with the housing flush.

9   Insert the retaining bolts, remembering to replace any fittings retained by them. Tighten the bolts progressively to the specified torque. Refit the plastic protector, actuating rod and return spring.

10 Refit the starter and left-hand engine mounting.

11 Refit the engine/transmission as described in Chapter 1.

12 Adjust the clutch as described in Section 2.

8 Clutch release mechanism – overhaul

1   The clutch actuating rod can be removed by slackening the operating adjustment and unhooking the return spring.

2   To remove or overhaul the withdrawal bearing and fork the flywheel housing must be removed. This is described in Section 5.

3   With the housing removed the withdrawal fork and bearing can be withdrawn from the output shaft for inspection.

4   Do not clean the bearing with solvent as it will harm the bearing. Wipe it clean and check for excessive wear or play. Always renew if in doubt.

5   Inspect the fork retaining ball stud and if obviously distorted or worn renew it. Drift the ball stud from the housing using a suitable diameter drift. Fit the new one together with a new rubber cup by driving it carefully into position using a soft faced hammer. Support the housing during this operation to prevent it being damaged.

6   Before reassembly, check the output (clutch) shaft oil seal. If it is leaking then the complete guide bush/seal assembly must be renewed as the seal is not supplied separately.

7   Press the guide bush out of the flywheel housing.

8   Press the new bush/seal assembly fully into its recess so that it seats firmly.

9   Any wear in the spigot bush which is located in the centre of the crankshaft rear flange (flywheel mounting) and supports the output shaft can be rectified by renewal of the bush as described in Chapter 1.

Fig. 5.2 Removing clutch release lever pivot balljoint (Sec 8)

10 To refit the fork, fit the spring blade so that it is located under the rubber cover as shown (photo).

11 Position the release bearing over the engine output and engage the retainers behind the fork fingers. The release bearing can be slid along the sleeve whilst holding the fork (photos).

12 Check the fork and bearing for correct operation and then refit the housing – see Section 5. Readjust the clutch operating clearance on completion – see Section 2.

8.10 Release arm and bearing

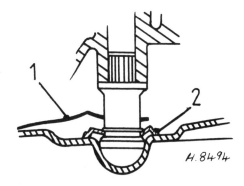

Fig. 5.3 Clutch release lever spring retaining clip (1) and rubber cover (2) (Sec 8)

8.11A Release bearing fixing clips

Fig. 5.4 Fitting release lever pivot balljoint rubber cover (4) (Sec 8)

9 Transfer gears – removal and refitting

1 The transfer gears are located under a cover plate at the end of the clutch/flywheel housing. Their purpose is to transmit power from the engine crankshaft and clutch to the transmission input shaft which lies below the engine.

2 The gears can only be removed after the engine/transmission has been withdrawn. Unbolt and remove the cover plate.

3 Unbolt and remove the transfer gear intermediate plate (1). The plate will probably require tapping off with a plastic-faced hammer. Take care that the intermediate gear (2) does not drop out as the plate is removed (Fig. 5.6).

4 Remove the intermediate gear.

5 Clean away all old gasket material and obtain a new one.

6 Examine the gear teeth for wear or damage and the bearings for wear or 'shake'.

7 If a ball bearing is to be renewed, use a pair of circlip pliers to fully

8.11B Release arm and bearing engaged on ballstud

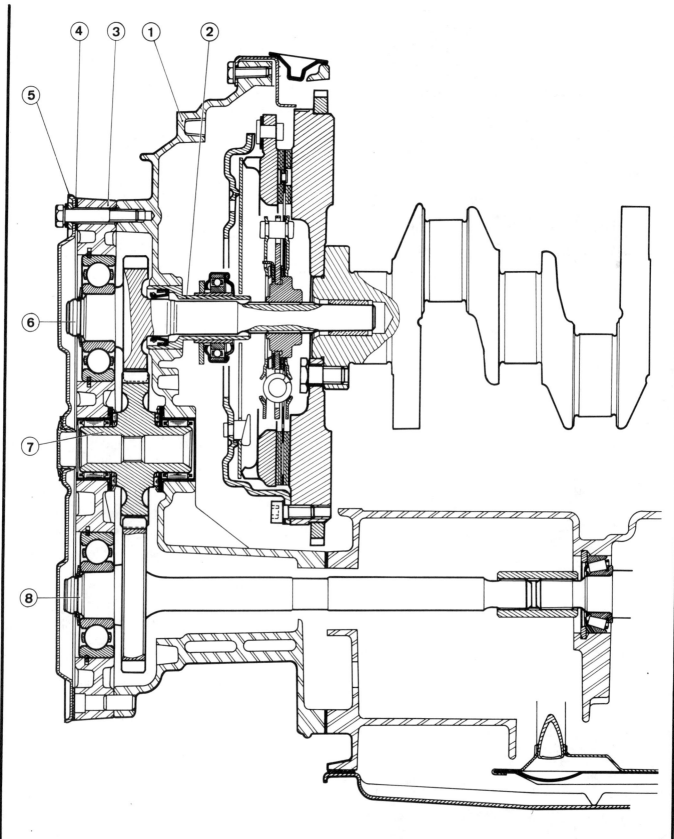

Fig. 5.5 Sectional view of power drivetrain (Sec 9)

1	Clutch/flywheel housing	3	Intermediate plate	5	Cover plate	7	Intermediate gear
2	Release bearing guide bush	4	Gasket	6	Output (clutch shaft)	8	Input shaft

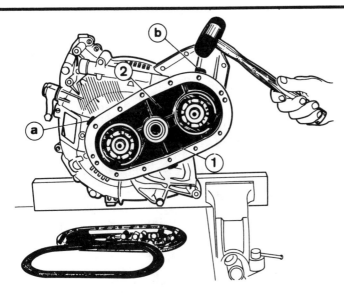

Fig. 5.6 Removing intermediate plate (Sec 9)

1   Intermediate plate
2   Intermediate gear

(a)   Casting boss (impact point)
(b)   Casting boss (impact point)

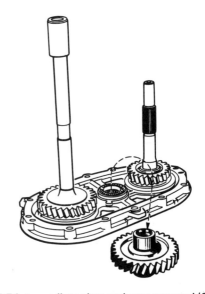

Fig. 5.7 Intermediate plate and gear removed (Sec 9)

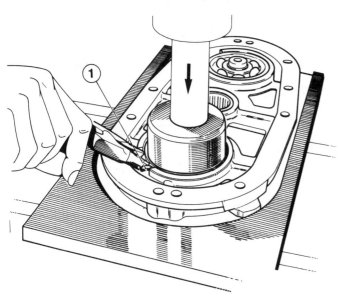

Fig. 5.8 Expanding circlip (1) and pressing out ball bearing from intermediate plate (Sec 9)

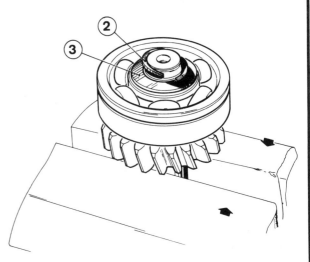

Fig. 5.9 Bearing circlip and Belleville washer (Sec 9)

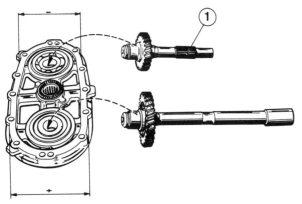

Fig. 5.10 Shaft identification (Sec 9)

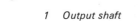

1   Output shaft

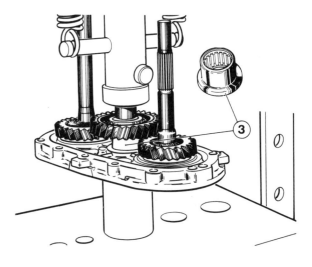

Fig. 5.11 Using intermediate gear to press needle roller bearing (3) into intermediate plate (Sec 9)

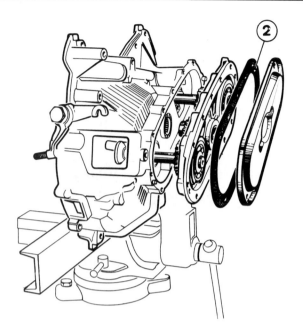

Fig. 5.12 Assembling transfer gears and cover plate (Sec 9)

2   Gasket

9.12 Transfer gears and intermediate plate

9.14 Fitting transfer gear cover and gasket

expand the circlip before pressing the shaft out of the bearing or the shaft/bearing out of the intermediate plate.

8   When reassembling, remember that the shorter shaft is located at the narrower end of the intermediate plate. Always use new circlips and support the plate adequately during the pressing operation.

9   Always use a new Belleville washer under the circlip so that its concave face is towards the bearing.

10 If the intermediate gear needle race is to be renewed in the intermediate plate, press the old one out and use the intermediate gear as an installation tool, but make sure that the gear teeth do not lock with those of the other gears during the pressing operation.

11 Lubricate the bearings and fit the intermediate gear.

12 Offer the transfer gears with intermediate plate to the flywheel housing. No gasket is used (photo).

13 Locate the cover plate and its gasket.

14 Fit the cover plate bolts and tighten to the specified torque wrench setting (photo).

10 Fault diagnosis – clutch

Symptom	Reason(s)
Judder when taking up drive	Loose engine or gearbox mountings Badly worn friction linings or contaminated with oil Worn splines on transfer shaft or driven plate hub Worn spigot bush in crankshaft flange
*Clutch spin (failure to disengage) so that gears cannot be meshed	Incorrect release bearing to pressure plate clearance Rust on splines (may occur after vehicle standing idle for long periods) Damaged or misaligned pressure plate assembly Cable stretched or broken
Clutch slip (increase in engine speed does not result in increase in vehicle road speed – particularly on gradients)	Incorrect release bearing to pressure plate finger clearance Friction linings worn out or oil contaminated
Noise evident on depressing clutch pedal	Dry, worn or damaged release bearing Incorrect pedal adjustment Weak or broken return spring Excessive play between driven plate hub splines and shaft splines
Noise evident as clutch pedal released	Distorted driven plate Broken or weak driven plate cushion coil springs Incorrect pedal adjustment Weak or broken clutch pedal return spring Distorted or worn transfer gear shaft Release bearing loose on retainer hub

*This condition may also be due to the driven plate being rusted to the flywheel or pressure plate. It is possible to free it by applying the handbrake, engaging top gear and operating the starter motor. If really badly corroded, then the engine will not turn over, but in the majority of cases the driven plate will free. Once the engine starts, rev it up and slip the clutch several times to clear the rust deposits.

Chapter 6 Transmission

For modifications, and information applicable to later models, see Supplement at end of manual

Contents

Specifications

Type .... BH 3/4 (four-speed) four forward speeds all with synchromesh, one reverse
BH 3/5 (five-speed) five forward speeds all with synchromesh, one reverse

Gear ratios
1st .... 3.883 : 1
2nd:
    All except S and Cabriolet .... 2.074 : 1
    S and Cabriolet .... 2.297 : 1
3rd:
    All except S and Cabriolet .... 1.377 : 1
    S and Cabriolet .... 1.502 : 1
4th:
    All except S and Cabriolet .... 0.944 : 1
    S and Cabriolet .... 1.124 : 1
5th (S and Cabriolet) .... 0.904 : 1
Reverse .... 3.569 : 1

Final drive
LE, LS, S, Roller .... 3.867 : 1
GL, Cabriolet .... 3.353 : 1
Convertible, GLS .... 3.562 : 1

Lubrication .... Common supply with engine

Torque wrench settings

	Nm	lbf ft
Primary shaft nut	45	33
Secondary shaft nut:		
4-speed	23	17
5-speed	95	70
Crownwheel bolt	65	48
Reverse lockplate (5-speed)	10	7
Detent ball plug	12	9
Oil filter screen bolt	10	7
Sump plate bolts	12	9
Drain plug	27	20
Reverse lamp switch	27	20
Selector lever bolt	13	10

Half casing bolts (refer to Section 9)
Primary shaft bearing preload on 4-speed transmission (refer to Section 9)

1 General description

The transmission is mounted transversely directly under and to the rear of the engine with which it shares a common lubrication system.

The transmission casing is constructed in light alloy and incorporates the final drive and differential.

Power from the engine crankshaft is transmitted through the output shaft then the transfer gears (refer to Chapter 5, Section 9) to the transmission input shaft.

Drive to the front roadwheels is transmitted through open driveshafts from the differential side gears.

The transmission may be of four or five speed type depending upon the vehicle model. Both types are similar except for the 5th gear located on the ends of the primary and secondary shafts.

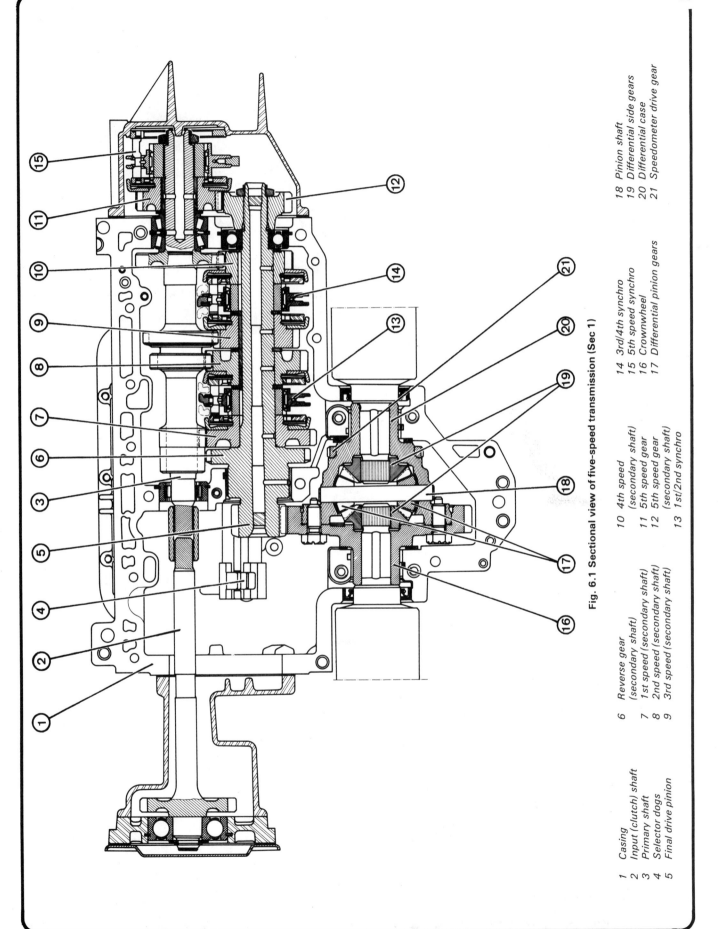

Fig. 6.1 Sectional view of five-speed transmission (Sec 1)

1 Casing
2 Input (clutch) shaft
3 Primary shaft
4 Selector dogs
5 Final drive pinion

6 Reverse gear
   (secondary shaft)
7 1st speed (secondary shaft)
8 2nd speed (secondary shaft)
9 3rd speed (secondary shaft)

10 4th speed
    (secondary shaft)
11 5th speed gear
12 5th speed gear
    (secondary shaft)
13 1st/2nd synchro

14 3rd/4th synchro
15 5th speed synchro
16 Crownwheel
17 Differential pinion gears

18 Pinion shaft
19 Differential side gears
20 Differential case
21 Speedometer drive gear

The transmission is of conventional two shaft constant-mesh layout. There are four pairs of gears, one for each forward speed. The gears on the primary shaft are fixed to the shaft, while those on the secondary or pinion shaft float, each being locked to the shaft when engaged by the synchromesh unit. The reverse idler gear is on a third shaft.

On five-speed units, the 5th speed gears are of fixed type with an extra synchromesh assembly.

The gear selector forks engage in the synchromesh unit; these slide axially along the shaft to engage the appropriate gear. The forks are mounted on selector shafts which are located in the base of the gearbox.

The helical gear on the end of the pinion shaft drives directly onto the crownwheel mounted on the differential unit. The latter differs from normal practice in that it runs in shell bearings and the end thrust is taken up by thrust washers in a similar manner to the engine crankshaft.

2 Gearchange linkage – adjustment

1   The gearchange linkage does not normally require adjustment. If new parts have been fitted however, set the balljointed link rods in accordance with the following dimensions:

Rod 1 (between centres of ball sockets) 73.0 to 87.0 mm (2.87 to 3.42 in)
Rod 2 (between centres of ball sockets) 171.0 to 173.0 mm (6.73 to 6.82 in)

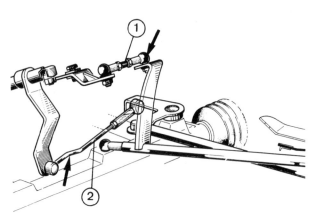

Fig. 6.2 Gearchange link rods (Sec 2)

1   Upper rod   *2   Lower rod*

Fig. 6.3 Location of gearchange link rod tension spring (3) (Sec 2)

2   If the linkage is not already fitted with a tension spring, fit one as shown in Fig. 6.3.
3   The gear lever can be removed after withdrawal of the centre console (Chapter 12) (photos).

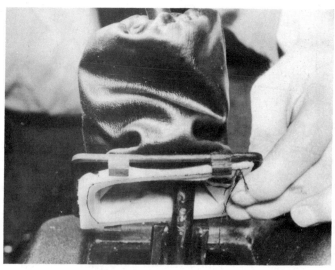

2.3A Removing gear lever gaiter

2.3B Gear lever/rod arrangement

3 Transmission – overhaul general

1   No work can be carried out to the transmission until the engine/transmission has been removed from the car as described in Chapter 1 and cleaned externally.
2   Remove the clutch/flywheel housing and transfer gears as described in Chapters 1 and 5. Drain the lubricating oil.
3   Unbolt and remove the timing chain cover and the flywheel as described in Chapter 1.
4   Unscrew and remove all the engine to transmission connecting bolts, making sure that the two bolts and one nut are removed from the flange joint adjacent to the flywheel mounting flange on the end of the crankshaft.
5   Prise the transmission from the engine using a length of wood as a lever.

4 Transmission – dismantling into major units

1   With the transmission on the bench unbolt and remove the protective plate and sump cover (photos).

4.1A Sump protective plate

4.1B Sump cover and gasket

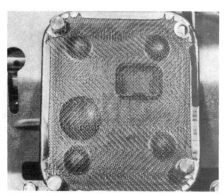

4.2 Oil pick-up screen

4.3 Speedometer drivegear

4.4 Reverse lamp switch

4.6 Primary shaft bearing ring nut cut-outs (four-speed)

4.7 Removing primary shaft (five-speed)

4.8 Removing secondary shaft

4.10 Transmission shaft bearing shells

2   Unbolt and remove the oil pick-up screen (photo).
3   Remove the speedometer drivegear (photo).
4   Unscrew and remove the reverse lamp switch (photo).
5   Release, but do not remove the nineteen bolts which hold the two transmission half casing sections together.

Four-speed unit
6   Unscrew and remove the primary shaft bearing ring nut by engaging a suitable tool in the nut cut-outs (photo).

All units
7   Remove the casing bolts, separate the casing sections and lift out the primary shaft (photo).
8   Lift out the secondary shaft (photo).
9   Lift out the final drive/differential.

10 Remove the bearing shells, identifying them in respect of location if they are to be used again (photo).
11 Examine all components for wear or damage and carry out further dismantling as necessary and as described in the following Sections.
12 If it is intended to renew the casing sections then they must both be renewed at the same time as a pair.
13 Clean old gasket material from the original casings without scoring the metal and clean out the oilways.

5   Primary shaft – overhaul

1   Only the bearings can be renewed as the gears cannot be removed from the shaft.

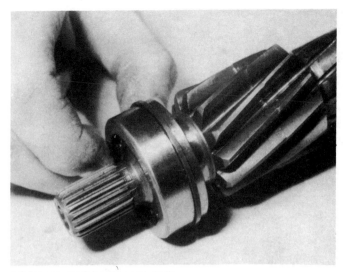

5.2 Primary shaft bearing and circlip

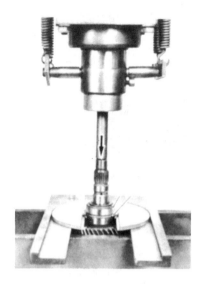

Fig. 6.5 Pressing primary shaft out of bearing (five-speed) (Sec 5)

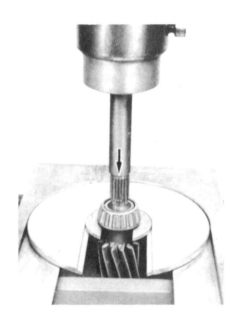

Fig. 6.4 Pressing primary shaft out of bearing (four-speed) (Sec 5)

5.6 Primary shaft nut (five-speed)

Four-speed unit
2   Either support the bearing and press the shaft from it or draw the bearing from the shaft using a two-legged puller (photo).
3   When fitting the bearing, apply pressure to the inner track only.

Five-speed unit
4   Mark the position of the 5th speed synchro sleeve in relation to the hub.
5   Grip the shaft in a vice fitted with jaw protectors.
6   Unscrew the nut (3), Fig. 6.6 (photo).
7   Withdraw 5th speed synchro sleeve from the shaft (photo).
8   Support the gear and press the shaft out of the synchro hub. Alternatively use a suitable puller, Fig. 6.7 (photo).
9   Remove 5th speed gear, bush and washer (photos).
10   Press the shaft out of the bearings or draw off the bearings using a suitable puller. Remove the washer (photo).
11   When refitting the bearings, apply pressure to the centre track only.

Fig. 6.6 Primary shaft nut (five-speed) (Sec 5)

5.7 Removing 5th speed synchro sleeve

5.8 Removing 5th speed synchro hub

5.9A 5th speed gear

5.9B 5th speed gear bush

5.9C 5th speed gear thrust washer

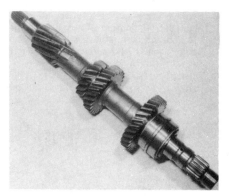

5.10 Primary shaft (five-speed)

Fig. 6.7 Pressing primary shaft from synchro hub (five-speed)
(Sec 5)

12 The bearings at the opposite end of the shaft are of single roller type.

13 When refitting the synchro hub use a new nut, tighten to the specified torque and stake the nut into the shaft groove to lock it.

Four and five-speed units

14 Never re-use a bearing which has been removed from a shaft.

15 Do not mix the components of one new bearing set with another and do not attempt to remove the original bearing grease.

Fig. 6.8 5th speed gear primary shaft components (Sec 5)

7 Washer   10 Synchro hub
8 Bush   11 Nut
9 5th speed gear

Fig. 6.9 Primary shaft (five-speed) double taper bearing (Sec 5)

3 Race and track   5 Washer
4 Bush   6 Race and track

Fig. 6.10 Primary shaft (five-speed) single taper roller bearing
(Sec 5)

6   Secondary shaft – overhaul

1   Secure the shaft in a vice fitted with jaw protectors and unscrew
the nut.
2   Using a press or a suitable puller remove the bearing (four-speed)
or bearing and 5th speed gear (five-speed) (photo).
3   Remove the spacer and 4th speed gear.
4   Mark the relationship of the hub to the sleeve of the 3rd/4th
synchro unit and then remove the synchro unit.
5   Remove the key (7) and spacer (8), Fig. 6.15.
6   Take off 3rd speed gear (9), Fig. 6.16.
7   Take off the spacer (10).
8   Remove 2nd speed gear (11) and the spacer.

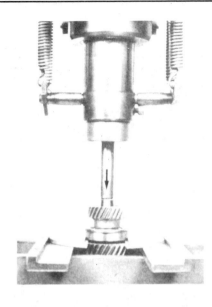

Fig. 6.12 Removing secondary shaft 5th speed gear and bearing
(Sec 6)

6.2 Removing secondary shaft bearing with 5th speed gear

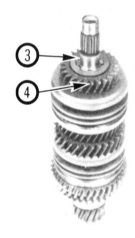

Fig. 6.13 Five-speed secondary shaft spacer (3) and 4th speed
gear (4) (Sec 6)

Fig. 6.11 Secondary shaft (five-speed) (Sec 6)

1   Nut

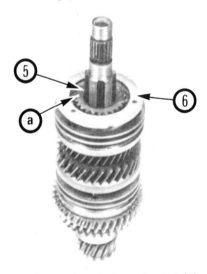

Fig. 6.14 Five-speed secondary shaft synchro hub (5) and sleeve
(6) (Sec 6)

a   Alignment marks

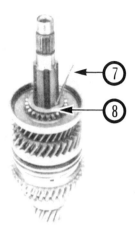

Fig. 6.15 Five-speed secondary shaft key (7) and spacer (8) (Sec 6)

9 Mark the relationship of the hub to the sleeve of the 1st/2nd synchro unit and then take off the synchro unit (13).
10 Remove 1st speed gear (15).

Reassembly
11 As work progresses, dip each component in clean engine oil (photo).
12 To the shaft fit 1st speed gear (photo).
13 Fit the 1st/2nd synchro hub (photo).
14 Fit the spacer and align its splines so that the key can be fitted (photo).
15 Fit the 1st/2nd synchro sleeve so that its mark made at dismantling aligns with the one on the hub. The lines on the spacer pins are towards 1st speed gear (photos).
16 Fit 2nd speed gear (photo).
17 Fit the spacer and align the splines so that the key can be fitted (photo).
18 Fit 3rd speed gear (photo).
19 Fit the spacer, once more aligning the splines so that the key can be fitted (photo).
20 Push the key into the widest shaft groove so that the chamfered edge on the key is at the bottom of the groove. Push the key until it is flush with the spacer (photo).
21 Fit the 3rd/4th synchro hub (photo).
22 Fit the 3rd/4th synchro sleeve so that its mark made at dismantling aligns with the one on the hub. The line on the spacer pin must be towards 3rd speed gear (photo).
23 Fit 4th speed gear (photo).
24 Fit the spacer (photo).
25 Press the bearing (four-speed) or the bearing and 5th speed gear (five-speed) onto the shaft (photos).
26 Engage a new circlip in the bearing outer track groove.
27 Screw on a new shaft nut to the specified torque and stake the nut into the groove in the shaft (photo).

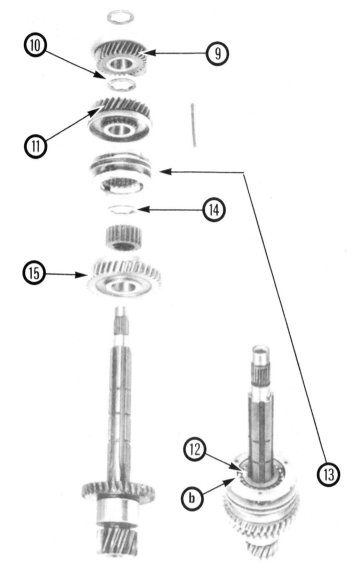

Fig. 6.16 Five-speed secondary shaft components (Sec 6)

9 *3rd speed gear*	13 *Synchro sleeve*
10 *Spacer*	14 *Spacer*
11 *2nd speed gear*	15 *1st speed gear*
12 *Synchro hub*	b *Alignment marks*

6.11 Secondary shaft stripped

6.12 Fitting 1st speed gear to secondary shaft

6.13 Fitting 1st/2nd synchro hub to secondary shaft

6.14 Fitting first spacer to secondary shaft

6.15A Fitting 1st/2nd synchro sleeve to secondary shaft

6.15B Lines on synchro spacer pins

6.16 Fitting 2nd speed gear to secondary shaft

6.17 Fitting second spacer to secondary shaft

6.18 Fitting 3rd speed gear to secondary shaft

6.19 Fitting third spacer to secondary shaft

6.20 Pushing key into shaft groove

6.21 3rd/4th synchro hub on secondary shaft

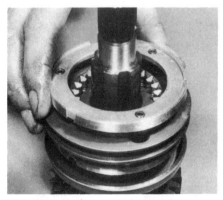

6.22 Fitting 3rd/4th synchro sleeve to secondary shaft

6.23 Fitting 4th speed gear to secondary shaft

6.24 Fitting 4th speed spacer

6.25A Fitting secondary shaft bearing

6.25B Fitting 5th speed gear to secondary shaft

6.27 Secondary shaft nut

7 Selector mechanism and reverse idler – dismantling and reassembly

1   Unscrew and remove the three threaded detent plugs and extract the coil springs and balls. If the plugs are very tight, tap their end-face hard using a rod and hammer.

Four-speed unit
2   Drive out the reverse fork roll pin (Fig. 6.17).

Fig. 6.17 Driving out reverse fork roll pin (four-speed) (Sec 7)

Five-speed unit
3   Knock out the roll pin and unscrew the bolt and remove the reverse fork ball lock plate. Extract the two balls (4), Fig. 6.18. Move the position of the selector shaft slightly to release the second ball.
4   Slide the 5th/reverse selector shaft so that the dog contacts the housing web (a) then drive out the roll pin which secures the dog.

All units
5   Withdraw the reverse selector shaft and retrieve the interlock disc (5), Fig. 6.19.
6   Drive out the roll pin which secures the 3rd/4th fork to the selector shaft. Remove the fork from the shaft.
7   Drive out the roll pin which secures the fork to the 1st/2nd selector shaft.

Five-speed unit
8   Drive out the roll pin which secures the dog to the 1st/2nd selector shaft. Before doing this, slide the shaft so that the dog is in contact with the housing web.

Fig. 6.18 Detent ball retaining plate (3) and detent balls (4) (Sec 7)

Fig. 6.19 Interlock disc (5) (five-speed) (Sec 7)

All units
9   Withdraw the 1st/2nd selector shaft.
10 Withdraw the 3rd/4th selector shaft.
11 Remove the 1st/2nd and reverse selector forks.
12 Drive out the reverse idler shaft roll pin (1) (Fig. 6.23).

Fig. 6.20 Driving out 3rd/4th selector fork roll pin (Sec 7)

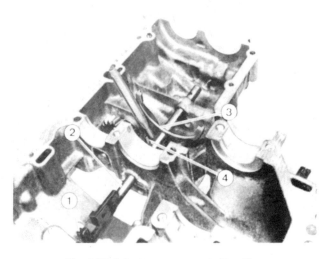

Fig. 6.21 Selector components (Sec 7)

1	1st/2nd selector shaft	3	1st/2nd selector fork
2	3rd/4th selector shaft	4	Reverse fork

Fig. 6.22 Removing 1st/2nd selector dog roll pin (Sec 7)

a   Casing web

Fig. 6.23 Reverse idler components (Sec 7)

1	Roll pin	3	Stop
2	Idler shaft		

13 Remove reverse idler shaft (2), the stop (3) and reverse idler gear.
14 Remove the pivot bolt and withdraw the selector lever (4) (Fig. 6.24).
15 Drive out the dual roll pins (5) at the selector finger (6) and remove the finger (Fig. 6.25).
16 Compress the coil spring using an open-ended spanner or forked tool and remove the cups (7) (Fig. 6.26).
17 Remove the remote control rod (8) and extract the oil seal (9) (Fig. 6.27).

Reassembly

18 Lubricate all components with clean engine oil as work proceeds. Renew all roll pins and the remote control rod O-ring.
19 Fit the O-ring into its recess in the remote control rod housing.
20 Fit the remote control rod together with spacer, spring and stop.
21 Compress the coil spring and fit the half cups.
22 Fit the selector finger, check for correct alignment and drive in the dual roll pins.
23 Using the pivot bolt, fit the gearchange rod lever. Tighten the pivot bolt to the specified torque.
24 Fit reverse idler gear, the stop and the idler shaft. Drive in the shaft roll pin (photos).
25 Place reverse fork in position and then fit the 1st/2nd selector shaft with its fork. The shaft will pass through the reverse fork cut-out (photos).

Fig. 6.24 Selector lever (4) and pivot bolt (Sec 7)

Fig. 6.25 Selector finger (6) and roll pin (5) (Sec 7)

Fig. 6.26 Compressing selector finger coil spring to remove cup (7) (Sec 7)

7.24A Reverse idler gear stop and shaft

7.24B Reverse idler shaft roll pin

7.25A 1st/2nd selector shaft with reverse fork viewed from oil pick-up screen side

7.25B 1st/2nd selector shaft with reverse fork viewed from inner side

Four-speed unit
26 Pin the fork to the 1st/2nd selector shaft.

Five-speed unit
27 Pin the dog to the 1st/2nd selector shaft (photo).

All units
28 Fit the 3rd/4th selector shaft with its fork and drive in the securing pin.

Five-speed unit
29 Secure the fork to the 1st/2nd selector shaft by driving in the roll pin.

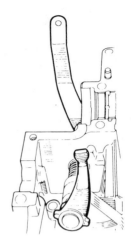

Fig. 6.29 Alignment of selector finger and lever bellcrank (Sec 7)

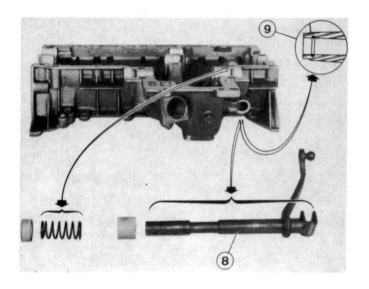

Fig. 6.27 Remote control rod (8) and casing oil seal (9) (Sec 7)

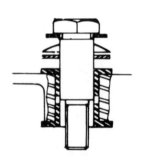

Fig. 6.30 Gearchange rod bellcrank pivot arrangement (Sec 7)

All units
30 Insert the reverse interlock disc so that it engages positively in the slots in the selector shafts (photo).
31 Slide the reverse selector shaft without disturbing the interlock disc.

Four-speed unit
32 Secure the reverse fork to the selector shaft with a roll pin (photo).

Five-speed unit
33 Fit 5th/reverse dog to its selector shaft and secure it with a roll pin (photos).
34 Place one detent ball in the reverse fork then fit the plate with the second ball (photos).
35 Tighten the plate fixing bolt to the specified torque.

All units
36 Fit the three detent balls and their springs. Apply thread locking fluid to clean threads of the detent plugs and tighten the plugs to the specified torque. Do not apply too much fluid or it will run down and cause the balls to seize (photos).

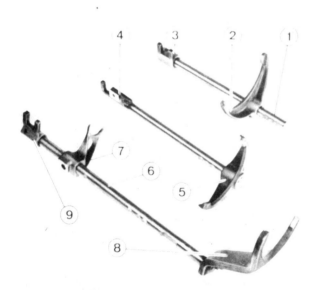

Fig. 6.28 Selector identification (Sec 7)

1	1st/2nd selector shaft	6	Reverse (4-speed)
2	1st/2nd selector fork		Reverse/5th (5-speed
3	1st/2nd selector dog		selector shaft)
4	3rd/4th selector shaft	7	Reverse selector fork
5	3rd/4th selector fork	8	5th speed selector shaft
		9	5th/reverse selector dog

8   Final drive/differential – dismantling and reassembly

1   Unscrew the fixing bolts and remove the crownwheel from the differential case.
2   Remove the pinion shaft, pinion gears with friction washers and side gears with thrust washers.
3   Clean all components and examine for worn or chipped gear teeth. Renew components as necessary.

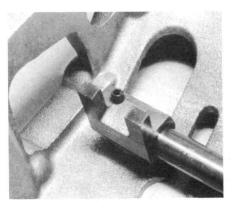

7.27 1st/2nd selector shaft dog and roll pin

7.30 Interlock disc

7.32 Reverse fork roll pin (four-speed shown)

7.33A 5th/reverse selector dog roll pin

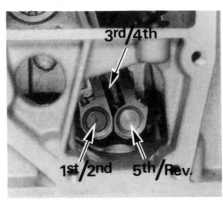

7.33B Selector shaft locations

7.34A Fitting first ball to reverse fork

7.34B Reverse fork second ball

7.34C Reverse fork lock plate

7.36A Using a pencil magnet to locate detent ball

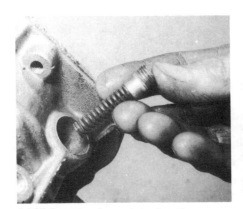

7.36B Detent spring and plug location

7.36C Location of remaining two detent springs and plugs

7.36D Allen key used to tighten detent plug

Fig. 6.31 Exploded view of final drive/differential (Sec 8)

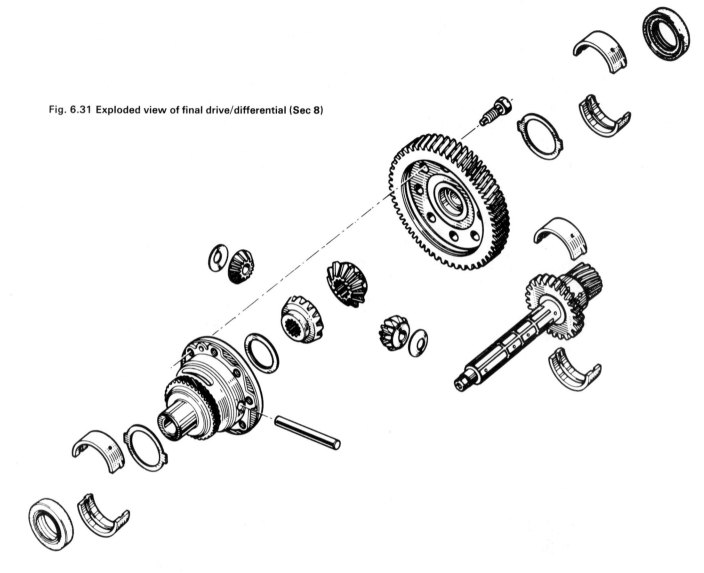

4   Commence reassembly by fitting the differential side gears and thrust washers. The grooved side of the washer must be towards the gear.

5   Fit the friction washers, pinion gears and push the pinion shaft into position.

6   Locate the crownwheel with the differential case, insert the connecting bolts and tighten to the specified torque. Make sure that the pinion shaft is retained by two of the crownwheel bolts.

9   Transmission – reassembly

1   Renew all gaskets and oil seals also the shaft nuts. As reassembly proceeds, apply clean engine oil to all components.

2   Check that the housing half casing positioning dowels are in place.

3   Make sure that new bearing shells are in their recesses in the casings. If the original shells are being used, check that they are returned to their original locations and their recesses and the shell backs are perfectly clean and free from grit.

4   The selector mechanism will already have been fitted as described in Section 7.

5   Fit the final drive/differential, together with the thrust washers, into the selector shaft half casing. Make sure that the copper side of the thrust washer is towards the crownwheel and the tabs offset upwards (photo).

9.5 Differential thrust washer with tabs offset

6   Fit the secondary shaft geartrain into the half casing making sure that the selector forks engage in the synchro sleeve grooves and the bearing circlip fits into its casing groove.
7   Fit the primary shaft geartrain, remembering that on four-speed units the shaft must be fitted with bearing outer tracks and thrust washer. On five-speed units, the 5th/reverse synchro assembly must be positioned on the shaft with the longer spacer pins towards the end of the shaft (photo).
8   Make sure that the casing locating dowels are in position and then apply jointing compound to the mating face of the half casings (photo).
9   Fit the casings together making sure that the selector finger engages in the selector shaft dog cut-outs.
10 Use new lock washers and screw in the connecting bolts finger tight. Note the location of the various bolt sizes and lengths, Fig. 6.32.
11 *On four-speed transmissions,* the primary shaft bearing preload must now be adjusted. Screw in the bearing ring nut finger tight and then tighten the casing internal bolts accessible through the sump plate aperture.
12 Engage any gear and turn the nut on the end of the secondary shaft to settle the bearings.
13 Tighten the ring nut to 15 lbf ft (20 Nm) then loosen it and retighten 7 lbf ft (9 Nm).
14 Finally stake the nut into the shaft groove. In order to be able to turn the ring nut, make up an adaptor (to engage in the nut cut-outs) to which a torque wrench can be connected.

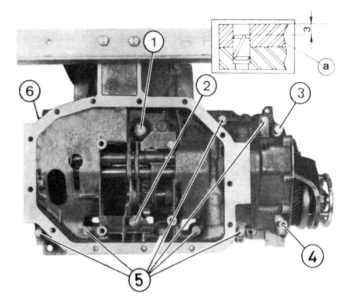

9.7 Geartrains and final drive (five-speed)

9.8 Applying jointing compound to casing flanges

Fig. 6.32 Transmission casing connecting bolt locations (Sec 9)

1	M10 x 1.50 x 75	6	M7 x 1.00 x 30
2	M8 x 1.25 x 55	7	M10 x 1.50 x 90
3	M8 x 1.25 x 55	8	M10 x 1.50 x 65
4	M8 x 1.25 x 55	9	M8 x 1.25 x 55
5	M7 x 1.00 x 75	10	M7 x 1.00 x 30

Note: *Inset on top illustration shows correct positioning of casing dowels.*

All units
15 Tighten the casing bolts in the order shown in Fig. 6.32 to the torque settings given in the table below.

Stage one
Bolts 2 – 3 – 4 – 9   9 Nm (7 lbf ft)
Bolts 5 – 6 – 10   12 Nm (9 lbf ft)
Bolts 1 – 7 – 8   20 Nm (15 lbf ft)

Stage two
Bolts 2 – 3 – 4 – 9   17 Nm (13 lbf ft)
Bolts 1 – 7 – 8   45 Nm (33 lbf ft)

9.18 Sump cover bolt with reinforcement washer

9.19 Oil drain plug showing magnet

9.22 Driveshaft oil seal at transmission

Fig. 6.33 Ring nut adaptor tool (Sec 9)

16 Fit the oil pick-up filter, tightening the bolts to the specified torque.
17 Refit the sump cover plate with a new gasket. Tighten the bolts to the specified torque. Fit the protective plate (photo).
18 Fit and tighten the drain plug (photo).
19 Refit the speedometer drive pinion with a new O-ring.
20 Screw in the reverse lamp switch.
21 If new driveshaft oil seals have not already been fitted drive them squarely into position now and fill their lips with grease (photo).

10 Differential/driveshaft oil seals – renewal

1 The differential oil seals can be removed and refitted with the engine/transmission unit in position in the car, but the driveshafts will obviously have to be removed. This operation is covered in Chapter 7.
2 With the driveshafts withdrawn the old oil seals can be extracted from the differential housing using a suitable screwdriver.
3 Clean out the seating before fitting a new seal. Lubricate the seal to assist assembly and drift carefully into position, with the lip facing inwards. Fill the seal lips with grease.
4 Always take care not to damage the oil seals when removing or refitting the driveshafts.

11 Fault diagnosis – transmission

Symptom	Reason(s)
Weak or ineffective synchromesh	Synchromesh units worn, or damaged
Jumps out of gear	Gearchange mechanism worn Synchromesh units badly worn Selector fork badly worn
Excessive noise	Incorrect grade of oil or oil level too low Gearteeth excessively worn or damaged Intermediate gear thrust washers worn allowing excessive end play Worn bearings
Difficulty in engaging gears	Clutch pedal adjustment incorrect
Noise when cornering	Wheel bearing or driveshaft fault Differential fault

Note: *It is sometimes difficult to decide whether it is worthwhile removing and dismantling the gearbox for a fault which may be nothing more than a minor irritant. Gearboxes which howl, or where the synchromesh can be 'beaten' by a quick gearchange, may continue to perform for a long time in this state. A worn gearbox usually needs a complete rebuild to eliminate noise because the various gears, if re-aligned on new bearings, will continue to howl when different wearing surfaces are presented to each other. The decision to overhaul therefore, must be considered with regard to time and money available, relative to the degree of noise or malfunction that the driver has to suffer.*

Chapter 7
Driveshafts, hub bearings, roadwheels and tyres

For modifications, and information applicable to later models, see Supplement at end of manual

Contents

Specifications

Driveshafts
Type .... Open with constant velocity joint at each end

Hub bearings
Front .... Twin ball
Rear .... Inner and outer tapered roller

Roadwheels
Type .... Pressed steel or light alloy
Size .... 4$\frac{1}{2}$ B 13, 5 B 13 or 5 B 14 (alloy only)

Tyres
Type .... Radial
Size .... 135 SR 13, 145 SR 13, 155/70 SR 13, 165/70 SR 13, 165/65 HR 14 (GLS option)

Tyre pressures

Normal loading	Front	Rear
135 SR 13	1.9 bar (28 lbf/in²)	2.0 bar (29 lbf/in²)
145 SR 13	1.8 bar (26 lbf/in²)	1.9 bar (28 lbf/in²)
155/70 SR 13	1.7 bar (25 lbf/in²)	1.9 bar (28 lbf/in²)
165/70 SR 13 (except Cabriolet)	1.7 bar (25 lbf/in²)	2.0 bar (29 lbf/in²)
165/70 SR 13 (Cabriolet)	1.8 bar (26 lbf/in²)	2.1 bar (30 lbf/in²)
165/65 HR 14 (GLS option)	1.8 bar (26 lbf/in²)	2.2 bar (32 lbf/in²)

High speed or heavy loading		
135 SR 13	2.1 bar (30 lbf/in²)	2.2 bar (32 lbf/in²)
145 SR 13	2.0 bar (29 lbf/in²)	2.1 bar (30 lbf/in²)
155/70 SR 13	1.8 bar (26 lbf/in²)	2.0 bar (29 lbf/in²)
165/70 SR 13 (except Cabriolet)	1.9 bar (28 lbf/in²)	2.2 bar (32 lbf/in²)
165/70 SR 13 (Cabriolet)	2.0 bar (29 lbf/in²)	2.3 bar (33 lbf/in²)
165/65 HR 14 (GLS option)	1.9 bar (28 lbf/in²)	2.2 bar (32 lbf/in²)

Torque wrench settings

	Nm	lbf ft
Driveshaft nut	245	180
Roadwheel nuts:		
Pressed steel	59	44
Light alloy	81	60
Track control arm pivot bolt	34	25
Anti-roll bar clamp bolts	43	32
Anti-roll bar end nut	54	40

1 Description and maintenance

1   The drive to the front wheels of the Samba is transmitted directly from the final drive unit to the front hubs by the driveshafts. Constant velocity universal joints are fitted at each end and accommodate the steering and suspension angular movements. The inner joints slide to absorb the changes of length that accompany suspension and steering movement.

2   The driveshafts are splined to the front hubs. These run on double row ball-races located in the hub carrier at the base of the MacPherson struts.

3   The rear hubs run on conventional taper-roller bearings on individual stub axles.

4   At the intervals specified in Routine Maintenance, check the driveshaft bellows for splits and leakage of grease, also the rear hub bearings for 'rock' or endfloat after having raised the roadwheels from the ground.

2 Driveshaft – removal and refitting

1   When the driveshaft is withdrawn from the transmission there will be some loss of oil so anticipate this by draining some of the engine/transmission oil or having a container ready to catch it. Raising the car sufficiently high on the side from which the shaft is being removed will prevent undue oil loss.

2   Disconnect the anti-roll bar clamp. Also disconnect the end of the bar from the track control arm on the side from which the driveshaft is being removed.

3   Turn the steering to full (outward) lock on the side being dismantled.

4   Raise the front of the car and support it securely. Remove the roadwheel.

Fig. 7.1 Separating hub carrier from driveshaft (Sec 2)

5   Unscrew the driveshaft nut. In order to prevent the hub from turning, either have an assistant apply the brakes fully or bolt a length of flat steel bar to two of the roadwheel studs to act as a lever (photo).

6   Disconnect the inboard end of the track control arm by unscrewing and removing the pivot bolt.

7   Pull the hub carrier assembly off the end of the driveshaft taking care not to strain the brake flexible hose.

8   Withdraw the driveshaft (photo).

9   Refitting is a reversal of removal, tighten all nuts and bolts to the specified torque. Stake the driveshaft nut into its shaft groove.

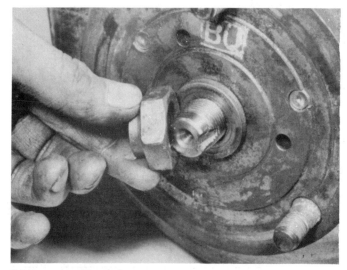

2.5 Removing driveshaft nut

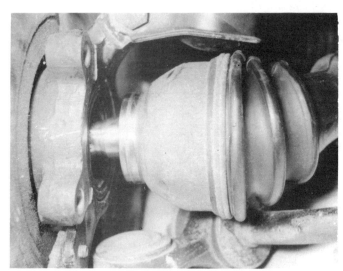

2.8 Separating driveshaft from hub carrier

3 Driveshaft joint bellows – renewal

Inboard joint

1   With the driveshaft removed from the car, prise back the lip of the cover and then tap the cover off to expose the tulip yoke.

2   Remove the tulip yoke, spring and thrust cup.

3   Wipe away as much of the original grease as possible.

4   If retaining circlips are not fitted, wind adhesive tape around the spider bearings to retain their needle rollers.

5   If it is now possible, borrow or make up a guide tool similar to the one shown. The defective bellows can be cut off and the new ones slid up the tool (well greased) so that they will expand sufficiently to ride over the joint and locate on the shaft (photo).

6   Where such a tool cannot be obtained, proceed in the following way.

7   Mark the relative position of the spider to the shaft.

8   Remove the spider retaining circlip.

9   Either support the spider and press the shaft from it or use a suitable puller to draw it from the shaft.

10   Remove the bellows/cover and the small rubber retaining ring.

11   Commence reassembly by smearing the inside of the cover with grease, fit the spacer to the new bellows which are supplied as a repair kit complete with grease sachet.

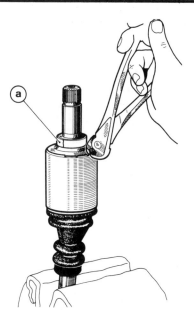

Fig. 7.2 Prising back driveshaft joint cover lip (Sec 3)

a   Oil seal rubbing surface

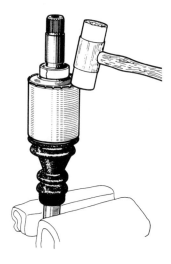

Fig. 7.3 Tapping off driveshaft joint cover (Sec 3)

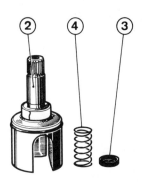

Fig. 7.4 Driveshaft inboard joint components (Sec 3)

2   Tulip   4   Spring
3   Thrust cup

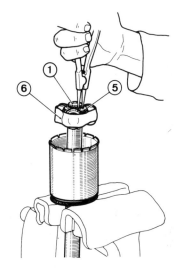

Fig. 7.5 Extracting spider circlip (Sec 3)

1   Shaft   6   Taped needle rollers
5   Needle roller cage

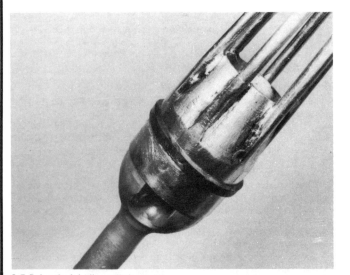

3.5 Driveshaft bellows fitting tool

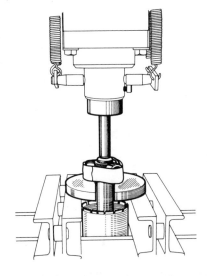

Fig. 7.6 Pressing shaft out of spider (Sec 3)

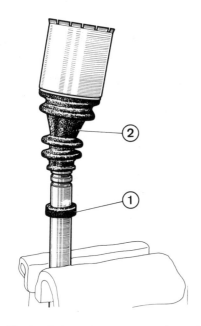

Fig. 7.7 Driveshaft inboard joint (Sec 3)

1   Rubber ring   2   Bellows

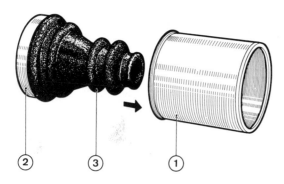

Fig. 7.8 Driveshaft inboard joint cover (1), spacer (2) and bellows (3) (Sec 3)

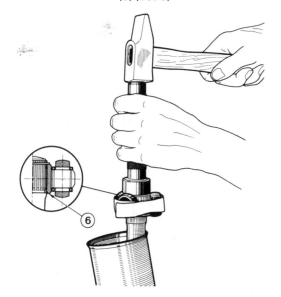

Fig. 7.9 Driving spider onto shaft (Sec 3)

6   Chamfered side

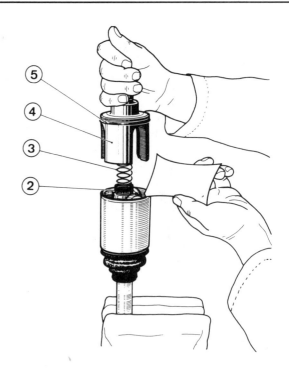

Fig. 7.10 Assembling inboard joint (Sec 3)

2   Thrust cup   4   Tulip
3   Spring   5   O-ring

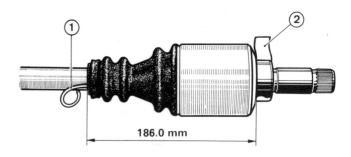

Fig. 7.11 Inboard joint bellows setting diagram (Sec 3)

1   Rod for air release   2   Protective tape

12 Insert the spacer/gaiter into the cover.
13 Slide the small rubber ring onto the shaft followed by the bellows/cover assembly.
14 Using a piece of tubing as a drift, align the marks made before dismantling and drive the spider onto the shaft. Note that the chamfered side of the spider should go onto the shaft first.
15 Fit a new spider retaining circlip.
16 Remove the bearing retaining tape.
17 Draw the cover over the spider and apply grease from the sachet to all components. Refit the tulip yoke with spring and thrust cap. Use a new O-ring seal.
18 Peen the rim of the cover evenly all around the yoke.
19 Engage the rubber retaining ring over the narrow end of the bellows.
20 Carefully insert a thin rod under the narrow end of the bellows and release trapped air.
21 Set the dimension as shown in the diagram by sliding the bellows or cover.

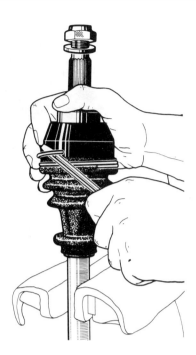

Fig. 7.12 Removing bellows clip from driveshaft outboard joint
(Sec 3)

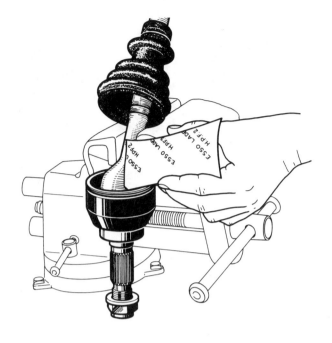

Fig. 7.14 Applying grease to outboard joint (Sec 3)

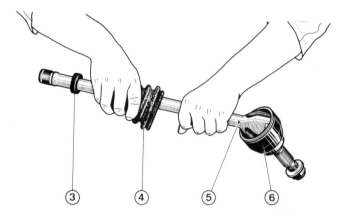

Fig. 7.13 Withdrawing outboard bellows (Sec 3)

3 Rubber ring   5 Shaft
4 Bellows   6 Stub axle

Outboard joint

22 If the guide tool mentioned in paragraph 5 is available, it is possible to cut the defective bellows from the shaft and fit the new bellows without dismantling the shaft. Where such a tool is not available, proceed in the following way.

23 With the driveshaft removed from the car and the inboard joint dismantled as previously described, take off the spring clip which retains the larger diameter end of the bellows.

24 Prise off the rubber ring from the smaller diameter end of the bellows and slide the bellows down the shaft.

25 Wipe away as much grease as possible from the joint and discard the defective bellows.

26 Apply the grease supplied with the repair kit evenly between the bellows and joint.

27 Locate the new bellows, clip and rubber ring.

28 Insert a thin rod under the narrow end of the bellows to release any trapped air.

29 Refit the inboard joint as previously described.

4 Driveshaft joints – overhaul

1 The outboard joint cannot be overhauled or repaired except for renewal of the bellows as previously described.

2 The inboard joint can be overhauled to the extent of renewing the spider which is supplied as a repair kit. The operations involved are covered in Section 3.

5 Front hub bearings – renewal

1 Remove the hub carrier as described in Chapter 11, Section 6.

2 Clean away external dirt and grease and prise out the oil seal from the inboard side (photo).

5.2 Removing hub carrier inboard oil seal

5.3 Extracting hub bearing circlip

5.4 Withdrawing front hub from bearings

5.5A Removing disc retaining socket-headed screw

5.5B Separating disc from hub

5.5C Removing hub carrier outboard oil seal

5.5D Removing hub bearing track

3   Extract the bearing circlip (photo).
4   Press or draw the hub out of the bearings. A slide hammer is the best tool to use (photo).
5   Unscrew the socket-headed screws and separate the disc from the hub. Remove the bearings and oil seal from the hub carrier (photos).
6   Renew the seals and circlips.
7   Inspect the hub for wear in the splines. Check that the seal rubbing surface is not grooved or pitted.

8   Make sure that the hub drain holes are clear.
9   Work some wheel bearing grease into the new bearings and draw them into the hub. Fit a new circlip.
10   Apply grease to the lips of the seals and fit them, lips towards bearing.
11   Draw the hub/disc into the bearing having tightened the disc socket-headed fixing screws to the specified torque.
12   Refit the hub carrier also as described in Chapter 11, Section 6.

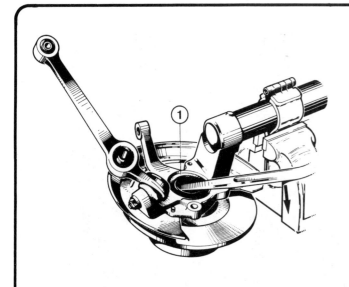

Fig. 7.15 Removing oil seal (1) from front hub (Sec 5)

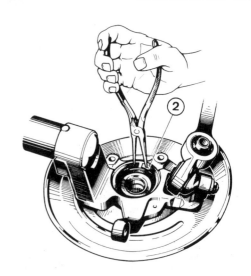

Fig. 7.16 Extracting front hub bearing circlip (2) (Sec 5)

Fig. 7.17 Unscrewing disc retaining screw (Sec 5)

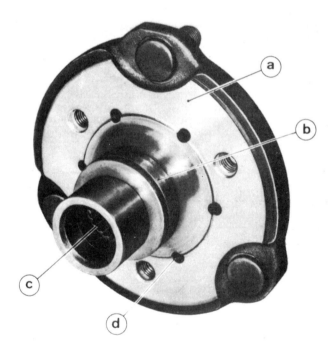

Fig. 7.18 Front hub (Sec 5)

a   Disc locating area   c   Driveshaft splines
b   Seal rubbing surface   d   Drain holes

6   Rear hub bearings – adjustment

1   If anything more than the slightest amount of endfloat or rock is detected when the roadwheel is raised and gripped at top and bottom then carry out the following adjustments.
2   With the wheel hanging free, remove the grease cap and its seal.
3   Unscrew the nut two or three turns and then spin the drum whilst tightening the nut to a torque of 30 Nm (22 lbf ft). Unscrew the nut and tighten with the fingers only.
4   Apply the footbrake two or three times and then unscrew the nut through 30°.

5   Without disturbing the setting of the nut, stake it into the groove in the axleshaft. Always use a new nut if a new area of the nut does not present itself for staking. It is often possible to swap the nuts from side to side in order to present new staking areas to the shaft groove.
6   Refit the grease cap (photo).

6.6 Rear hub grease cap

7   Rear hub bearings – renewal

1   Failure to adjust the rear hub bearings satisfactorily will be due to worn bearings which must be renewed in the following way.
2   Raise the rear of the car and remove the roadwheel.
3   Remove the brake drum as described in Chapter 9.
4   Prise out the inner oil seal and take out the bearing race. The outer bearing race will have been displaced when the drum was being removed. The oil seal may also have been left on the stub axle (photo).
5   Using a suitable extractor or a bolt with plates and distance pieces, draw both bearing tracks from the hub.
6   Wipe out the old grease.
7   Fit the new tracks. If both sides of the car are being dismantled, do not mix up the components of the individually packed bearing sets.
8   Pack the space between the two tracks one third full with wheel bearing grease, fit the inner race and a new oil seal.

7.4 Rear hub oil seal

7.9A Rear hub bearing thrust washer

7.9B Fitting rear hub nut

9   Fit the drum/hub to the stub axle and fit the outer bearing race, the thrust washer and nut (photos).
10 Adjust the bearings as described in Section 6.

8   Roadwheels and tyres

1   On cars with pressed-steel wheels, clean them (inner and outer surfaces) at regular intervals and keep them free from rust by repainting periodically if necessary.
2   Keep alloy wheels clean and free from corrosion using a proprietary product.
3   Avoid kerbing or rubbing kerbs when parking.
4   Apart from keeping the tyres correctly inflated, it is recommended that every few thousand miles the roadwheels are moved between front and rear on the same side of the car as a means of evening out tyre wear. Do not move wheels with radial tyres from side to side or diagonally.
5   Whilst the wheels are removed, take the opportunity to remove embedded flints, inspect the tyre carcass for splits and bulges and for tread wear.
6   Renew the tyre when the tread has worn down to the legal limit or the tread wear indicator bars are visible.
7   When new tyres are fitted, have the wheels balanced and whenever steering vibration or judder indicates the need for re-balancing.
8   Always tighten roadwheel nuts to their specified torque.
9   On certain models with 165/70 tyres the spare wheel is stowed under the bonnet in a deflated condition. A compressor is supplied with the car to inflate the tyre by plugging in to the cigar lighter socket.

9   Fault diagnosis – driveshafts, hub bearings, roadwheels and tyres

Symptom	Reason(s)
Vibration	Driveshaft bent Worn universal joints Out-of-balance roadwheels
'Clonk' on taking up drive or on overrun	Worn universal joints Worn splines on shaft, hub carrier or differential side gears Loose driveshaft nut Loose roadwheels bolts
Noise or roar especially when cornering	Worn hub bearings Incorrectly adjusted hub bearings

Chapter 8 Steering system

Contents

Specifications

Type .... Rack and pinion with universally jointed safety column

Turning circle (between kerbs) .... 9.3 m (30.5 ft)

Number of turns of steering wheel, lock to lock 3.92

Steering angles (car at kerb weight)
Camber (non-adjustable)
  All models except Rallye .... 0° 30′ ± 30′ positive
  Rallye .... 2° 30′ negative
Toe-in (total) .... 1.2 mm ± 2 mm (0.047 ± 0.078 in)

Rack lubricant .... Molybdenum disulphide grease

Torque wrench settings

	Nm	lbf ft
Rack housing mounting bolts	34	25
Flexible coupling pinch-bolts	15	11
Gearchange lever pivot bolt	12	9
Tie-rod end balljoint taper pin nut	34	25
Tie-rod balljoint locknut	43	32
Steering column bracket bolts	24	18
Steering wheel nut	49	36
Roadwheel nuts		
Steel wheel	59	44
Alloy wheel	81	60

---

1 General description

The steering system is of rack and pinion type. Movement is transmitted to the roadwheels through balljointed tie-rods which are connected to steering arms on the hub carrier.

The steering column is of safety type having a universally jointed lower shaft and a flexible coupling to the steering gear pinion.

2 Maintenance

1 Maintenance consists mostly of regular visual inspection of all steering components.

2 Check the rack bellows for splits or evidence of leakage of lubricant. Expand the bellows and examine the base of the grooves particularly carefully as this is the most likely place for splits to occur.

3 With an assistant turning the steering wheel through a few degrees from lock to lock, check the tie-rod end balljoints for wear. This is indicated when the balljoint 'rocks' or moves slightly without any corresponding movement of the hub carrier arm or roadwheel.

4 Where such movement is evident, renew the balljoint as described in Section 4.

5 Any movement of the steering wheel without corresponding movement of the front roadwheels (lost motion) may also be due to worn rack and pinion teeth on high mileage cars.

6 The steering shaft flexible coupling should be examined for deformation or general deterioration and renewed if necessary (Section 9).

3 Steering rack bellows – renewal

1 Release the tie-rod end balljoint locknut through a quarter of a turn and then count the number of exposed threads between the shoulder on the balljoint socket and the locknut. Record the number.
2 Unscrew the balljoint taper pin nut, but do not remove it.
3 Using a suitable extractor 'split' the balljoint from the eye of the steering arm on the hub carrier (photo).
4 Remove the taper pin nut, release the balljoint from the steering arm and unscrew it from the tie-rod.
5 Release the spring clip from the larger diameter end of the bellows and slide the bellows off the end of the tie-rod. These operations will be made easier if the roadwheel is first removed and the steering turned to full lock, but it is not essential.
6 If the bellows have been split for some time, wipe all the old grease and dirt from the rack and liberally apply specified lubricant to the rack teeth (extended).
7 Slide the new bellows up the tie-rod, fit the clip to the larger diameter end of the bellows (photo).
8 Screw the balljoint over the end of the tie-rod until the number of exposed threads is as recorded at removal.
9 Connect the balljoint taper pin to the steering arm eye, tighten the nut to the specified torque. **Note:** *If difficulty is experienced in loosening or tightening a balljoint taper pin nut due to the taper pin turning in the eye, apply pressure with a jack or long lever to the balljoint socket to force the taper pin into its conical seat.*
10 However carefully the tie-rod end balljoint is screwed back onto the tie-rod, always check the front wheel alignment (toe-in) as described in Section 12.

4 Tie-rod end balljoint – removal and refitting

1 The operations are described in paragraphs 1 to 4 and 8 to 10 of the preceding Section.

5 Steering wheel – removal and refitting

1 Set the front roadwheels in the straight-ahead position. The steering wheel spokes should be in the lower half of the steering wheel with the top bar of the Talbot motif in the steering wheel hub horizontal.
2 Prise out the motif and then using a socket, unscrew and remove the steering wheel nut (photos).

3.3 Disconnecting a tie-rod end balljoint

5.2A Removing steering wheel centre motif

3.7 Steering bellows clip

5.2B Steering wheel nut

3 If the steering wheel does not simply pull off its shaft splines, thump the rear of the rim at opposite points using the palms of the hands.

4 Refitting is a reversal of removal, but apply a smear of grease to the splines of the shaft before pushing the steering wheel into place.

5 Make sure that the alignment of the spokes is correct with the roadwheels in the straight-ahead position and then tighten the retaining nut to the specified torque.

6 Press the motif into the steering wheel hub.

6 Steering column lock – removal and refitting

1 Disconnect the battery negative lead.

2 Remove the lower steering column shroud.

3 Turn the ignition key to the A position.

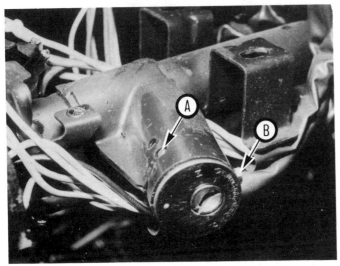

6.4 Steering lock/ignition switch

A Plunger *B Retaining bolt*

4 Unscrew and remove the small bolt which retains the lock/ignition switch in the steering column housing (photo).

5 Using a small rod depress the plunger which is visible through the cut-out in the lock housing and withdraw the lock/switch assembly.

6 Disconnect the wiring harness plug.

7 The ignition switch may be separated from the steering lock by extracting the two small screws.

8 Refitting is a reversal of removal.

7 Steering column – removal and refitting

1 Disconnect the battery.

2 Remove the steering column lower shroud after extracting the securing screws. The upper shroud can only be removed after the column is lowered (photo).

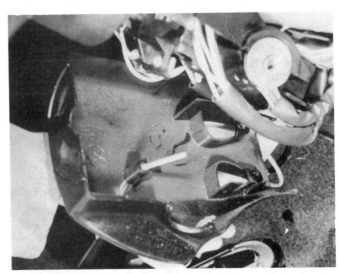

7.2 Steering column lower shroud removed

3 Remove the steering wheel (Section 5).

4 Disconnect the wiring plugs and remove the column switches as described in Chapter 10.

5 Unscrew and remove the pinch-bolt from the upper clamp of the flexible coupling (photo).

6 Unscrew the steering column mounting bracket nuts and withdraw the column complete with universally-jointed intermediate shaft (photos).

7 Refitting is a reversal of removal. Make sure that the coupling is so positioned that the pinch-bolt passes smoothly through the cut-out in the splined shaft.

8 Tighten all bolts to the specified torque.

8 Steering column – overhaul

1 Remove the steering column (Section 7).

2 The steering column bushes may be renewed after carefully tapping the shaft out of the tube using a plastic-faced hammer. The lower bush will come out with the shaft.

7.5 Steering shaft flexible coupling

7.6A Steering column brackets

7.6B Partially splined end of steering shaft

3   Fit the lower bush to the shaft and then tap the bush into the lower end of the tube using a piece of tubing as a drift. Stake the tube to retain the bush.
4   Tap the upper bush into the tube.

9 Steering shaft flexible coupling – renewal

1   The flexible coupling may be renewed without the need to remove either the column or steering gear.
2   Disconnect the ball-jointed gearchange link rods (1) and (2) (Fig. 8.1).
3   Disconnect the exhaust bracket (3).

Fig. 8.1 Steering shaft flexible coupling disconnection points (Sec 9)

1   Gearchange link rod
2   Gearchange link rod
3   Exhaust bracket
4   Flexible coupling pinch bolt
5   Rack housing mounting bolts

Fig. 8.2 Removing steering shaft flexible coupling (Sec 9)

Fig. 8.3 Pinion oil seal (1) (Sec 9)

a   Lip

4   Unscrew and remove both pinch-bolts (4) from the flexible coupling.
5   Unscrew and remove the steering rack mounting bolts (5) and retain any spacers.
6   Prise open the jaws of the flexible coupling clamps very slightly then pull the rack housing downwards so that the coupling can be slid off the splined pinion and intermediate shaft.
7   Check the condition of the pinion oil seal. If necessary, remove the spacer and oil seal and renew the seal. The seal lip (a) should be lightly greased and face downward when installed.
8   Fit the new flexible coupling to the intermediate shaft, push the rack housing upwards and engage the pinion shaft with the coupling. Fit the pinch-bolts.
9   Refit the rack housing mounting bolts and spacers.
10 Reconnect the exhaust bracket.
11 Reconnect the gearchange link rods.
12 Tighten all nuts and bolts to the specified torque wrench settings.

10 Steering gear – removal and refitting

1   Unscrew and remove the gearchange lever pivot bolt (1) (photo).
2   Unscrew and remove the upper pinch-bolt from the flexible coupling.

10.1 Gearchange lever pivot on steering gear housing

Fig. 8.4 Gearchange lever pivot bolt (1) (Sec 10)

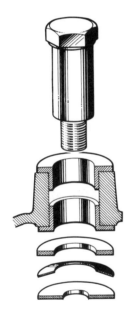

Fig. 8.5 Sequence for fitting of gearchange lever pivot components (Sec 10)

3   Unscrew, but do not remove, the nuts from the tie-rod end balljoint taper pins and then using a suitable extractor, 'split' the balljoints from the steering arms on the hub carrier. Remove the nuts.
4   Unscrew and remove the rack housing mounting bolts together with washers and spacers.
5   Withdraw the steering gear downwards and then out from under the wheel arch.
6   Refitting is a reversal of removal, tighten all nuts and bolts to the specified torque and check the front wheel alignment (Section 12) on completion.
7   Make sure that the fitted sequence of the gearchange lever pivot components is as shown in Fig. 8.5.

11 Steering gear – overhaul

1   The steering gear has a very long life before any wear becomes evident always provided that the bellows are kept in good order to maintain adequate lubrication.
2   In view of the special tools and gauges required to overhaul the steering gear, it is recommended that when the need for this arises, the assembly should be changed for a new or factory reconditioned one rather than dismantle the worn unit.

12 Steering angles and front wheel alignment

1   Accurate front wheel alignment is essential to provide good steering and roadholding characteristics and to ensure slow and even tyre wear. Before considering the steering angles, check that the tyres are correctly inflated, that the front wheels are not buckled, the hub bearings are not worn or incorrectly adjusted and that the steering linkage is in good order, without slackness or wear at the joints.
2   Wheel alignment consists of four factors: *Camber,* is the angle at which the road wheels are set from the vertical when viewed from the front or rear of the vehicle. Positive camber is the angle (in degrees) that the wheels are tilted outwards at the top from the vertical. *Castor,* is the angle between the steering axis and a vertical line when viewed from each side of the vehicle. Positive castor is indicated when the steering axis is inclined towards the rear of the vehicle at its upper end. *Steering axis inclination,* is the angle when viewed from the front or rear of the vehicle between vertical and an imaginary line drawn between the upper and lower strut mountings.
     Camber, castor and steering axis inclination are set during production of the car and any deviation from specified tolerance must therefore be due to gross wear in the suspension mountings or collision damage. *Toe,* is the amount by which the distance between the front inside edges of the roadwheel rims differs from that between the rear inside edges. If the distance between the front edges is less than that at the rear, the wheels are said to toe-in. If the distance between the front inside edges is greater than that at the rear, the wheels toe-out.
3   To check the front wheel alignment, first make sure that the lengths of both tie-rods are equal when the steering is in the straight-ahead position.
4   Release the tie-rod balljoint locknuts and rotate the tie rods until the distance between the end of the tie-rod and the centre of the ball socket is 59.0 mm (2.3 in). This operation will set the roadwheels parallel. Check that the rack bellows are not twisted.
5   Obtain a tracking gauge. These are available in various forms from accessory stores or one can be fabricated from a length of steel tubing suitably cranked to clear the sump and bellhousing and having a setscrew and locknut at one end.
6   With the gauge, measure the distance between the two wheel inner rims (at hub height) at the rear of the wheel. Push the vehicle forward to rotate the wheel through 180° (half a turn) and measure the distance between the wheel inner rims, again at hub height, at the front of the wheel. This last measurement should differ from the first by the appropriate toe-in according to specification (see Specifications Section).
7   Where the toe-in is found to be incorrect, release the tie-rod balljoint locknuts and turn the tie-rods equally. Only turn them a quarter of a turn at a time before re-checking the alignment. Do not grip the threaded part of the tie-rod balljoint during adjustment and make sure that the bellows outboard clip is released otherwise the bellows may twist as the tie-rod is rotated. Rotating a tie-rod through a quarter turn will alter the toe at the wheel rim by 0.5 mm (0.020 in).
8   Always turn each tie-rod in the same direction (clockwise or anti-clockwise) when viewed from the centre line of the car otherwise the lengths of the rods will become unequal. This would cause the steering wheel spoke position to alter and cause problems on turns with tyre scrubbing.
9   On completion, tighten the tie-rod locknuts without disturbing their setting, check that the balljoint is at the centre of its arc of travel.
10   Refer to Chapter 11 for details of rear wheel alignment.

Fault diagnosis appears overleaf

13 Fault diagnosis – steering gear

Symptom	Reason(s)
Stiff action	Lack of rack lubrication Seized tie-rod end balljoints Siezed track control arm swivel joint
Free movement at steering wheel	Wear in tie-rod balljoints Wear in rack teeth
Tyre squeal when cornering or severe wear at tyre shoulders	Incorrect wheel alignment Worn hub bearings
Knocking when traversing rough surfaces	Worn column or rack bushes Incorrectly adjusted rack slipper or broken coil spring

Chapter 9 Braking system

Contents

Specifications

Type	Four-wheel hydraulic dual-circuit, discs front, drums rear with automatic adjusters. Servo assistance certain models only. Handbrake, mechanical to rear wheels. Pressure regulating valve in hydraulic circuit

Disc brakes

Type	DBA or Teves
Disc diameter	241.0 mm (9.4 in)
Disc thickness	10.0 mm (0.39 in)
Minimum thickness after regrind	8.5 mm (0.33 in)
Maximum disc run-out	0.07 mm (0.0028 in)
Disc pad (friction lining) wear limit:	
DBA	2.5 mm (0.098 in)
Teves	2.0 mm (0.079 in)

Drum brakes

Type	DBA or Girling
Drum internal diameter	180.0 mm (7.09 in)
Maximum internal diameter after regrind	181.0 mm (7.13 in)
Maximum drum out of round	0.10 mm (0.0039 in)
Minimum shoe friction lining wear limit	2.5 mm (0.098 in)

Hydraulic units

Master cylinder diameter	19.0 mm (0.75 in)
Caliper piston	48.0 mm (1.89 in)
Wheel cylinder diameter	22.0 mm (0.87 in)

Vacuum servo unit

Diameter	152.4 mm (6.0 in)

Torque wrench settings

	Nm	lbf ft
Brake pedal pivot bolt	27	20
Caliper mounting bolts (Teves)	68	50
Caliper mounting socket screws (DBA)	83	61
Roadwheel nuts:		
Pressed steel	59	44
Alloy	81	60
Disc securing bolts	64	47
Master cylinder mounting nuts	10	7

1 General description

The braking system is of four-wheel hydraulic type with discs on the front and drums on the rear.

The hydraulic circuit is of dual type, the front and rear brakes operating independently.

A pressure regulating valve reduces the hydraulic pressure to the rear brakes under heavy applications of the brake pedal in order to prevent rear wheel lock-up.

The rear brakes incorporate automatic adjusters.

The handbrake is cable-operated to the rear wheels.

On certain models, vacuum servo assistance is provided.

2 Maintenance

1   Although the master fluid reservoir is fitted with a low level switch it is as well to check the fluid level at the weekly service check (photo).

2   Maintain the level of the fluid between the 'Minimum' and 'Maximum' marks. Always top up with clean fluid of specified type which has been stored in an air-tight tin.

3.3 Disc pad wear sensor earth lead at strut

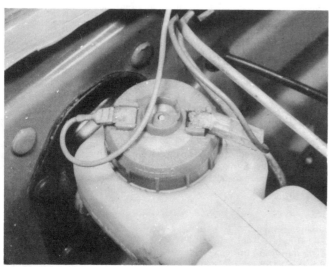

2.1 Master cylinder fluid reservoir cap and low level warning switch

3   The need for frequent topping up will indicate a leak somewhere in the system and this must be traced and rectified without delay.

4   At the specified intervals, renew the hydraulic fluid by bleeding (see Section 13).

5   If there is evidence of hydraulic fluid weeping from the master cylinder, wheel cylinder or caliper pistons, then the seals must be renewed immediately.

6   At the specified intervals, check the wear of the disc pads and brake linings also the condition of the fluid pipes and hoses as described in later Sections of this Chapter.

7   Although the handbrake travel is automatically taken up by the action of the automatic adjusters, if movement of the hand control lever becomes excessive, tension the cable as described in Section 15.

3 Disc pads – inspection and renewal

1   Raise the front of the car and support it securely.

2   Remove the roadwheels.

3   If upon inspection, the friction material has worn down to 2.0 mm (0.079 in) (this is indicated if the groove in the pad has disappeared) then the pads must be renewed as an axle set. The removal and refitting operations will vary according to the type of caliper. On later models, a pad wear sensor is fitted (photo).

DBA disc caliper

4   Remove the clips from the ends of the sliding keys.

5   Tap out the upper and lower sliding keys.

6   Free the cylinder housing and tie it to one side out of the way.

7   Remove the disc pads.

8   Clean away all dust and dirt taking care not to inhale the dust which may be injurious to health.

9   Check the piston for signs of brake fluid leakage. If evident, the cylinder must be overhauled as described later in this Chapter.

10 Before fitting the new pads, smear their backs with a product such as Copaslip or Permatex to prevent squeal.

11 Fit the pads noting very carefully the position of the stops and how the springs are engaged in the notches.

12 In order to accommodate the new thicker pads, the piston must be fully depressed into its bore. This action will cause the fluid level in the

Fig. 9.1 DBA caliper (Sec 3)

1   Key retaining clips

Fig. 9.2 Removing sliding keys (2) and (3) from DBA caliper (Sec 3)

Fig. 9.5 DBA disc pads refitted (Sec 3)

1 Springs

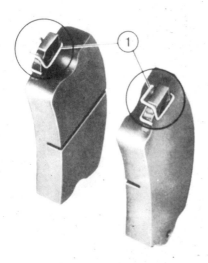

Fig. 9.3 DBA disc pads with springs (1) (Sec 3)

Fig. 9.4 DBA disc pad spring (a) and locating notch (b) (Sec 3)

master cylinder reservoir to rise so anticipate this by syphoning some fluid from the reservoir using a poultry baster or (clean) battery hydrometer.

13 Fit the cylinder and the sliding keys. These should have been smeared with the faintest trace of Copaslip or high melting point grease.

14 Fit new spring clips.

15 Make sure that the arms of the pad retaining clips are located under the slide grooves and are not caught between the sliding keys and caliper housing.

Teves disc caliper

16 Drive the pad retaining pins out of the caliper towards the centre of the car (photo).

17 Extract the anti-rattle spring.

3.16 Teves type caliper disc pad retaining pin

3.18 Removing inboard disc pad

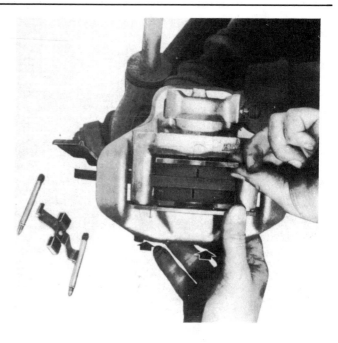

Fig. 9.7 Removing inboard disc pad (Teves caliper) (Sec 3)

18 Push back the sliding caliper and take out the inboard disc pad (photo).

19 Pull back the sliding caliper until the recess on the outboard pad backplate can be freed and the pad withdrawn.

20 Fully depress the piston into the cylinder housing. This action will cause the fluid level in the master cylinder reservoir to rise, so anticipate this by syphoning some fluid from the reservoir using a poultry baster or (clean) battery hydrometer.

21 Check the piston for sign of brake fluid leakage. If evident the cylinder must be overhauled as described later in this Chapter.

22 Clean away all dust and dirt, taking care not to inhale the dust which may be injurious to health.

23 Before fitting the new pads, smear their backs with a product such as Copaslip or Permatex to prevent squeal.

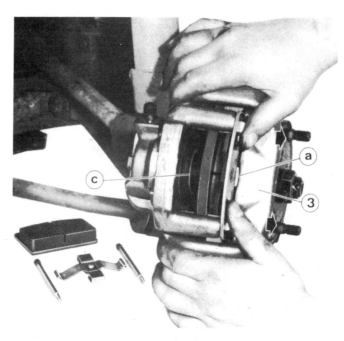

Fig. 9.8 Freeing outboard disc pad (Teves caliper) (Sec 3)

3   Sliding caliper   a   Pad retaining boss
                                  c   Piston

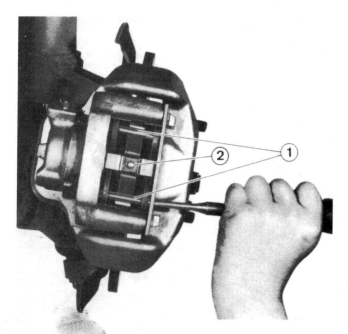

Fig. 9.6 Removing pad retaining pins (Teves caliper) (Sec 3)

1   Pin   2   Anti-rattle spring

24 Align the spigot (a) with the face (b) of the caliper bracket.

25 Locate the outboard disc pad so that its backplate recess engages with the boss (photo).

26 Fit the inboard pad.

27 Refit the anti-rattle spring with the two retaining pins.

3.25 Pair of disc pads (Teves)

Fig. 9.9 Aligning spigot (a) with face (b) of Teves type caliper bracket (Sec 3)

DBA and Teves calipers

28 Repeat the operations on the opposite disc caliper.
29 Apply the footbrake several times to position the pads against the discs.
30 Top up the master cylinder reservoir to its correct level.
31 Refit the roadwheels and lower the car to the ground.

4 Rear shoe linings (DBA brake) – inspection and renewal

1 Raise the rear of the car and support it securely.
2 Remove the roadwheels, release the handbrake.
3 Tap off the grease cap and then unscrew the staked nut from the end of the axle and remove the thrust washer.
4 Remove the hub/drum taking care that the outboard bearing does not drop out (photo).
5 Should the drum be stuck, this may be due to the shoes having worn grooves in the drum in which case, remove the plug from the brake backplate, insert a screwdriver and push the handbrake lever to one side thus freeing the thrust spigot and drum (photo).
6 Wipe the axleshaft free from grease and clean away all dust and dirt from the brake shoes. Take care not to inhale the dust as this may be injurious to health.
7 Inspect the thickness of the friction material on the shoes. If it has worn down to, or nearly down to, the rivet heads or in the case of bonded linings the thickness has been reduced to 2.5 mm (0.099 in) then the shoes should be renewed. Always obtain new or factory re-lined shoes. Attempting to re-line the original shoes seldom proves satisfactory (photo).

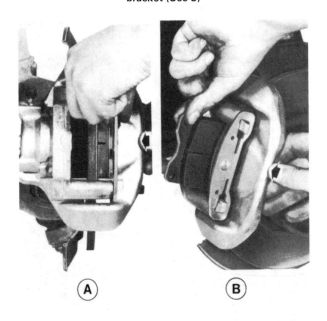

Fig. 9.10 Fitting Teves disc pads (Sec 3)

A   Outboard pad   *B   Inboard pad*

4.4 Brake drum removed

4.5 Brake backplate plug

4.7 Drum brake arrangement

Fig. 9.11 DBA drum brake assembly (Sec 4)

6   Shoe steady spring   (a) Seal lips
7   Oil seal

4.11 Shoe steady spring showing hook at rear of shoe

Fig. 9.12 Serrated automatic adjuster lever (8) and link rod (9) –
DBA (Sec 4)

Fig. 9.13 Leading brake shoe – DBA (Sec 4)

4   Serrated automatic adjuster lever   5   Retaining clip

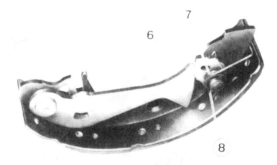

Fig. 9.14 Automatic adjuster pawl (6), spring (7) and
circlip (8) – DBA (Sec 4)

8   Disconnect the shoe upper return spring.
9   Fully release the handbrake cable adjustment and disconnect the
cable from the shoe lever. Note the position of the shoes as to which
is leading and trailing. The leading shoe is the one nearest the front of
the car whilst the trailing shoe is the one to which the handbrake cable
is attached. It is very important to observe the correct positioning of
the shoes with reference to their leading and trailing ends as indicated
by the length of exposed shoe which the lining does not cover.
10   If both brakes are being dismantled at the same time, do not mix
up the automatic adjuster struts as they are not interchangeable.
11   Remove the shoe steady springs. These are of tapered coil type
and are removed by inserting a screwdriver and rotating the spring to
release it (photo).

12   Move the serrated automatic adjuster lever towards the centre of
the brake backplate and then free the link rod.
13   Move the serrated lever back to its original position, expand the
shoes and remove them both from the backplate, together with the
shoe lower return spring.

Fig. 9.15 Trailing shoe – DBA (Sec 4)

9   Handbrake lever   10 Retaining clip

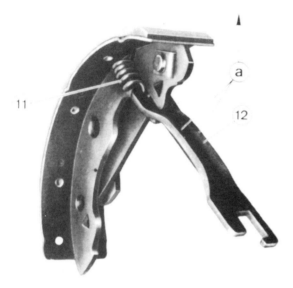

Fig. 9.16 Link rod (12) and spring (11) (Sec 4)

(a) Turned over edges

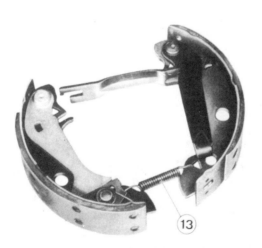

Fig. 9.17 Shoes with lower return spring (13) connected – DBA (Sec 4)

Fig. 9.18 Shoes being fitted to backplate – DBA (Sec 4)

1   Lower return spring   2   Shoe anchor plate

14 Check that the wheel cylinder is not leaking. If it is, overhaul the cylinder as described in Section 8.
15 Whilst the shoes are removed, do not depress the brake pedal or the wheel cylinder pistons will be ejected.
16 With the shoes removed to the bench, transfer the automatic adjuster serrated lever to the new leading shoe. Note that it is located on the outboard side of the shoe. Use a new spring retaining clip on the lever pivot pin.
17 Now fit the adjuster pawl, spring and a new retaining circlip to the shoe.
18 Fit the handbrake actuating lever to the outboard side of the trailing shoe and use a new clip to secure it.
19 Transfer the tension spring and link to the trailing shoe making sure that the turned over edges of the link are towards the actuating lever pivot clip.
20 Set the shoes on the bench in their correct location and engage the shoe lower return spring.
21 Apply a smear of Copaslip or high melting point grease to the shoe rubbing high points on the backplate.
22 Offer the brake shoes to the backplate, expand them against the tension of the shoe return spring and locate them on the backplate. Make sure that the shoe lower return spring is behind the bottom anchor plate (photo).

4.22 Shoe lower return spring, anchor plate and handbrake cable end fitting

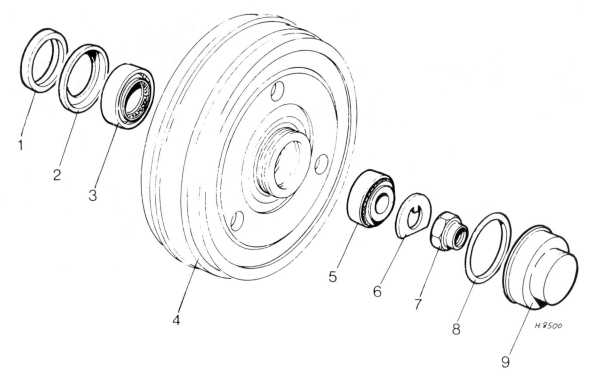

Fig. 9.19 Rear hub and drum components (Sec 4)

1	Oil seal	4	Brake drum	7	Axle nut
2	Thrust cup	5	Outer roller bearing	8	Grease cap seal
3	Inner roller bearing	6	Thrust washer	9	Grease cap

23 Move the serrated adjuster lever towards the centre of the backplate and engage the link rod between the shoes.
24 Move the serrated adjuster lever into contact with the leading shoe and then connect the upper return spring.
25 Fit the shoe steady springs so that the anchor lug is horizontal.
26 Fit a new oil seal (lips visible) if the seal was left on the axleshaft as the drum was removed.
27 Clean the interior of the drum and refit it having replenished the grease between the bearings to compensate for that removed at dismantling.
28 With the outboard bearing in position, fit the thrust washer and screw on a new nut.
29 Spin the brake drum whilst tightening the nut to 22 lbf ft (30 Nm). Unscrew the nut and tighten finger tight until any endfloat just disappears.
30 Apply the footbrake two or three times and then unscrew the nut through 30°.
31 Without disturbing the setting of the nut, stake it into the axle groove. Tap the grease cap and seal into position.
32 Repeat all the operations on the opposite brake, refit the road-wheels and lower the car to the ground.
33 Apply the footbrake several times to bring the shoes into close contact with the drums.
34 Adjust the handbrake as described in Section 15.

5 Rear shoe linings (Girling brake) – inspection and renewal

1 Carry out the operations described in paragraphs 1 to 7 in the preceding Section.
2 Fully slacken the handbrake cable and unhook it from the shoe lever.
3 Remove the shoe upper return spring.
4 Remove the shoe steady springs. To do this, grip the spring retaining cup with a pair of pliers. Depress the cup and turn it through 90° then release it so that the tee head of the steady pin passes through the cut-out in the spring cup.

5 Prise the upper ends of the shoes apart and remove the star wheel adjuster strut.
6 Remove the shoes from the lockplate, noting the position of the leading and trailing shoes as described in paragraphs 9 and 10 of the preceding Section.
7 Check that the wheel cylinder is not leaking. If it is, overhaul the cylinder as described in Section 8.
8 Whilst the shoes are removed, do not depress the brake pedal or the wheel cylinder pistons will be ejected.

Fig. 9.20 Handbrake cable (arrowed) on Girling brake (Sec 5)

1   Shoe upper return spring

Fig. 9.21 Handbrake lever (3) on Girling brake (Sec 5)

(b) Backplate inspection hole   (c) Lever locating spigot

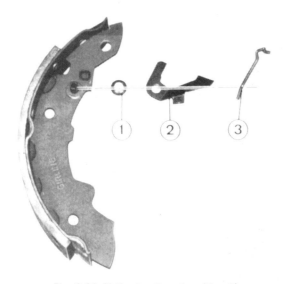

Fig. 9.22 Girling leading shoe (Sec 5)

1 Spacer   3 Clip
2 Automatic adjuster pawl

9   With the shoes removed to the bench, transfer the automatic adjuster spacer, lever and clip to the new leading shoe.
10 Set the shoes in their correct location on the bench and connect the lower return spring.
11 Apply a smear of Copaslip or high melting point grease to the shoe rubbing high points on the backplate.
12 Offer the brake shoes to the backplate, expand them against the

Fig. 9.23 Initial setting of Girling brake shoes (Sec 5)

tension of the shoe return spring and locate them on the backplate. Connect the handbrake cable.
13 Make sure that the shoe lower return spring is behind the shoes and the shoe anchor plate.
14 Clean and lightly lubricate the threads on the star wheel adjuster and set it in its fully retracted state.
15 Engage the adjuster strut between the shoes and connect the remaining springs to the shoes and automatic adjuster mechanism.
16 Fit the shoe steady pins, springs and cups.
17 Turn the star wheel adjuster to expand the shoes to the point where the drum will only just pass over them. The shoes must be concentric within the backplate. If a suitable pair of calipers are available, expand the shoes until their outside diameter is 179.5 mm (7.1 in).
18 Fit a new oil seal (lips visible) if the seal was left on the axleshaft when the drum was removed.
19 Carry out the operations described in Section 4, paragraphs 27 to 34.

6   Caliper – removal, overhaul and refitting

1   Raise the car and support it securely.
2   Remove the roadwheel and disc pads (Section 3).
3   Unscrew the two bolts or socket-headed mounting screws and withdraw the caliper (photo).

6.3 Unscrewing caliper fixing bolt

4   On Teves calipers, hold the flats of the flexible hose end fitting in an open-ended spanner and unwind the caliper from it. Quickly cap the end of the hose to prevent loss of fluid.
5   On DBA (light alloy) calipers, the flexible hose connection is by means of a banjo type union. In order to prevent loss of fluid when this union is disconnected, place a rubber disc on each side of the banjo and seal them with a pair of self-locking grips.

Teves caliper — overhaul
6   Clean away external dirt and then separate the cylinder from the sliding caliper using a soft-faced mallet.
7   Remove the dust excluder, apply air pressure from a hand or foot-operated type pump to the cylinder fluid union and eject the piston.
8   Examine the surfaces of the piston and cylinder bore. If they are scored, corroded or metal-to-metal rubbed areas are evident, renew the piston/cylinder assembly complete.
9   If the components are in good condition clean them in methylated spirit or hydraulic fluid then pick out the seal from the cylinder groove and discard it. Obtain a repair kit which will contain all the necessary new seals and other renewable items.

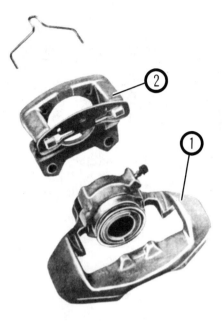

Fig. 9.26 Teves caliper (Sec 6)

1   Sliding caliper   2   Bracket

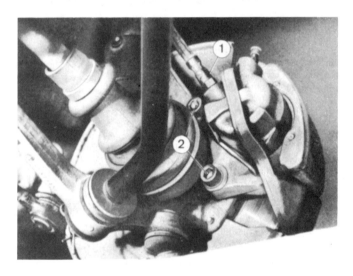

Fig. 9.24 Teves type caliper socket-head mounting screws (Sec 6)

1   Flexible hose union   2   Mounting screws

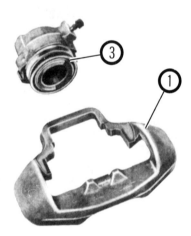

Fig. 9.27 Teves sliding caliper (1) with cylinder (3) separated (Sec 6)

10 Manipulate the new seal into its groove using the fingers only, dip the piston in clean hydraulic fluid and insert it into the cylinder.
11 Twist the piston so that the step on the piston is located as shown in Fig. 9.28 in relation to the bleed screw. The left-hand caliper is illustrated. The right-hand unit is handed with the step reversed.
12 Clean the caliper slides and fit the cylinder to the sliding caliper.

DBA caliper — overhaul
13 Clean away external dirt and separate the cylinder from its sliding caliper. To do this, the sliding caliper must be lightly held in a vice and the flanges spread using the tool (978830) or something similar made up to do the job.
14 With the flanges spread, drive out the spigot using a punch.
15 Remove the cylinder.
16 If the slides are corroded, renew the caliper complete.
17 Refer to paragraphs 7 to 10 of this Section and carry out the operations described.
18 Reconnect the cylinder to the sliding caliper by spreading the flanges and making sure that the spigot engages.

Fig. 9.25 DBA type caliper mounting bolts (Sec 6)

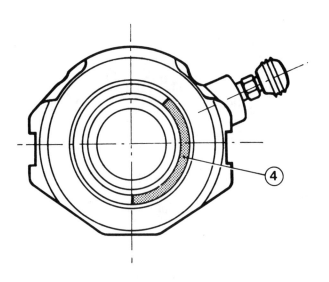

Fig. 9.28 Location of step (4) on Teves caliper piston (Sec 6)

Fig. 9.31 Driving out DBA caliper spigot (Sec 6)

Refitting

19 Clean the mounting bolt threads and apply thread locking fluid to them. Locate the caliper, connect it to the flexible hose and then screw in the mounting bolts and tighten them to the specified torque.

20 Fit the disc pads (Section 3).

21 Bleed the front hydraulic circuit as described in Section 13.

22 Fit the roadwheel and lower the car to the ground.

---

7   Disc – inspection and renovation

---

1   Whenever the disc pads are being inspected for wear, check the condition of the disc for deep scoring or cracks. Light scoring is a normal condition.

2   It is possible to have the discs ground to remove deep grooves provided both faces are ground by a similar amount and the thickness of the disc is not reduced below that specified.

Fig. 9.29 Caliper flange spreading tool (Sec 6)

Fig. 9.30 Spreading DBA caliper flanges (Sec 6)

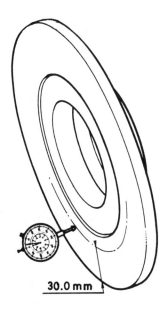

30.0 mm

Fig. 9.32 Disc run-out measuring point (Sec 7)

3   If disc distortion is suspected check the disc run-out. To do this, raise the car and remove the front roadwheel. Using a dial gauge or feeler blades between the disc and a fixed point, turn the disc and record the run-out. If the disc run-out exceeds the specified maximum tolerance, it may be possible to bring it within tolerance by moving the disc to one of the two alternative fixing positions on the hub.
4   Removal and refitting of the disc is described in Chapter 7, Section 5.

8   Rear brake wheel cylinder – removal, overhaul and refitting

1   Raise the rear of the car and support it securely. Remove the roadwheel and brake drum.
2   Prise the upper ends of the brake shoes apart so that the shoe webs no longer make contact with the pistons. If this proves difficult, remove the shoes from the backplate as described in Section 4 (photo).
3   Brush away dirt and dust from the backplate and then unscrew the hydraulic pipe union and disconnect the pipe from the wheel cylinder. Quickly cap the end of the pipe to prevent loss of fluid. Bleed nipple dust caps are useful for this purpose (photo).

8.3 Hydraulic pipe connection at wheel cylinder

8.2 Rear wheel cylinder

4   Unscrew and remove the two cylinder mounting bolts and remove the cylinder from the backplate.
5   Clean the outside of the cylinder and pull off the dust excluders.
6   Extract the pistons, seals and return spring. These components can be ejected by applying air from a tyre pump to the fluid union hole on the cylinder or by tapping the cylinder on a piece of hard wood. Note carefully the fitted direction of the seal lips (photos).
7   Inspect the surface of the cylinder bore and piston. If there is evidence of scoring, corrosion or metal-to-metal rubbed areas, renew the cylinder complete.
8   If the components are in good condition, discard the seals and obtain a repair kit which will contain all the new seals and other renewable components.
9   Clean the piston and cylinder using only methylated spirit or clean brake hydraulic fluid, then dip each component in brake fluid and reassemble.
10 Bolt the cylinder to the backplate, connect the brake pipe and tighten the union.
11 If the shoes were removed, reassemble them as described in Section 4 or 5.
12 Refit the brake drum (Section 4).

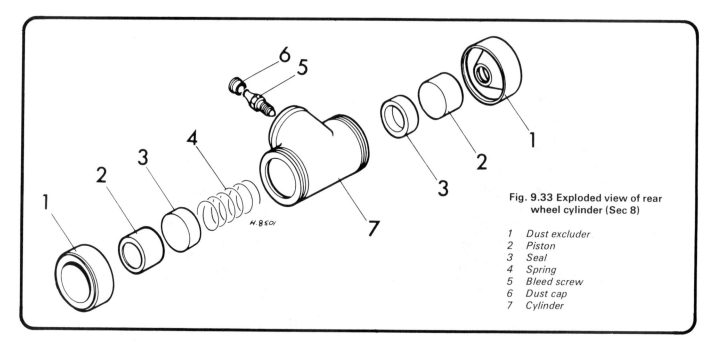

Fig. 9.33 Exploded view of rear wheel cylinder (Sec 8)

1   Dust excluder
2   Piston
3   Seal
4   Spring
5   Bleed screw
6   Dust cap
7   Cylinder

8.6A Extracting wheel cylinder piston with dust excluder

8.6B Wheel cylinder seals and spring

8.6C Exploded view of a rear wheel cylinder

13 Bleed the rear brake hydraulic circuit as described in Section 13.
14 Refit the roadwheel and lower the car to the ground.

9 Brake drum – inspection and renovation

1 Whenever the brake drum is removed to check the linings, take the opportunity to inspect the interior of the drum.
2 If the drum is grooved owing to failure to renew worn linings or after a very high mileage has been covered, then it may be possible to regrind it, provided the maximum internal diameter is not exceeded.
3 Even if only one drum is in need of grinding both drums must be reground to the same size in order to maintain even braking characteristics.
4 Judder or a springy pedal felt when the brakes are applied can be caused by a distorted (out of round) drum. Here again it may be possible to regrind the drums otherwise a new drum will be required.

10 Master cylinder – removal, overhaul and refitting

1 Syphon the fluid from the master cylinder reservoir.
2 Disconnect the hydraulic pipes from the master cylinder by unscrewing the unions. Cap the open ends of the pipes to prevent loss of fluid and entry of dirt (photo).
3 On master cylinders with remote type fluid reservoirs, disconnect the fluid feed hoses.
4 Unscrew the nuts and pull the master cylinder off the mounting studs on the bulkhead or the front face of the vacuum servo unit (if fitted).

5 Unfortunately the master cylinder cannot be overhauled as the piston stop roll pins cannot be extracted and repair kits are not supplied (photo).
6 If the master cylinder is faulty or leaking, renew it, but retain the original fluid reservoir (photos).

10.5 Master cylinder piston stop pin

10.2 Hydraulic pipes disconnected and master cylinder removed

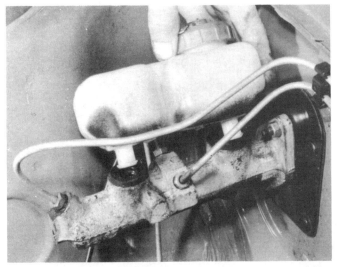

10.6A Removing fluid reservoir from master cylinder

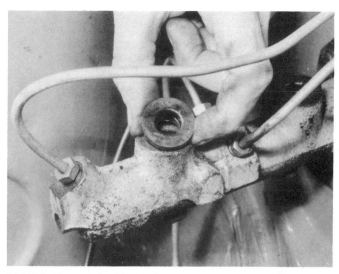

10.6B Fluid reservoir rubber seal

7   Refitting is a reversal of removal.
8   Bleed the complete brake system (both circuits) as described in Section 13.

11 Pressure regulating valve – removal and refitting

1   The valve is not repairable, but in the event of it not operating correctly as proved by rear wheel lock up occurring during heavy braking, it should be removed and a new valve fitted.
2   Disconnect the fluid lines from the valve and cap them to prevent loss of fluid (photo).

11.2 Brake hydraulic pressure regulator

3   Unbolt and remove the valve and fit the new one.
4   Reconnect the fluid pipes.
5   Bleed the hydraulic system as described in Section 13.

12 Flexible and rigid hydraulic lines – inspection and renewal

1   Examine first all the unions for signs of leaks. Then look at the flexible hoses for signs of fraying and chafing (as well as for leaks). This is only a preliminary inspection of the flexible hoses as exterior condition does not necessarily indicate interior condition which will be considered later.
2   The steel pipes must be examined equally carefully. They must be thoroughly cleaned and examined for signs of dents or other percussive damage, rust and corrosion. Rust and corrosion should be scraped off and, if the depth of pitting in the pipes is significant, they will need renewal. This is most likely in those areas underneath the chassis and along the rear suspension arms where the pipes are exposed to the full force of road and weather conditions.
3   Rigid pipe removal is usually quite straightforward. The unions at each end are undone and the pipe drawn out of the connection. The clips which may hold it to the car body are bent back and it is then removed. Underneath the car exposed unions can be particularly stubborn, defying the efforts of an open ended spanner. As few people will have the special split ring spanner required, a self-grip wrench is the only answer. If the pipe is being renewed new unions will be provided. If not then one will have to put up with the possibility of burring over the flats on the union and use a self-grip wrench for replacement also.
4   Flexible hoses are always fitted to a rigid support bracket where they join a rigid pipe, the bracket being fixed to the chassis or rear suspension arm. The rigid pipe unions must first be removed from the flexible union. Then the locknut securing the flexible pipe to the bracket must be unscrewed, releasing the end of the pipe from the bracket. As these connections are usually exposed they are more often than not rusted up and a penetrating fluid is virtually essential to aid removal. When undoing them, both halves must be supported as the bracket is not strong enough to support the torque required to undo the nut and can easily be snapped off. On some models, a clip is used to secure the hose end fitting (photo).

12.4 Brake hose support bracket and clip

5   Depending upon the make of the particular caliper, the flexible hose may be connected simply by screwing it into its tapped hole or by using a hollow bolt with banjo end fitting. Use a new copper sealing washer on each side of the banjo union.
6   Once the flexible hose is removed examine the internal bore. If clear of fluid it should be possible to see through it. Any specks of rubber which come out, or signs of restriction in the bore, mean that the inner lining is breaking up and the hose must be renewed.
7   Rigid pipes which need replacement can usually be purchased at any local garage where they have the pipe, unions and special tools to make them up. They will need to know the pipe length required and the type of flare used at the ends of the pipe. These may be different at each end of the same pipe.
8   Installation of the pipes is a reversal of the removal procedure. The pipe profile must be pre-set before fitting. Any acute bends must be put in by the garage on a bending machine otherwise there is the possibility of kinking them and restricting the fluid flow.
9   All hose and pipe threads and unions are to metric standards.

Screw in new components by hand initially to ensure that the threads are compatible.

10 Remember that a metric hose end fitting seals at the tip of its threaded section and will leave a gap between the hexagon of the end fitting and the surface of the component. Do not attempt to overtighten the hose end fitting in order to eliminate the gap.

11 The hydraulic system must be bled on completion of hose or rigid pipe renewal.

13 Hydraulic system – bleeding

1 If the master cylinder or pressure regulating valve have been removed and refitted, both hydraulic circuits must be bled. If only a component of one circuit has been disturbed then only that particular circuit need be bled.

2 If the entire system is being bled, the sequence of bleeding should be carried out by starting at the bleed screw furthest from the master cylinder and finishing at the one nearest to it. Unless the pressure bleeding method is being used, do not forget to keep the fluid level in the master cylinder reservoir topped up to prevent air from being drawn into the system which would make any work done worthless.

3 Before commencing operations, check that all system hoses and pipes are in good condition with unions tight and free from leaks.

4 Take great care not to allow hydraulic fluid to come into contact with the vehicle paintwork as it is an effective paint stripper. Wash off any spilled fluid immediately with cold water.

5 On models with a vacuum servo, destroy the vacuum by giving several applications of the brake pedal in quick succession.

Bleeding – two man method

6 Gather together a clean glass jar and a length of rubber or plastic tubing which will be a tight fit on the brake bleed screws.

7 Engage the help of an assistant.

8 Push one end of the bleed tube onto the first bleed screw and immerse the other end in the glass jar which should contain enough hydraulic fluid to cover the end of the tube (photo).

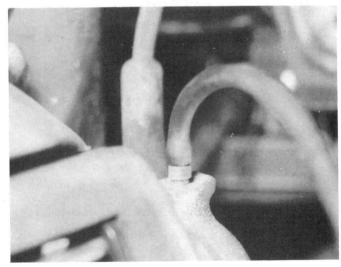

13.8 Bleed nipple and tube

9 Open the bleed screw one half a turn and have your assistant depress the brake pedal fully then slowly release it. Tighten the bleed screw at the end of each pedal downstroke to obviate any chance of air or fluid being drawn back into the system.

10 Repeat this operation until clean hydraulic fluid, free from air bubbles, can be seen coming through into the jar.

11 Tighten the bleed screw at the end of a pedal downstroke and remove the bleed tube. Bleed the remaining screws in a similar way.

Bleeding – using one-way valve kit

12 There is a number of one-man, one-way brake bleeding kits available from motor accessory shops. It is recommended that one of these kits is used wherever possible as it will greatly simplify the bleeding operation and also reduce the risk of air or fluid being drawn back into the system, quite apart from being able to do the work without the help of an assistant.

13 To use the kit, connect the tube to the bleed screw and open the screw one half a turn.

14 Depress the brake pedal fully then slowly release it. The one-way valve in the kit will prevent expelled air from returning at the end of each pedal downstroke. Repeat the operation several times to be sure of ejecting all the air from the system. Some kits include a translucent container which can be positioned so that the air bubbles can actually be seen being ejected from the system.

15 Tighten the bleed screw, remove the tube and repeat the operations on the remaining brakes.

16 On completion, depress the brake pedal. If it still feels spongy, repeat the bleeding operations as air must still be trapped in the system.

Bleeding – using a pressure bleeding kit

17 These kits too are available from motor accessory shops and are usually operated by air pressure from the spare tyre.

18 By connecting a pressurised container to the master cylinder fluid reservoir, bleeding is then carried out simply by opening each bleed screw in sequence and allowing the fluid to run out, rather like turning on a tap, until no air is visible in the expelled fluid.

19 By using this method, the large reserve of hydraulic fluid provides a safeguard against air being drawn into the master cylinder during bleeding which may occur if the fluid level in the reservoir is allowed to fall too low.

20 Pressure bleeding is particularly useful when bleeding the complete system at time of routine fluid renewal.

All methods

21 When bleeding is completed, check and top up the fluid level in the master cylinder reservoir.

22 Check the feel of the brake pedal. If it feels at all spongy, air must still be present in the system and the need for further bleeding is indicated. Failure to bleed satisfactorily after a reasonable repetition of the bleeding operations may be due to worn master cylinder seals.

23 Always discard brake fluid which has been bled from the system. It is almost certain to be contaminated with moisture, air and dirt, making it unsuitable for further use.

24 Clean fluid should always be stored in an airtight container as it absorbs moisture readily (hygroscopic) which lowers its boiling point and could affect braking performance under severe conditions.

14 Vacuum servo unit – description, testing, maintenance, removal and refitting

Description

1 The vacuum servo unit is fitted into the brake hydraulic circuit in series with the master cylinder to provide power assistance to the driver when the brake pedal is depressed.

2 The unit operates by vacuum obtained from the engine induction manifold and consists of, basically, a booster diaphragm and non-return valve.

3 The servo unit and the master cylinder are connected so that the servo piston rod acts as the master cylinder pushrod.

4 The driver's braking effort is transmitted from the brake pedal to the servo unit piston and its integral control system.

5 The forward chamber of the servo unit is held under vacuum at all times whilst the rear chamber is held under vacuum conditions only when the brake pedal is in the released position. When the pedal is depressed, the rear chamber opens to atmospheric pressure which causes the servo piston to move forward and so operate the master cylinder pushrod.

6 It is emphasised that a servo unit provides assistance only and should a fault occur, the normal hydraulic braking system is unaffected except that the need for higher pedal pressures will be noticed.

Testing

7 With the engine switched off, depress the brake pedal several times. The distance by which the pedal moves should not alter over all applications.

8 Depress the brake pedal fully and hold it down then start the engine. The pedal should be felt to move downward slightly.
9 Hold the pedal depressed with the engine running, switch off the ignition and continue to hold the pedal depressed for 30 seconds during which period the pedal should neither rise nor drop.
10 Start the engine whilst the brake pedal is released, run it for a minute and switch off. Give several applications of the brake pedal. The pedal travel should decrease with each application.
11 Failure of the brake pedal to act in the way described will indicate a fault in the servo unit.
12 The servo unit should not be serviced or overhauled beyond the operations described in this Section and in the event of a fault developing, renew the servo complete.
13 Periodically check the condition of the vacuum hose and security of the clips.
14 Renew the hose if necessary.
15 If the servo hose right-angled non-return valve is loose in its sealing grommet, or if the grommet shows evidence of cracking or perishing, renew it. Apply some hydraulic fluid to the rubber to facilitate fitting.

Air filter – renewal
16 Although not a specified operation, the air filter through which the pushrod passes at the rear of the servo can become clogged after a high mileage. Disconnect the rod from the pedal, cut the filter diagonally having slipped the dust excluder off the rod. Fit the new filter.

Removal and refitting
17 Remove the master cylinder as described in Section 10. Disconnect the servo vacuum hose.
18 Working inside the car, disconnect the pushrod from the brake pedal.
19 Unscrew the servo mounting nuts from the bulkhead just above the pedals.
20 Withdraw the servo unit into the engine compartment.
21 Refitting is a reversal of removal.

15 Handbrake – adjustment

1 The handbrake is normally kept adjusted by the action of the automatic adjusters on the rear brake shoes. However, in due course, the cables will stretch and will have to be adjusted in order to fully apply the handbrake.
2 To adjust, first place the handbrake lever onto the third notch.
3 Working under the car release the locknuts, at the cable adjusters, at the point where the cables are only a short distance from entering the floor pan (photo).

15.3 Handbrake cable adjuster

4 Turn the adjusters equally until, with the rear wheel raised, the shoes can just be felt to bind when the wheels are turned.
5 Check the setting of the compensator at the handbrake lever when the handbrake is fully applied. If it is not at right-angles to the handbrake lever slightly adjust the cables to correct the setting.
6 Tighten the adjuster locknuts and lower the car.

16 Handbrake cables – renewal

1 Disconnect and remove the finisher panel from the floor at the rear of the handbrake control lever.
2 Completely slacken the cable adjuster nut from the cable which is to be removed.
3 Unbolt the handbrake control lever from the floor and disconnect the cable from the equaliser.
4 Remove the brake drum and disconnect the cable from the handbrake lever on the shoe.
5 Withdraw the cable from its trailing arm clip and from the grommet in the floor.
6 Refit the new cable by reversing the removal operations.
7 Adjust the hub bearing (Section 4) and adjust the handbrake (Section 15).

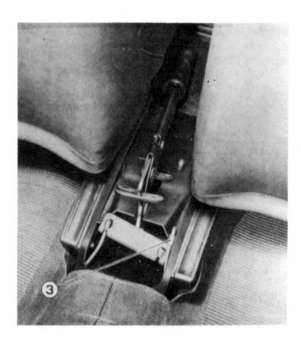

Fig. 9.34 Handbrake cable end fitting at equaliser (Sec 16)

3   Cable end fitting

17 Brake pedal – removal and refitting

1 The brake pedal operates on a common pivot bolt with the clutch pedal. Refer to details of removal and refitting described in Chapter 5.

18 Stop-lamp switch – adjustment

1 The stop-lamp switch at the brake pedal should be adjusted by means of the locknuts so that when the brake pedal is finally released, the switch plunger projects by 1.5 mm (0.059 in).

19 Fault diagnosis – braking system

Before diagnosing faults from the following chart, check that any braking irregularities are not caused by:
- *(a)   Uneven and incorrect tyre pressures*
- *(b)   Incorrect mix of radial and crossply tyres*
- *(c)   Wear in the steering mechanism*
- *(d)   Misalignment of the chassis geometry*

Symptom	Reason/s
Pedal travels a long way before the brakes operate	Brake shoes set too far from the drums due to faulty self-adjusting mechanism
Stopping ability poor, even though pedal pressure is firm	Linings/pads and/or drums/disc badly worn or scored One or more wheel hydraulic cylinders or caliper pistons seized resulting in some brake shoes/pads not pressing against the drums/discs Brake linings/pads contaminated with oil Wrong type of linings/pads fitted (too hard) Brake shoes/pads wrongly assembled Faulty servo unit (where fitted)
Car veers to one side when the brakes are applied	Brake linings/pads on one side are contaminated with oil Hydraulic wheel cylinder(s)/caliper on one side partially or fully seized A mixture of lining materials fitted between sides Unequal wear between sides caused by partially seized wheel cylinders/pistons
Pedal feels spongy	Air in the hydraulic system
Pedal feels springy when the brakes are applied	Brake linings/pads not bedded into the drums/discs (after fitting new ones) Master cylinder or brake backplate mounting bolts loose Out of round drums or discs with excessive run-out
Pedal travels right down with little or no resistance and brakes are virtually non-operative	Leak in hydraulic system resulting in lack of pressure for operating wheel cylinders/caliper pistons If no signs of leakage are apparent the master cylinder internal seals are failing to sustain pressure
Binding, juddering, overheating	One or a combination of causes given in the foregoing sections Handbrake over-adjusted Handbrake cable(s) seized
Lack of servo assistance	Vacuum hose leaking Non-return valve defective or leaking grommet Servo internal fault

Chapter 10 Electrical system

For modifications, and information applicable to later models, see Supplement at end of manual

Contents

Specifications

System type .... 12V negative earth, alternator, battery and pre-engaged starter

Battery .... 28 Ah or 36 Ah depending on model

Alternator
Type .... Ducellier, Motorola, Paris-Rhone or SEV-Marchal
Output .... 33A or 35A depending on model
Regulated voltage at 20°C .... 13.8 to 14.8V

Starter motor
Type .... Ducellier or Paris-Rhone pre-engaged
Minimum brush length .... 12.7 mm (0.5 in)
Starter drive pinion to stop clearance with solenoid energised .... 1.5 mm (0.059 in)

Fuses

No	Circuit protected	Rating
1	Front parking and tail lamps, instrument panel lamps, heater illumination, rear number plate	5A
2	Interior lamp, clock, cigar lighter	16A
3	Direction indicator flasher unit	16A
4	Rear foglamps	10A
5	Reversing lamps, heated tailgate heater blower, stop-lamp switch	16A
6	Windscreen wiper, tailgate wiper	10A

Bulbs

	Wattage
Headlamps	40/45 or 55/60 Halogen
Front parking lamps	5
Direction indicator lamps	21
Reversing lamps	21
Rear foglamps	21
Stop/tail lamps	5/21
Rear number plate lamps	5
Interior lamp	5
Luggage compartment lamp	4

Torque wrench settings

	Nm	lbf ft
Alternator mounting bolt	45	33
Alternator adjuster link bolt	17	13
Starter motor mounting nuts	12	9
Starter motor mounting bolts	16	12

1 General description

The electrical system is of the 12 volt negative earth type and the major components consist of a battery of which the negative terminal is earthed, an alternator which is driven from the crankshaft pulley, and a starter motor.

The battery supplies a steady amount of current for the ignition, lighting and other electrical circuits and provides a reserve of electricity when the current consumed by the electrical equipment exceeds that being produced by the alternator.

The alternator is controlled by a regulator which ensures a high output if the battery is in a low state of charge or the demand from the electrical equipment is high, and a low output if the battery is fully charged and there is little demand for the electrical equipment.

When fitting electrical accessories it is important, if they contain silicone diodes or transistors, that they are connected correctly, otherwise serious damage may result to the components concerned. Items such as radios, tape recorders, electronic ignition systems, electronic tachometer, automatic dipping etc, should all be checked for correct polarity.

It is important that both battery leads are always disconnected if the battery is to be boost charged; also if body repairs are to be carried out using electric arc welding equipment the alternator must be disconnected otherwise serious damage can be caused to the more delicate instruments. Whenever the battery has to be disconnected it must always be reconnected with the negative terminal earthed.

2 Battery – maintenance and inspection

1   The modern battery seldom requires topping up but nevertheless, the electrolyte level should be inspected weekly as a means of providing the first indication that the alternator is overcharging or that the battery casing has developed a leak. The battery plates should always be covered to a depth of 6.0 mm (0.25 in) with electrolyte.

2   When topping up is required, use only distilled water or melted ice from a referigerator (frosting not ice cubes).

3   Acid should never be required if the battery has been correctly filled from new, unless spillage has occurred.

2.4 Battery tray

4   Inspect the battery terminals and mounting tray for corrosion. This is the white fluffy deposit which grows at these areas. If evident, clean it away and neutralise it with ammonia or baking soda. Apply petroleum jelly to the terminals and paint the battery tray with anti-corrosive (photo).

5   Keep the top surface of the battery casing dry.

6   An indication of the state of charge of a battery can be obtained by checking the electrolyte in each cell using a hydrometer. The specific gravity of the electrolyte for fully charged and fully discharged conditions at the electrolyte temperature indicated, is listed below.

Fully discharged	Electrolyte temperature	Fully charged
1.098	38°C (100°F)	1.268
1.102	32°C (90°F)	1.272
1.106	27°C (80°F)	1.276
1.110	21°C (70°F)	1.280
1.114	16°C (60°F)	1.284
1.118	10°C (50°F)	1.288
1.122	4°C (40°F)	1.292
1.126	−1.5°C (30°F)	1.296

7   There should be very little variation in the readings between the different cells, but if a difference is found in excess of 0.025 then it will probably be due to an internal fault indicating impending battery failure. This assumes that electrolyte has not been spilled at some time and the deficiency made up with water only.

8   If electrolyte is accidently spilled at any time, mop up and neutralise the spillage at once. Electrolyte attacks and corrodes metal rapidly; it will also burn holes in clothing and skin. Leave the addition of acid to a battery cell to your dealer or service station as the mixing of acid with distilled water can be dangerous.

9   Never smoke or allow naked lights near the battery; the hydrogen gas which it gives off is explosive.

10   With normal motoring, the battery should be kept in a good state of charge by the alternator and never need charging from a mains charger.

11   However, if the daily mileage is low with much use of starter and electrical accessories, it is possible for the battery to become discharged owing to the fact that the alternator is not in use long enough to replace the current consumed.

12   Also as the battery ages, it may not be able to hold its charge and some supplementary charging may be needed. Before connecting the charger, disconnect the battery terminals or better still, remove the battery from the vehicle.

13   Specially rapid 'boost' charges which are claimed to restore the power of the battery in 1 to 2 hours are most dangerous as they can cause serious damage to the battery plates through overheating.

14   While charging the battery note that the temperature of the electrolyte should never exceed 100°F (37.8°C).

3 Battery – removal and refitting

1   The battery is located on a tray on the left-hand side towards the front of the engine compartment (photo).

2   Disconnect the battery leads. The negative lead used as original equipment has a wing type terminal nut which if unscrewed two or three turns will isolate the battery without the need for complete

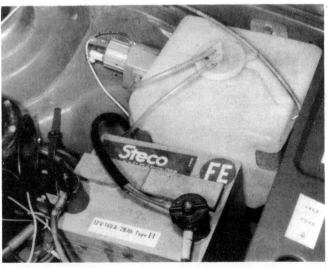

3.1 Battery location

disconnection. This is a useful facility when undertaking routine electrical jobs on the car.
3   Release the battery clamp and lift the battery carefully from the engine compartment (photos).
4   Refitting is a reversal of removal, smear the terminals with petroleum jelly on completion.

3.3A Battery clamp and bolt

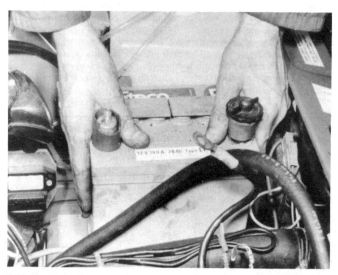

3.3B Removing battery

4   Alternator – general description and maintenance

1   All models covered by this manual are fitted with alternators. The alternator generates alternating current (AC) which is rectified by diodes into direct current (DC) and is the current needed for charging the battery.
2   The main advantage of the alternator lies in its ability to provide a high charge at low revolutions. Driving slowly in heavy traffic with a dynamo invariably means no charge is reaching the battery. In similar conditions even with the heater, wiper, lights and perhaps radio switched on the alternator will ensure a charge reaches the battery.
3   The alternator is of the rotating field ventilated design and comprises principally a laminated stator on which is wound the output winding, a rotor carrying the field winding and a diode rectifier.

4   The rotor is belt-driven from the engine through a pulley keyed to the rotor shaft. A fan adjacent to the pulley draws air through the unit. Rotation is clockwise when viewed from the drive end.
5   The voltage regulator is mounted externally on the rear cover of the alternator.
6   The equipment has been designed for the minimum amount of maintenance in service, the only items subject to wear being the brushes and bearings.
7   Brushes should be examined after about 120 000 km (75 000 miles) and renewed if necessary. The bearings are pre-packed with grease for life, and should not require further attention.
8   Regularly check the drivebelt tension and if slack adjust as described in Chapter 2.

5   Alternator – removal and refitting

1   Isolate the battery negative terminal.
2   Remove the spare wheel and air cleaner.
3   Remove the alternator drivebelt.
4   Disconnect the alternator mounting and adjuster bolts. Take care that the alternator does not swing and damage the radiator.
5   Note that the adjuster link has the engine lifting lug incorporated in it (photo).
6   Disconnect the electrical leads from the rear of the alternator. If there is any doubt as to their position when reconnecting, mark them (photo).
7   Lift the alternator from its mounting lugs.
8   Refitting is a reversal of removal. Tension the drivebelt on completion as described in Chapter 2.

6   Alternator – brush renewal

1   As previously explained, renewal of the voltage regulator or brushes should be regarded as the limit of overhaul on an alternator. If more extensive repair is required, obtain a new or factory reconditioned exchanged unit which will prove more economical than attempting to repair the original.
2   The following operations apply to a Motorola alternator but the procedure for other makes is similar.
3   With the alternator removed, extract the two screws which hold the voltage regulator to its rear cover (photo).
4   Pull the voltage regulator far enough away to be able to disconnect the wires.
5   Extract the single screw and withdraw the brush holder (photo).
6   With the brush holder removed, check the condition of the slip rings. If they are blackened, clean them with a fuel moistened rag. If they are deeply scored or grooved then it will probably indicate that the alternator is coming to the end of its life (photo).
7   Fit the new brush holder which is supplied complete with brushes and then screw on the voltage regulator.

7   Starter motor – description and testing

1   The starter motor is mounted on the front of the engine and is of the pre-engaged type, where the drive pinion is brought into mesh with the starter ring gear on the flywheel before the main current is applied.
2   When the starter switch is operated, current flows from the battery to the solenoid which is mounted on the top of the starter motor body. The plunger in the solenoid moves inwards, so causing a centrally pivoted lever to push the drive pinion into mesh with the starter ring gear. When the solenoid plunger reaches the end of its travel, it closes an internal contact and full starting current flows to the starter field coils. The armature is then able to rotate the crankshaft, so starting the engine.
3   A special freewheel clutch is fitted to the starter drive pinion so that as soon as the engine fires and starts to operate on its own it does not drive the starter motor.
4   When the starter switch is released, the solenoid is de-energised and a spring moves the plunger back to its rest position. This operates the pivoted lever to withdraw the drive pinion from engagement with the starter ring.

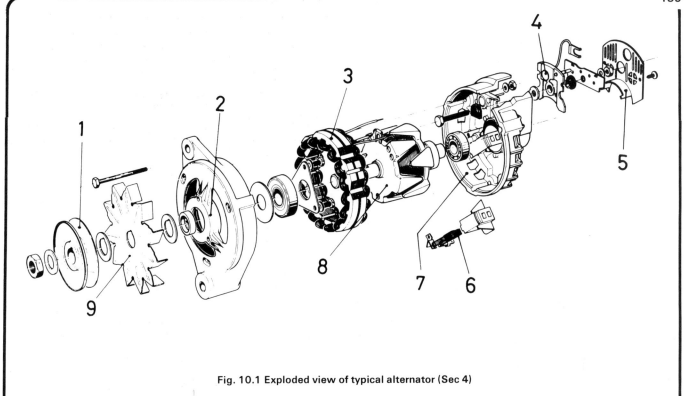

Fig. 10.1 Exploded view of typical alternator (Sec 4)

1	Drive pulley	4	Isolating diode	7	Brush end cover
2	Drive end bracket	5	Rear end cover	8	Rotor
3	Stator	6	Brushes/regulator	9	Fan

5.5 Alternator showing adjuster link with engine lifting lug

5.6 Alternator wiring connections

6.3 Removing alternator regulator

6.5 Removing alternator brush assembly

6.6 Alternator slip rings

5   If the starter motor fails to turn the engine when the switch is operated there are four possible reasons why:

(a) *The battery is discharged or faulty*
(b) *The electrical connections between switch, solenoid, battery and starter motor are somewhere failing to pass the necessary current from the battery, through the starter to earth*
(c) *The solenoid has an internal fault*
(d) *The starter motor is electrically defective*

6   To check the battery, switch on the headlights. If they go dim after a few seconds the battery is discharged. If the lamp glows brightly next operate the ignition/starter switch and see what happens to the lights. If they do dim it is indicative that power is reaching the starter motor but failing to turn it. If the starter should turn very slowly go on to the next check.

7   If, when the ignition/starter switch is operated the lights stay bright, then the power is not reaching the starter motor. Check all connections from the battery to solenoid for cleanliness and tightness. With a good battery fitted this is the most usual cause of starter motor problems. Check that the earth cable between the engine and body is also intact and cleanly connected. This can sometimes be overlooked when the engine is taken out.

8   If no results have yet been achieved turn off the headlights, otherwise the battery will soon be discharged. It may be possible that a clicking noise was heard each time the ignition/starter switch was operated. This is the solenoid switch operating but it does not necessarily follow that the main contact is closing properly. (If no clicking has been heard from the solenoid it is certainly defective). The solenoid contact can be checked by putting a voltmeter or bulb between the main cable connection on the starter side of the solenoid and earth. When the switch is operated there should be a reading or a lighted bulb. If not the switch has a fault.

8   Starter motor – removal and refitting

1   Isolate the battery by disconnecting the negative lead.
2   Disconnect the lead from the starter solenoid terminals (photo).
3   Unscrew and remove the two bolts from the front end bracket.
4   Unscrew the three bolts from the flywheel housing end. Two of these bolts will have to remain in position as they cannot be removed.
5   Withdraw the starter motor (photo).
6   Refitting is a reversal of removal, but it is important to tighten the bolts in the following sequence.

Starter drive end flange to flywheel housing
Brush end bracket to engine crankcase
Brush end bracket to starter motor (photos)

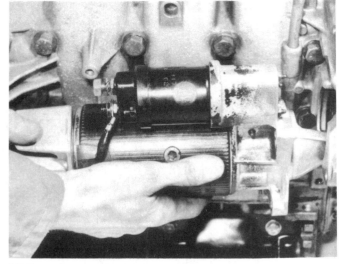

8.5 Removing starter motor

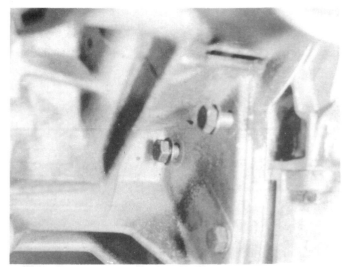

8.6A Starter drive end mounting bolts

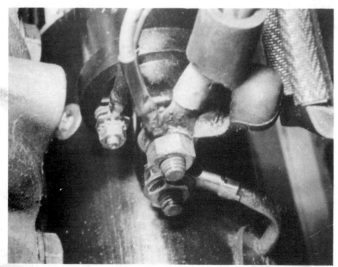

8.2 Starter solenoid connections

8.6B Starter brush end bracket bolts and nut

A To crankcase   B To starter motor

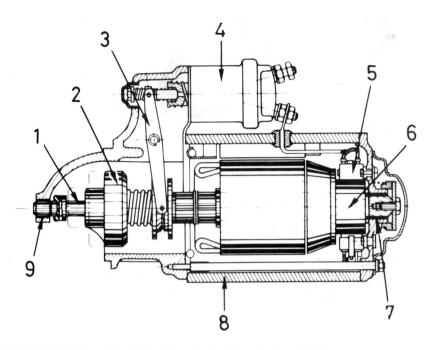

Fig. 10.2 Cutaway view of typical starter motor (Sec 9)

1 Armature shaft
2 Freewheel clutch
3 Engagement fork
4 Solenoid
5 Brushes
6 Commutator
7 Rear end bearing
8 Yoke
9 Drive end bearing

9 Starter motor – overhaul

1 With the starter removed from the car, disconnect the solenoid leads (photo).
2 Unscrew the nuts and remove the brush end bracket (photo).
3 Unscrew the three nuts and remove the solenoid (photos).

4 Prise the plastic cap from the endplate (photo).
5 Unscrew the two tie-rod nuts.
6 Mark the set position of the head of the engagement lever pivot pin. The pin is of eccentric type and its rotation and final setting controls the end stop clearance.
7 Tap out the pivot pin (photo).

9.1 Starter field coil to solenoid lead

9.2 Removing brush end bracket

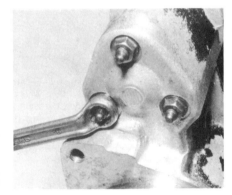
9.3A Starter solenoid nuts

9.3B Withdrawing starter solenoid

9.4 Removing cap from starter endplate

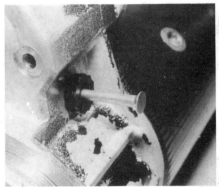
9.7 Starter engagement lever pivot pin

9.8A Removing starter drive end housing

9.8B Shim inside starter drive end housing

9.9 Starter engagement fork

9.10 Starter armature endplate bolt

9.11 Removing starter endplate

9.12 Starter armature

8   Withdraw the drive end housing complete with tie bolts. Note the internal shaft shim.
9   Lift off the engagement fork (photo).
10   Depress and then unscrew the armature endplate bolt. Note the wave and plain washers (photo).
11   Remove the endplate noting that located under it are a wave washer, two plain washers and a fibre washer (photo).
12   Withdraw the armature noting the shim, wave washer, shim and fibre washer (in that order) located against the commutator end face (photo).
13   If the brushes are worn down they can be renewed. The brush lead

from the field coil must be cut and the new one soldered on. Take care not to allow heat to damage the field coils nor to allow solder to run down the lead or their flexibility will be ruined (photo).
14   Undercut the separators of the commutator using an old hacksaw blade to a depth of about 0.02 to 0.03 in (0.5 to 0.8 mm). The commutator may be further surface cleaned using a strip of very fine glass paper. Do not use emery cloth for this purpose as the carborundum particles will become embedded in the copper surfaces.
15   Testing of the armature is best left to an auto electrician but if an ohmmeter is available it can be done by placing one probe on the armature shaft and the other on each of the commutator segments in turn. If there is a reading indicated at any time during the test, then the armature is defective and must be renewed.
16   The field coil can also be tested using an ohmmeter. Connect one probe to the field coil positive terminal and the other to the positive brush holder. If there is no indication of a reading then the field coil circuit has a break in it.
17   Connect one lead of the meter to the field coil positive lead and the other one to the yoke. If there is a low resistance then the field coil is earthed due to a breakdown in the insulation. If this proves to be the case the field coils must be renewed. As field coil replacement requires special tools and equipment it is a job that should be entrusted to your auto-electrician. In fact it will probably prove more economical and beneficial to exchange the starter motor for a reconditioned unit.
18   If the starter drive is faulty, it can be removed if the sleeve is tapped up the shaft, using a piece of tubing, to expose the jump ring. Remove the jump ring and starter drive (photo).
19   Once the starter drive has been refitted with its jump ring, draw the covering sleeve over it using a small puller of claw type (photo).
20   Reassembly is a reversal of dismantling, but observe the following points.
21   Apply high melting point grease to the armature shaft bearings.
22   Note the locating pip on the yoke which aligns with the notch in the rim of the endplate (photo).
23   If the setting of the engagement lever pivot pin was not marked at dismantling, energise the starter solenoid and check that the clearance between the end face of the pinion shaft and the stop button within

9.13 Starter motor brushes

9.18 Starter drive jump ring

9.19 Drawing jump ring cover sleeve over jump ring

9.22 Yoke/endplate alignment 'pip' and notch

the drive end housing is 1.5 mm (0.059 in). If not, withdraw the eccentric type pivot pin from the engagement lever and rotate it a few splines then re-check the clearance.

10 Fuses

1   The fuse box is located under the left-hand side of the facia panel (photo).

10.1 Fuse box

2   Six fuses protect the electrical circuits with space in the fuse block for spares.
3   Should a fuse blow, replace it only with one of identical rating and if the new one blows again immediately, trace and rectify the cause, usually due to a bare wire touching the bodywork due to the insulation having chafed.

11 Direction indicator/hazard warning flasher unit

1   The unit is located under the facia panel and controls both the direction indicator and hazard warning function (photo).

11.1 Flasher unit

2　In the event of either system not operating or one lamp flashing very quickly, carry out the following checks before renewing the flasher unit itself.

3　Inspect the circuit fuse and renew it if it is blown.

4　Check the condition of all wiring and the security of the connections.

5　Check the lamp, which is malfunctioning, for a broken bulb.

6　Make sure that the lamp casing or bulb earth connection is making a good contact.

12 Steering column switch – removal and refitting

1　Isolate the battery by means of the negative lead.

2　Refer to Chapter 8 and remove the steering wheel.

3　Disconnect the column switch wiring harness plugs.

4　Remove the fixing screws and withdraw the combination switch off the end of the steering column shaft.

5　Refitting is a reversal of removal.

13 Facia-mounted switches – removal and refitting

1　Prise off the plastic cover (photo).

2　Reach up behind the panel and compress the switch retaining tabs.

3　Withdraw the switch and pull it from its connecting plug (photo).

4　Refitting is a reversal of removal.

14 Courtesy lamp switch – removal and refitting

1　This switch is secured to the door hinge pillar by a self-tapping screw.

2　Peel the rubber cover from the switch, extract the screw and withdraw the switch and leads (photo).

3　If the leads are disconnected, tape them to the pillar to prevent them from slipping inside the pillar cavity.

4　It is recommended that the metal contacts of the switch are smeared with petroleum jelly as a precaution against corrosion.

5　Refit by reversing the removal operation.

15 Instrument panel – removal and refitting

1　Disconnect the battery.

2　Push a thin screwdriver blade into the rectangular opening under the bottom edge of the panel and release the retaining clip.

3　Release the clip at the upper aperture in a similar way (photo).

4　Withdraw the instrument panel. At the same time have an assistant feed the speedometer drive cable through the bulkhead grommet.

5　As soon as the panel has been withdrawn sufficiently, disconnect the speedometer cable by prising the connector tabs apart.

6　Disconnect the wiring plugs from the rear of the panel and remove it (photo).

7　The instrument glass can be separated from the panel by prising off the clips.

8　The individual instruments can be removed for repair by a specialist or renewal after extracting their fixing screws or nuts. Take care not to damage the printed circuit (photo).

9　Refitting is a reversal of removal.

16 Speedometer cable – renewal

1　Withdraw the instrument panel sufficiently far to be able to disconnect the speedometer drive cable as described in the preceding Section.

2　Unscrew the lockbolt and withdraw the cable from the transmission (photo).

3　Withdraw the cable assembly through the bulkhead grommet (photo).

4　Fit the new cable by reversing the removal operations.

13.1 Facia switch cover

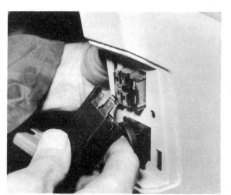
13.3 Removing a facia-mounted switch

14.2 Courtesy lamp switch

15.3 Releasing instrument panel clip

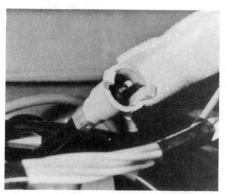
15.5 Speedometer cable connector

15.6 Rear view of instrument panel

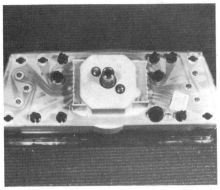
15.8 Instrument panel showing printed circuit board, warning lamp bulbholders and instrument fixing screws

16.2 Releasing speedometer cable from transmission

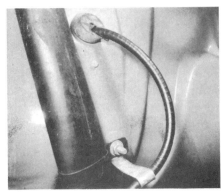
16.3 Speedometer cable at bulkhead

17 Bulbs (exterior) – renewal

Headlamps
1 Open the bonnet and pull the wiring plug from the rear of the headlamp (photo).
2 Peel off the rubber protective cover.
3 Release the spring clips and withdraw the bulbholder (photo).
4 Fit the new bulb so that the positioning lug on the holder engages in the cut-out.
5 Secure the holder, with the spring clip, fit the rubber cover and the wiring plug.

Front parking lamps
6 The bulb is located in the lower part of the headlamp bowl.
7 Pull the bulbholder from the headlamp and renew the bulb (photo).

Front direction indicator lamps
8 Access to the bulb is obtained by extracting the lens screws and removing the lens (photo).

Rear lamp cluster
9 Access to the tail, stop, reverse and direction indicator lamp bulbs is obtained by extracting the screws and removing the lens (photos).
10 The lamp connections, printed circuit board and fixing nuts are accessible from within the luggage compartment (photo).

Rear number plate lamp
11 Extract the screws and separate the lamp into its component parts (photo).
12 Remove the bulb from its holder and fit a new one.

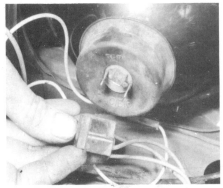
17.1 Disconnecting headlamp wiring plug

17.3 Removing headlamp bulbholder

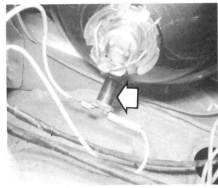
17.7 Front parking lamp bulb

17.8 Removing front direction indicator lens

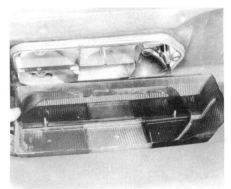
17.9A Rear lamp cluster lens

17.9B Rear lamp cluster bulbs

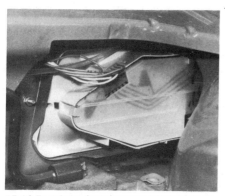

17.10 Rear lamp from luggage compartment

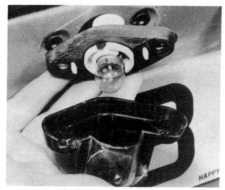

17.11 Rear number plate lamp

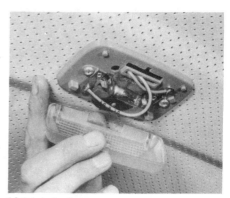

18.1 Interior lamp

18 Bulbs (interior) – renewal

Interior lamp
1   Prise off the lens for access to the festoon type bulb (photo).

Instrument panel lamps
2   Partially withdraw the instrument panel as described in Section 15.
3   The bulbholders can then be twisted and pulled from the rear of the panel (photo).
4   The bulbs are of wedge base type and are simply pulled from their holders.

19 Headlamp – removal and refitting

1   Open the bonnet and pull the spring clip from the face of the load adjuster lever. Disconnect the headlamp wiring plug (photo).
2   Release the front direction indicator lamp by unscrewing its retaining bolt inside the engine compartment (photos).
3   Pull the headlamp sharply to release its lower ball-headed stud from its socket and remove the lamp (photos).

20 Headlamp – beam adjustment

1   It is recommended that the adjustment of the headlamp beams is left to a service station having suitable equipment.

18.3 Instrument panel warning lamp bulb

19.1 Headlamp retaining clip

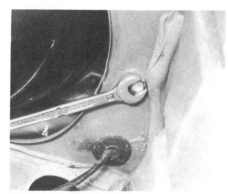

19.2A Front direction indicator lamp retaining bolt

19.2B Removing front direction indicator lamp

19.3A Removing headlamp unit

19.3B Headlamp ball-stud fixing socket

2   In an emergency the beam adjustment knobs can be turned to adjust the light pattern.
3   With a normal load, push the load control lever, which is located at the top of the headlamp, fully clockwise before adjusting the beam.

21 Windscreen wiper blades and arms – removal and refitting

1   Whenever the wiper blades fail to clean the screen, the blades or their rubber inserts should be renewed.
2   To remove a blade, pull the arm from the glass, swivel the blade, pinch the two sides of the U-shaped plastic block together and slide the assembly out of the hook of the arm (photo).
3   When refitting note the pivot pin in the blade is offset to allow the blade to swivel fully against the glass. Make sure, therefore, that the blade is fitted the right way round so that the 'pip' on the plastic block locates in the cut-out in the hook of the wiper arm.
4   Before removing a wiper arm, stick some masking tape along the edge of the blade so that its position on the glass can be restored when the arm is being refitted to its spindle splines.
5   Flip up the plastic cover, unscrew the nut and pull the arm from the spindle splines (photo).
6   Refitting is a reversal of removal.

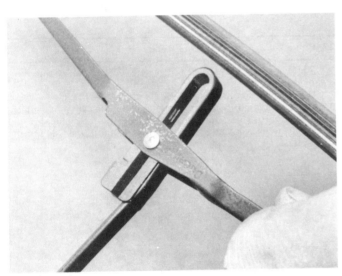

21.2 Wiper blade attachment

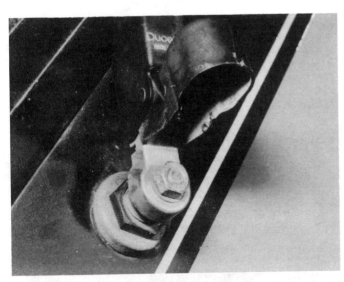

21.5 Wiper arm attachment

22 Windscreen wiper motor and linkage – removal and refitting

1   Remove the wiper blades and arms as previously described.
2   Disconnect the battery.
3   Prise out the long plastic panel from the engine compartment rear bulkhead (photo).
4   Unscrew the nuts from the wiper spindles.
5   Disconnect the wiper motor electrical plug.
6   Unscrew the wiper motor mounting nuts and withdraw the motor with linkage through the scuttle aperture.
7   The motor can be separated from the linkage by removing the nut from the crankcase.
8   Refitting is a reversal of removal.
9   It is essential that the wiper motor/linkage compartment (scuttle) is kept clear of dirt. Periodically clean the large drain hose, if this becomes blocked, water can enter the car interior.

22.3 Wiper motor/linkage access panel detached

23 Tailgate wiper motor – renewal and refitting

1   Remove the wiper arm and blade as described for the windscreen in Section 21.
2   Remove the cover from inside the tailgate just below the glass.
3   Unscrew the spindle nut and the motor mounting screws and lift the assembly from the tailgate. Disconnect the leads (photos).
4   Refitting is a reversal of removal.

23.3A Tailgate wiper motor cover

23.3B Tailgate wiper motor and tailgate striker

In winter add some methylated spirit to the fluid to prevent freezing. Never use cooling system anti-freeze as it will damage the paintwork.

25 Tailgate heated window

1   Take great care not to scratch the heater elements with carelessly stacked luggage or the rings on the fingers.
2   Avoid sticking labels over the elements and clean the glass interior surface with warm water and a little detergent wiping in the same direction as the elements run.
3   Should an element be scratched so that the current is interrupted, it can be repaired using one of the silver paint products now available for the purpose.
4   The electrical contact blocks on the tailgate and luggage compartment side panel provide the electrical connections to the rear accessories so avoiding the use of continually flexing cables (photos).

26 Electrically-operated front windows

1   On models fitted with this facility, access to the window lift motors is obtained by removing the door trim panel as described in Chapter 12.
2   The control switches are locate one on either side of the radio.

24 Washer system

1   The washer fluid reservoir is located on the left-hand side of the engine compartment with the electric washer pump adjacent to it (photo).
2   On some models, a tailgate washer is fitted.
3   The washer jets are adjustable by inserting a pin into their nozzles and moving them to give an acceptable pattern on the glass (photo).
4   The use of a good quality screen wash product is recommended.

27 Radio

1   Some models are supplied complete with a radio and roof-mounted aerial.
2   On less expensive models, these items may be fitted.
3   The accepted position for the radio is under the centre of the facia panel. A supplementary mounting panel is to be recommended and holes already exist for attaching the panel to the lower edge of the facia (photo).

24.1 Washer fluid reservoir and pump

24.3 Tailgate washer jet

25.4A Tailgate contact block on body

25.4B Tailgate contact block on tailgate

27.3 Radio

4   The recommended location for the aerial is on the roof, 50.0 mm (2.0 in) to the rear of the centre top edge of the windscreen.
5   Drill a pilot hole, remove the interior mirror.
6   Widen the hole to accept the aerial base and then feed the cable along over the windscreen and down the body pillar and along under the facia panel. Replace the mirror.
7   Take power from the wire provided (see Wiring Diagram) and attach the radio casing to a good earthing point.
8   The speakers now remain to be fitted and connected. The location for the speakers is one of personal choice, but cutting and

fitting them into the side panels at the front footwells just ahead of the front doors will be the most conventional choice. Alternatively, the speakers may be fitted at the rear or on the front parcel shelves.
9   All models are suppressed against ignition interference during production, but additional suppressors may be required for the alternator and wiper motors as experience dictates. Fit a fuse in the power feed line.
10   Finally remember that the aerial will require trimming in accordance with the radio manufacturer's instructions.

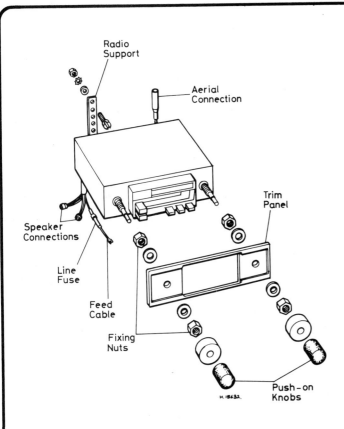

Fig. 10.3 Typical radio mounting and connections (Sec 27)

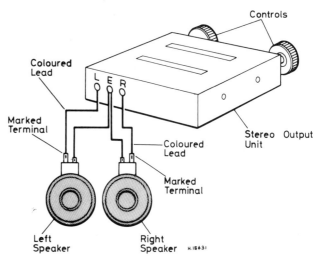

Fig. 10.5 Typical speaker connections (Sec 27)

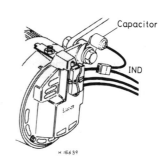

Fig. 10.6 Alternator suppressor (Sec 27)

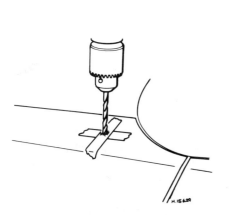

Fig. 10.4 Using masking tape to protect paintwork when drilling for aerial (Sec 27)

Fig. 10.7 Wiper motor suppressor (Sec 27)

28 Fault diagnosis – electrical system (general)

Symptom	Reason(s)
Starter fails to turn engine	Battery discharged Battery defective internally Battery terminal leads loose or earth lead not securely attached to body Loose or broken connections in starter motor circuit Starter motor switch or solenoid faulty Starter brushes badly worn, sticking, or brush wires loose Commutator dirty, worn or burnt Starter motor armature faulty Field coils earthed
Starter turns engine very slowly	Battery in discharged condition Starter brushes badly worn, sticking or brush wires loose Loose wires in starter motor circuit
Starter spins but does not turn engine	Starter motor pinion sticking on the screwed sleeve Pinion or flywheel gear teeth broken or worn
Starter motor noisy or excessively rough engagement	Pinion or flywheel gear teeth broken or worn Starter motor retaining bolts loose
Battery will not hold charge for more than a few days	Battery defective internally Electrolyte level too low or electrolyte too weak due to leakage Plate separators no longer fully effective Battery plates severely sulphated Drivebelt slipping Battery terminal connections loose or corroded Alternator not charging Short in lighting circuit causing continual battery drain Regulator unit not working correctly
Ignition light fails to go out, battery runs flat in a few days	Drivebelt loose and slipping or broken Alternator brushes worn, sticking, broken or dirty Alternator brush springs weak or broken Internal fault in alternator Regulator faulty

Failure of individual electrical equipment to function correctly is dealt with alphabetically, item-by-item, under the headings below

Horn

Horn operates all the time	Horn push either earthed or stuck down Horn cable to horn push earthed
Horn fails to operate	Cable or cable connection loose, broken or disconnected Horn has an internal fault Blown fuse
Horn emits intermittent or unsatisfactory noise	Cable connections loose

Lights

Lights do not come on	If engine not running, battery discharged Wire connections loose, disconnected or broken Light switch shorting or otherwise faulty
Lights come on but fade out	If engine not running, battery discharged Wire connections loose Light switch shorting or otherwise faulty
Lights work erratically – flashing on and off, especially over bumps	Battery terminals or earth connections loose Lights not earthing properly Contacts in light switch faulty

Wipers

Wiper motor fails to work	Blown fuse Wire connections loose, disconnected or broken Brushes badly worn Armature worn or faulty
Wiper motor works very slowly and takes excessive current	Commutator dirty, greasy or burnt Armature bearings dirty or unaligned Armature badly worn or faulty

Symptom	Reason(s)
Wiper motor works slowly and takes little current	Brushes badly worn Commutator dirty, greasy or burnt Armature badly worn or faulty
Wiper motor works but wiper blades remain static	Wiper motor gearbox parts badly worn

Wiring diagrams commence overleaf

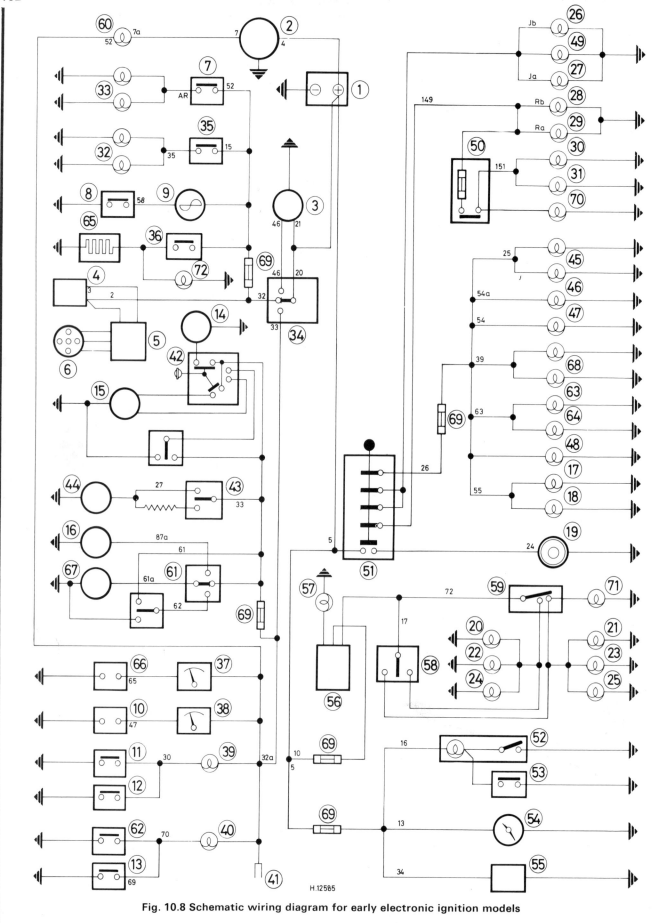

Fig. 10.8 Schematic wiring diagram for early electronic ignition models

H.12585

Key to schematic wiring diagram for early electronic ignition models

1 Battery
2 Alternator
3 Starter motor
4 Ignition coil
5 Electronic ignition control box
6 Distributor
7 Reverse lamp switch
8 Fan thermostatic switch
9 Engine cooling fan
10 Coolant temperature gauge sender unit
11 Oil pressure warning light sender unit
12 Coolant level sender unit
13 Brake fluid level sender unit
14 Windscreen washer pump
15 Windscreen wiper motor
16 Rear screen washer pump
17 LH front sidelamp
18 RH front sidelamp
19 Horn
20 Front LH direction indicator
21 Front RH direction indicator
22 LH indicator repeater (where fitted)
23 RH indicator repeater (where fitted)
24 Rear LH direction indicator
25 Rear RH direction indicator
26 LH headlamp main beam
27 RH headlamp main beam
28 LH headlamp dipped beam
29 RH headlamp dipped beam
30 LH rear foglamp
31 RH rear foglamp
32 Stop lamps
33 Reversing lamps
34 Starter/ignition switch
35 Stop lamp switch

36 Heated rear screen switch
37 Fuel gauge
38 Coolant temperature gauge
39 Oil pressure and coolant level warning light
40 Handbrake and brake fluid level warning light
41 Radio supply
42 Windscreen wiper control on steering column switch
43 Heater blower switch
44 Heater blower motor
45 Instrument panel illumination
46 Clock illumination
47 Heater control illumination
48 Sidelamps 'on' warning light
49 Headlamp main beam warning light
50 Rear foglamps switch
51 Lights and horn switch on steering column
52 Interior roof lamp
53 Interior lamp switch
54 Clock
55 Cigar lighter
56 Direction indicators flasher unit
57 Directions indicators 'on' warning light
58 Direction indicators control lever
59 Hazard warning switch
60 Ignition warning light
61 Rear screen wiper switch
62 Handbrake warning switch
63 LH tail lamp
64 RH tail lamp
65 Heated rear screen
66 Fuel tank unit
67 Rear screen wiper motor
68 Number plate lamps
69 Fuses

Note: *The component numbers are shown encircled; the remaining numbers and letters are wire identification codes and can be found on a tag attached to each wire.*

Chapter 11 Suspension

Contents

Specifications

Front suspension .... Independent, Macpherson struts, coil springs, anti-roll bar

Rear suspension .... Independent, trailing arms, telescopic hydraulic struts with coil springs. Anti-roll bar, GLS, Cabriolet, S and Rallye

Wheelbase .... 2340.0 mm (92.1 in)

Front track .... 1292.0 mm (50.8 in)

Rear track .... 1272.0 mm (50.0 in)

Rear wheel alignment (vehicle at kerb weight)
Camber (non-adjustable) .... 1° 40′ ± 30′ negative
Toe-in (total) .... 2.2 mm ± 2 mm (0.086 ± 0.078 in)

Torque wrench settings	Nm	lbf ft
Front suspension		
Strut upper mounting nuts	12	9
Strut piston rod nut	43	32
Strut base clamp pinch-bolts	68	50
Anti-roll bar clamp bolts	43	32
Anti-roll bar end nut	54	40
Strut gland nut	79	58
Driveshaft nut	245	180
Track control arm pivot bolt	34	25
Track control arm balljoint nut	74	55
Tie-rod balljoint nut	74	25
Brake caliper bolts (Teves)	68	50
Brake caliper bolts (DBA)	83	61

Rear suspension

Strut upper mounting nuts	10	7
Strut lower mounting nut	36	27
Strut lower mounting bolt	36	27
Trailing arm mounting nuts	34	25
Centre support bolts	31	23
Cross-tube pivot spindle nuts	54	40
Anti-roll bar bolts	34	25
Roadwheel nuts:		
Steel	59	44
Alloy	81	60

1 Description and inspection

1 The suspension is of four-wheel independent type.

2 The front suspension is of Macpherson strut design incorporating coil springs. An anti-roll bar is fitted on all models.

3 The rear suspension is of trailing arm type incorporating coil springs and telescopic hydraulic shock absorbers. On GLS and Cabriolet models an anti-roll bar is fitted at the rear.

4 At the intervals specified in Routine Maintenance inspect the suspension struts (shock absorbers) for fluid leaks. If anything more than a slight weep is visible on the strut or shock absorber casing around the piston rod gland, the unit must be renewed.

5 Check the rear suspension arm flexible pivot bushes and the shock absorber lower mounting bushes for wear or deformation. Renew if necessary.

6 Check the track control arm flexible bushes and balljoint for wear.

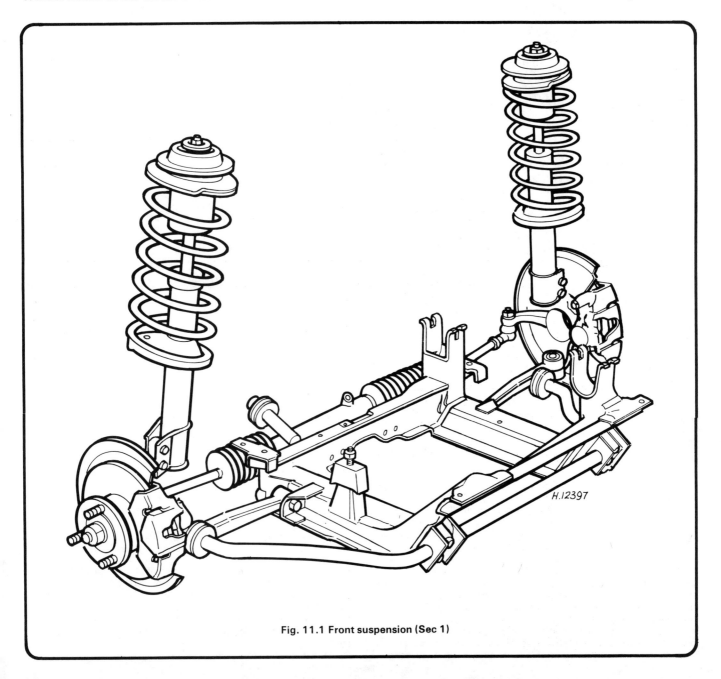

Fig. 11.1 Front suspension (Sec 1)

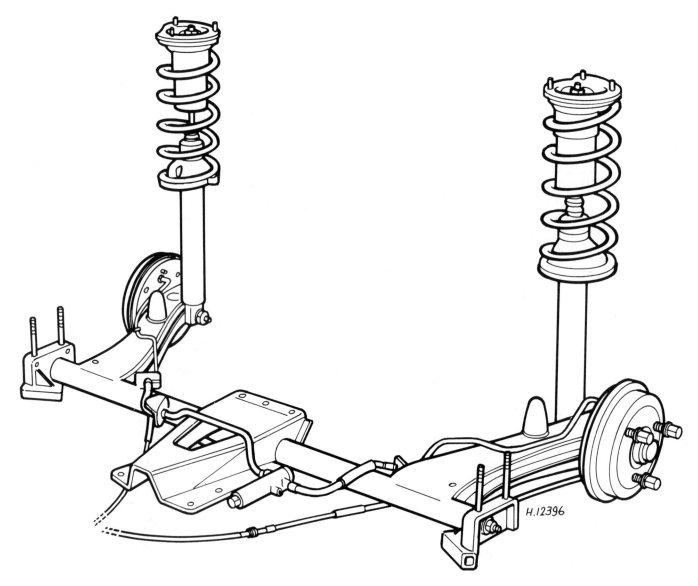

Fig. 11.2 Rear suspension (Sec 1)

2 Anti-roll bar – removal and refitting

1   Unscrew the bolts from the clamps which hold the anti-roll bar to the bodyframe.
2   Unscrew the nuts which hold the ends of the anti-roll bar to the track control arms or rear trailing arms (GLS and Cabriolet). Withdraw the anti-roll bar.
3   Refitting is a reversal of removal, tighten all nuts and bolts to the specified torque.
4   Note the sequence of the end fitting components.

3 Front suspension strut – removal and refitting

1   Unbolt the front anti-roll bar fixing clamps.
2   Unscrew the nut which holds the end of the anti-roll bar to the track control arm on the side from which the strut is being removed.
3   Raise the front of the car and support it securely. Remove the roadwheel.
4   Support the hub/disc on a block of wood and then unscrew and remove the two pinch-bolts which hold the base of the suspension strut to the stub axle (hub) carrier. Do not apply outward pressure to

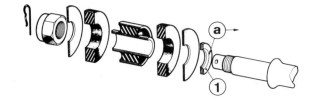

Fig. 11.3 Front anti-roll bar end fitting (Sec 2)

1   Washer   a   Chamfer

the hub/disc or the driveshaft may come out of the differential housing.
5   Open the bonnet. Release, but on no account remove, the piston rod nut. Hold the rod against rotation by engaging a large screwdriver in its slot.
6   Unscrew and remove the three strut upper mounting nuts.
7   Lower the stub axle carrier/hub and release the bottom end of the strut.
8   Withdraw the strut from under the front wing.

Fig. 11.4 Front strut clamp pinch-bolts (Sec 3)

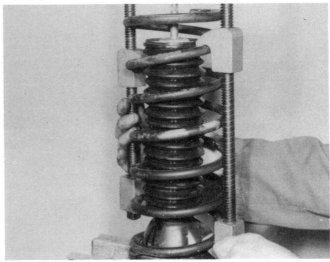

4.3 Spring compressors in position

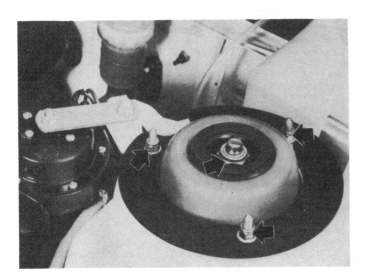

Fig. 11.5 Front strut upper mounting and piston rod nuts (Sec 3)

Fig. 11.6 Withdrawing piston from front strut (Sec 4)

9   If the coil spring must be removed from the strut refer to the next Section.
10 Refitting is a reversal of removal, tighten all nuts to the specified torque.

***

4   Front suspension strut – overhaul

1   With the strut removed, clean away external dirt.
2   To remove the coil spring, spring compressors must be used. These can be hired or purchased at most motor parts stores.
3   Engage the claws of the compressors over several spring coils and tighten the compressors evenly until the spring frees from the upper mounting (photo).
4   Remove the piston rod nut, take off the mounting and the spring with compressors. The spring may remain in the compressed state ready for refitting to the strut. If the spring is to be renewed, release

Fig. 11.7 Tapping off compensator valve (3) from piston (2) (Sec 4)

4.4A Releasing strut piston rod nut

4.4D Strut gaiter

4.4B Removing piston rod nut

the compressors very gently and evenly until they can be removed and fitted to the new spring. Remove the gaiter (photos).

5   If the strut shows signs of fluid seepage around the piston rod then the seals at least will have to be renewed.

6   To test the performance of the strut (without spring), fit the upper mounting to the piston rod and use the mounting to fully extend and contract the rod several times. There should be firm resistance in both directions. If there is no resistance or the movement is jerky, or the unit is seized, the strut must be renewed or overhauled.

7   A faulty strut can be put right in one of three ways.

   a   Fit a new strut
   b   Retain the original strut casing and fit a sealed cartridge
   c   Obtain a repair kit and rebuilt the original unit

8   If a cartridge is going to be used, follow the instructions supplied by the manufacturer after having first removed the strut internal components as described in the following paragraphs.

4.4C Removing strut upper mounting

Fig. 11.8 Strut piston rod stop (1) and upper bush (2) (Sec 4)

(a) Cupped side

9   Using suitable semi-circular protective packings, grip the strut vertically in the jaws of a vice.
10   Unscrew the gland nut from the top of the strut. A pin wrench or C spanner or other suitable tool will be required for this.
11   Withdraw the rod/piston assembly slowly to avoid oil spillage.
12   Withdraw the cylinder and tap off the compensator valve using a plastic-faced hammer.
13   The repair kit will contain a new piston rod nut, dust excluding gaiter, seal and O-ring.
14   Observe scrupulous cleanliness and commence reassembly by tapping the compensator valve into the end of the cylinder.
15   Insert the cylinder into the strut and pour in 320 cc of specified fluid (supplied in kit).
16   To the piston rod fit the expansion stop (1) and the upper bush (2) so that the cupped side (a) faces upward.
17   Insert the piston assembly very slowly into the cylinder so that the fluid is not displaced.
18   Tap the upper bush downward so that it is 1.5 mm (0.059 in) below the rim of the strut.
19   Fit the new O-ring smeared with rubber grease.
20   Dip the new gland seal in fluid and having taped the piston rod threads to prevent them cutting the seal lips, fit the seal so the lip is uppermost.
21   Fully extend the piston rod, fit the thrust washer (if originally fitted) and tighten the gland nut to the specified torque. Locate the spring lower insulator (photo).

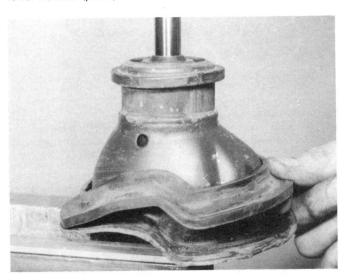

4.21 Strut coil spring lower insulator

Fig. 11.9 Strut seal (1) and lip (a) (Sec 4)

22   Fit the coil spring using the compressors.
23   Fit the upper mounting and screw on the piston rod nut, but do not fully tighten it until the strut is back in the car.
24   Gently release the spring compressors.

5   Track control arm – removal and refitting

1   On the side of the suspension being dismantled, release the anti-roll bar clamp and remove the nut which secures the anti-roll bar to the track control arm.
2   Raise the front of the car so that the roadwheels hang free. Support securely.
3   Disconnect the anti-roll bar from the track control arm.
4   Turn the steering to full lock on the side opposite to that being dismantled.
5   Unscrew and remove the pivot bolt from the inboard end of the track control arm.
6   Remove the roadwheel.
7   Unscrew and remove the driveshaft nut. In order to prevent the hub from turning as the nut is unscrewed, either have an assistant apply the brakes fully or bolt a length of steel bar to two of the wheel studs for use as a lever.
8   Pull the hub outwards and draw it off the outboard end of the driveshaft. Do not separate the joints or the driveshaft from the transmission during this operation.
9   Unscrew the nut from the track control arm balljoint taper pin, but do not remove it completely.
10   Using a suitable extractor separate the balljoint taper pin from the stub axle carrier. Remove the nut and withdraw the track control arm.
11   The flexible bushes in the control arm can be renewed using a press or bolt, nut and distance pieces. The balljoint is not renewable, if worn, renew the arm complete.
12   Refitting is a reversal of removal, tighten all nuts and bolts to the specified torque.
13   Stake the driveshaft nut into its groove.

Fig. 11.10 Track control arm pivot bolt (1) (Sec 5)

6   Front suspension hub carrier – removal, overhaul and refitting

1   Raise the front of the car and remove the roadwheel.
2   Unscrew the driveshaft nut. This is very tight and in order to prevent the hub turning, either have an assistant fully apply the brakes or bolt a length of steel bar to two of the wheel studs and use it as a lever. Disconnect the anti-roll bar from the appropriate side.
3   Unbolt the brake caliper and tie it up out of the way. There is no need to disconnect the hydraulic hose.
4   Using a balljoint extractor, disconnect the steering tie-rod from the arm on the hub carrier.

5   Unscrew and remove the pivot bolt from the inboard end of the track control arm.

6   Unscrew the two pinch-bolts from the base of the suspension strut (photo).

7   Pull the hub/disc downwards amd outwards out of the strut clamp jaws and off the driveshaft. Take care not to separate the driveshaft joints or the driveshaft from the transmission. Remove the hub carrier complete with track control arm to the bench. If required, the track control arm can be removed by unscrewing the balljoint taper pin nut and using a balljoint extractor.

8   Refer to Chapter 7 for details of overhaul of the hub carrier.

9   Commence refitting by offering the hub assembly to the driveshaft and then slide it onto the shaft.

10 Push the hub upwards and engage the carrier in the jaws of the strut clamp. Insert the pinch-bolts.

11 Reconnect the inboard end of the track control arm.

12 Refit the brake caliper.

13 Reconnect the anti-roll bar.

14 Tighten all nuts and bolts to the specified torque including the one for the driveshaft, which should then be staked into the shaft groove.

15 Fit the roadwheel and lower the car. **Note**: *If difficulty is experienced in loosening or tightening a balljoint taper pin nut, due to the taper pin turning in the eye, apply pressure with a jack or long lever to the balljoint socket to force the taper pin into its conical seat.*

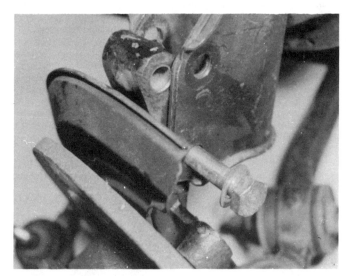

6.6 Hub carrier to strut fixing bolts

---

7   Rear suspension strut – removal and refitting

1   Remove the rear parcels shelf and release the seat back locking devices on the strut turrets.

2   Raise the rear of the car and support it under the jacking point with the roadwheel hanging free.

3   Place blocks under the (free) wheel tyre to just take its weight without compressing the strut.

4   Remove the bolt and sleeve from the base of the suspension strut.

5   Working inside the car, unscrew the strut upper mounting nuts from the suspension turret. These also hold the seat back locking devices.

6   Release the strut from its mountings and withdraw it downwards from under the car.

7   Remove the coil spring from the strut using compressors as described in Section 4.

8   If there is seepage of fluid from around the piston rod seal then the strut should be renewed, no repair being possible.

9   To test the action of the strut, remove the coil spring, fit the upper mounting to the piston rod and then fully extend and contract the rod several times. There should be firm resistance in both directions. If there is no resistance, or the movement is jerky or the rod is seized solid, renew the strut.

Fig. 11.11 Rear wheel supported (Sec 7)

2   Axle stand   3   Blocks

10 Fit the coil spring (compressed) to the strut.

11 Locate the upper mounting and screw on the piston rod nut.

12 Offer the strut to its mountings. Use new washers and screw on the top mounting nuts to the specified torque (photo).

7.12 Withdrawing rear suspension strut

13 Screw in the lower mounting bolt with its sleeve. Lower the car to the ground (photo).

14 Compress the rear suspension until the centre point of the roadwheel is 245.0 mm (9.65 in) above the floor surface. Load the luggage area or have people sit on the ledge of the tailgate opening to achieve the necessary loading.

15 With the suspension in this compressed state, tighten the strut lower mounting bolt and nut to the specified torque.

7.13 Rear strut lower mounting bolt and threaded sleeve

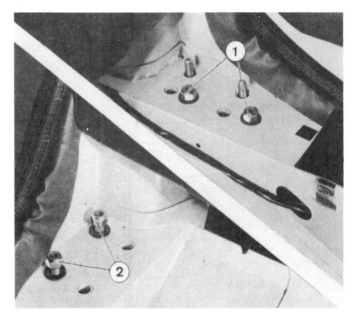

Fig. 11.13 Rear trailing arm mounting nuts (Sec 8)

1   Nuts removed (dismantled side)   2   Nuts slackened

10 On the side being dismantled, disconnect the rear strut lower mounting and pull the base of the strut off the arm pivot.
11 Mark the outline of the centre support on the underside of the floorpan. The position of the centre support influences the rear wheel alignment.
12 Unscrew and remove the centre support bolts (1) and pull the trailing arm downwards.
13 Disengage the outer support studs from the body.
14 Lift the trailing arm assembly from the car.
15 Where necessary, remove the drum brake assembly as described in Chapter 9.
16 Unbolt and remove the brake backplate.
17 The trailing arm flexible bushes can be renewed using a press or a length of studding and spacers. This is a difficult job without the special tools and it is really best left to your dealer.

Fig. 11.12 Rear strut lower mounting (Sec 7)

4   Bolt   5   Nut

8   Rear suspension trailing arm — removal and refitting

1   Working inside the car, remove the rear seat squab (Chapter 12).
2   Remove the nuts (1) from the side being dismantled and slacken, but do not remove, the nuts (2) on the opposite side.
3   Unbolt the handbrake control lever from the floor and disconnect the cable on the side being dismantled.
4   Raise the rear of the car and support it by placing axle stands under the support plates. Remove the roadwheel.
5   Disconnect the exhaust system rear mountings.
6   Working on the side being dismantled, withdraw the handbrake cable through the floor grommet.
7   Disconnect the brake hydraulic hose and seal the opening to prevent loss of fluid.
8   Unscrew and remove the inboard cross-tube spindle nut on the side being dismantled.
9   Slacken the remaining cross-tube spindle nuts.

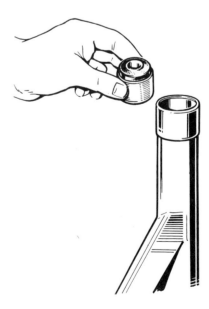

Fig. 11.14 Cross-tube inboard bush (Sec 8)

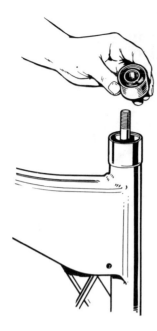

Fig. 11.15 Cross-tube outboard bush (Sec 8)

18 Before commencing reassembly, renew all lockwashers and self-locking nuts.
19 Offer the trailing arm into position and after fitting plain washers, tighten the nuts at the side of the seat squab inside the car to the specified torque.
20 Working under the car, screw on the self-locking nut at the inboard end of the pivot tube, but leave it slack.

21 Screw the four centre support bolts (3) in finger tight using internally toothed star washers.
22 Connect the suspension strut to the trailing arm by fitting the plain washer and screwing in the nut finger tight.
23 Tighten the pivot tube spindle nuts at each end to the specified torque.
24 Tighten the anti-roll bar nuts and bolts finger tight (GLS models).
25 Connect the brake hose, the handbrake cable and the exhaust pipe mounting.
26 Bolt the handbrake control lever to the floor. Refit the roadwheel.
27 Lower the car to the ground and tighten all nuts and bolts to the specified torque with the car loaded as described in Section 7 and the centre support set in its original position.
28 Bleed the rear brake hydraulic circuit as described in Chapter 9.
29 Check the rear wheel alignment as described in Section 10.

9 Rear axle – removal and refitting

1   The operations are very similar to those described in the preceding Section except that the operations must be duplicated on both sides of the car so that the trailing arms and centre support can be removed as an assembly.

10 Rear wheel alignment

1   The car should be standing on level ground at normal kerb weight.
2   Using a tracking gauge in a similar way to that described in Chapter 8 for the front wheels, check that the toe-in is as specified at the beginning of this Chapter.
3   If it is not, slacken the centre support bolts one complete turn and move the centre support forwards or backwards. Movement of the support through 1.0 mm (0.039 in) will alter the wheel alignment by 1.5 mm (0.059 in).
4   When the correct adjustment has been obtained, tighten the centre support bolts to the specified torque.
5   The rear wheel camber is not adjustable.

11 Fault diagnosis – suspension

Symptom	Reason(s)
Car wanders	Worn rear trailing arm bushes Incorrect wheel alignment Worn track control arm balljoints
Wheel wobble or vibration	Roadwheels buckled Incorrect wheel alignment Faulty suspension strut Weak coil spring
Excessive pitching or rolling on corners	Faulty strut Weak coil spring
Tyre squeal when cornering	Incorrect wheel alignment Incorrect tyre pressures

Chapter 12 Bodywork and fittings

Contents

Specifications

Type	Unitary construction, three-door hatchback or two-door convertible

For dimensions and weights, refer to the Introductory Section of this Manual

1 General description

The models in the Samba range have a very substantial body structure which is built up of a number of steel pressings welded to form a rigid shell. The shell is specially designed to have a non-deformable passenger compartment with the front and rear progressively collapsible to absorb impact.

Apart from the hinged components (doors, bonnet and tailgate) which are straightforward to renew, the two front front wings are bolt-on panels and can be renewed without welding or jigging if the need arises.

The cavities of the lower bodyshell sections have been injected with special anti-corrosive sealants to prevent rusting in and around the respective structural joints and panels.

2 Maintenance – bodywork and underframe

The general condition of a vehicle's bodywork is the one thing that significantly affects its value. Maintenance is easy but needs to be regular. Neglect, particularly after minor damage, can lead quickly to further deterioration and costly repair bills. It is important also to keep watch on those parts of the vehicle not immediately visible, for instance the underside, inside all the wheel arches and the lower part of the engine compartment.

The basic maintenance routine for the bodywork is washing – preferably with a lot of water, from a hose. This will remove all the loose solids which may have stuck to the vehicle. It is important to flush these off in such a way as to prevent grit from scratching the finish. The wheel arches and underframe need washing in the same way to remove any accumulated mud which will retain moisture and tend to encourage rust. Paradoxically enough, the best time to clean the underframe and wheel arches is in wet weather when the mud is thoroughly wet and soft. In very wet weather the underframe is usually cleaned of large accumulations automatically and this is a good time for inspection.

Periodically, except on vehicles with a wax-based underbody protective coat, it is a good idea to have the whole of the underframe of the vehicle steam cleaned, engine compartment included, so that a thorough inspection can be carried out to see what minor repairs and renovations are necessary. Steam cleaning is available at many garages and is necessary for removal of the accumulation of oily grime which sometimes is allowed to become thick in certain areas. If steam cleaning facilities are not available, there are one or two excellent grease solvents available which can be brush applied. The dirt can then be simply hosed off. Note that these methods should not be used on vehicles with wax-based underbody protective coating or the coating will be removed. Such vehicles should be inspected annually, preferably just prior to winter, when the underbody should be washed down and any damage to the wax coating repaired. Ideally, a completely fresh coat should be applied. It would also be worth considering the use of such wax-based protection for injection into door panels, sills, box sections etc, as an additional safeguard against rust damage.

After washing paintwork, wipe off with a chamois leather to give an unspotted clear finish. A coat of clear protective wax polish will give added protection against chemical pollutants in the air. If the paintwork sheen has dulled or oxidised, use a cleaner/polisher combination to restore the brilliance of the shine. This requires a little effort, but such dulling is usually caused because regular washing has been neglected. Care needs to be taken with metallic paintwork, as special non-abrasive cleaner/polisher is required to avoid damage to the finish. Always check that the door and ventilator opening drain holes and pipes are completely clear so that water can be drained out. Bright work should be treated in the same way as paintwork. Windscreens and windows can be kept clear of the smeary film which often appears by the use of a proprietary glass cleaner. Never use any form of wax or other body or chromium polish on glass (photos).

Most later model vehicles are well protected with underseal and wax injection in the underframe box-sections. However, a regular underbody cleaning is recommended periodically so that any protective coating can be inspected amd damage made good. A further application of a wax compound into the box-sections and door cavities with also serve to delay the start of corrosion.

2.4A Door drain

2.4B Sill drain

3   Maintenance – upholstery and carpets

Mats and carpets should be brushed or vacuum cleaned regularly to keep them free of grit. If they are badly stained remove them from the vehicle for scrubbing or sponging and make quite sure they are dry before refitting. Seats and interior trim panels can be kept clean by wiping with a damp cloth. If they do become stained (which can be more apparent on light coloured upholstery) use a little liquid detergent and a soft nail brush to scour the grime out of the grain of the material. Do not forget to keep the headlining clean in the same way as the upholstery. When using liquid cleaners inside the vehicle do

not over-wet the surfaces being cleaned. Excessive damp could get into the seams and padded interior causing stains, offensive odours or even rot. If the inside of the vehicle gets wet accidentally it is worthwhile taking some trouble to dry it out properly, particularly where carpets are involved. *Do not leave oil or electric heaters inside the vehicle for this purpose.*

4   Minor body damage – repair

The photographic sequences on pages 166 and 167 illustrate the operations detailed in the following sub-sections.

Repair of minor scratches in bodywork

If the scratch is very superficial, and does not penetrate to the metal of the bodywork, repair is very simple. Lightly rub the area of the scratch with a paintwork renovator, or a very fine cutting paste, to remove loose paint from the scratch and to clear the surrounding bodywork of wax polish. Rinse the area with clean water.

Apply touch-up paint to the scratch using a fine paint brush; continue to apply fine layers of paint until the surface of the' paint in the scratch is level with the surrounding paintwork. Allow the new paint at least two weeks to harden: then blend it into the surrounding paintwork by rubbing the scratch area with a paintwork renovator or a very fine cutting paste. Finally, apply wax polish.

Where the scratch has penetrated right through to the metal of the bodywork, causing the metal to rust, a different repair technique is required. Remove any loose rust from the bottom of the scratch with a penknife, then apply rust inhibiting paint to prevent the formation of rust in the future. Using a rubber or nylon applicator fill the scratch with bodystopper paste. If required, this paste can be mixed with cellulose thinners to provide a very thin paste which is ideal for filling narrow scratches. Before the stopper-paste in the scratch hardens, wrap a piece of smooth cotton rag around the top of a finger. Dip the finger in cellulose thinners and then quickly sweep it across the surface of the stopper-paste in the scratch; this will ensure that the surface of the stopper-paste is slightly hollowed. The scratch can now be painted over as described earlier in this Section.

Repair of dents in bodywork

When deep denting of the vehicle's bodywork has taken place, the first task is to pull the dent out, until the affected bodywork almost attains its original shape. There is little point in trying to restore the original shape completely, as the metal in the damaged area will have stretched on impact and cannot be reshaped fully to its original contour. It is better to bring the level of the dent up to a point which is about $\frac{1}{8}$ in (3 mm) below the level of the surrounding bodywork. In cases where the dent is very shallow anyway, it is not worth trying to pull it out at all. If the underside of the dent is accessible, it can be hammered out gently from behind, using a mallet with a wooden or plastic head. Whilst doing this, hold a suitable block of wood firmly against the outside of the panel to absorb the impact from the hammer blows and thus prevent a large area of the bodywork from being 'belled-out'.

Should the dent be in a section of the bodywork which has a double skin or some other factor making it inaccessible from behind, a different technique is called for. Drill several small holes through the metal inside the area – particularly in the deeper section. Then screw long self-tapping screws into the holes just sufficiently for them to gain a good purchase in the metal. Now the dent can be pulled out by pulling on the protruding heads of the screws with a pair of pliers.

The next stage of the repair is the removal of the paint from the damaged area, and from an inch or so of the surrounding 'sound' bodywork. This is accomplished most easily by using a wire brush or abrasive pad on a power drill, although it can be done just as effectively by hand using sheets of abrasive paper. To complete the preparation for filling, score the surface of the bare metal with a screwdriver or the tang of a file, or alternatively, drill small holes in the affected area. This will provide a really good 'key' for the filler paste.

To complete the repair see the Section on filling and re-spraying.

Repair of rust holes or gashes in bodywork

Remove all paint from the affected area and from an inch or so of the surrounding 'sound' bodywork, using an abrasive pad or a wire brush on a power drill. If these are not available a few sheets of abrasive paper will do the job just as effectively. With the paint removed you will be able to gauge the severity of the corrosion and therefore decide whether to renew the whole panel (if this is possible) or to repair the affected area. New body panels are not as expensive as most people think and it is often quicker and more satisfactory to fit a new panel than to attempt to repair large areas of corrosion.

Remove all fittings from the affected area except those which will act as a guide to the original shape of the damaged bodywork (eg headlamp shells etc). Then, using tin snips or a hacksaw blade, remove all loose metal and any other metal badly affected by corrosion. Hammer the edges of the hole inwards in order to create a slight depression for the filler paste.

Wire brush the affected area to remove the powdery rust from the surface of the remaining metal. Paint the affected area with rust inhibiting paint; if the back of the rusted area is accessible treat this also.

Before filling can take place it will be necessary to block the hole in some way. This can be achieved by the use of aluminium or plastic mesh, or aluminium tape.

Aluminium or plastic mesh is probably the best material to use for a large hole. Cut a piece to the approximate size and shape of the hole to be filled, then position it in the hole so that its edges are below the level of the surrounding bodywork. It can be retained in position by several blobs of filler paste around its periphery.

Aluminium tape should be used for small or very narrow holes. Pull a piece off the roll and trim it to the approximate size and shape required, then pull off the backing paper (if used) and stick the tape over the hole; it can be overlapped if the thickness of one piece is insufficient. Burnish down the edges of the tape with the handle of a screwdriver or similar, to ensure that the tape is securely attached to the metal underneath.

Bodywork repairs – filling and re-spraying

Before using this Section, see the Sections on dent, deep scratch, rust holes and gash repairs.

Many types of bodyfiller are available, but generally speaking those proprietary kits which contain a tin of filler paste and a tube of resin hardener are best for this type of repair. A wide, flexible plastic or nylon applicator will be found invaluable for imparting a smooth and well contoured finish to the surface of the filler.

Mix up a little filler on a clean piece of card or board – measure the hardener carefully (follow the maker's instructions on the pack) otherwise the filler will set too rapidly or too slowly.

Using the applicator apply the filler paste to the prepared area; draw the applicator across the surface of the filler to achieve the correct contour and to level the filler surface. As soon as a contour that approximates to the correct one is achieved, stop working the paste – if you carry on too long the paste will become sticky and begin to 'pick up' on the applicator. Continue to add thin layers of filler paste at twenty-minute intervals until the level of the filler is just proud of the surrounding bodywork.

Once the filler has hardened, excess can be removed using a metal plane or file. From then on, progressively finer grades of abrasive paper should be used, starting with a 40 grade production paper and finishing with 400 grade wet-and-dry paper. Always wrap the abrasive paper around a flat rubber, cork, or wooden block – otherwise the surface of the filler will not be completely flat. During the smoothing of the filler surface the wet-and-dry paper should be periodically rinsed in water. This will ensure that a very smooth finish is imparted to the filler at the final stage.

At this stage the 'dent' should be surrounded by a ring of bare metal, which in turn should be encircled by the finely 'feathered' edge of the good paintwork. Rinse the repair area with clean water, until all of the dust produced by the rubbing-down operation has gone.

Spray the whole repair area with a light coat of primer – this will show up any imperfections in the surface of the filler. Repair these imperfections with fresh filler paste or bodystopper, and once more smooth the surface with abrasive paper. If bodystopper is used, it can be mixed with cellulose thinners to form a really thin paste which is ideal for filling small holes. Repeat this spray and repair procedure until you are satisfied that the surface of the filler, and the feathered edge of the paintwork are perfect. Clean the repair area with clean water and allow to dry fully.

The repair area is now ready for final spraying. Paint spraying must be carried out in a warm, dry, windless and dust free atmosphere. This condition can be created artificially if you have access to a large indoor working area, but if you are forced to work in the open, you will have

to pick your day very carefully. If you are working indoors, dousing the floor in the work area with water will help to settle the dust which would otherwise be in the atmosphere. If the repair area is confined to one body panel, mask off the surrounding panels; this will help to minimise the effects of a slight mis-match in paint colours. Bodywork fittings (eg chrome strips, door handles etc) will also need to be masked off. Use genuine masking tape and several thicknesses of newspaper for the masking operations.

Before commencing to spray, agitate the aerosol can thoroughly, then spray a test area (an old tin, or similar) until the technique is mastered. Cover the repair area with a thick coat of primer; the thickness should be built up using several thin layers of paint rather than one thick one. Using 400 grade wet-and-dry paper, rub down the surface of the primer until it is really smooth. While doing this, the work area should be thoroughly doused with water, and the wet-and-dry paper periodically rinsed in water. Allow to dry before spraying on more paint.

Spray on the top coat, again building up the thickness by using several thin layers of paint. Start spraying in the centre of the repair area and then, using a circular motion, work outwards until the whole repair area and about 2 inches of the surrounding original paintwork is covered. Remove all masking material 10 to 15 minutes after spraying on the final coat of paint.

Allow the new paint at least two weeks to harden, then, using a paintwork renovator or a very fine cutting paste, blend the edges of the paint into the existing paintwork. Finally, apply wax polish.

5   Major body damage – repair

1   Because the car is built without a separate chassis frame and the body is therefore integral with the underframe, major damage must be repaired by competent mechanics with the necessary welding and hydraulic straightening equipment.
2   If the damage has been serious it is vital that the body is checked for correct alignment as otherwise the handling of the car will suffer and many other faults such as excessive tyre wear and wear in the transmission and steering may occur.
3   There is a special body jig which most large body repair shops have, and to ensure that all is correct it is important that the jig be used for all major repair work.

6   Bumpers – removal and refitting

Front

1   Unscrew the mounting screws which hold the ends of the bumpers to the front wings.
2   Unscrew and remove the bolts which hold the bumper brackets to the bodyframe side-members (photo).
3   Remove the bumper assembly together with its brackets.

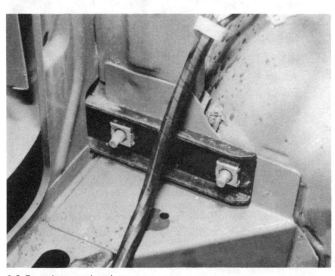

6.2 Front bumper bracket screw

This sequence of photographs deals with the repair of the dent and paintwork damage shown in this photo. The procedure will be similar for the repair of a hole. It should be noted that the procedures given here are simplified — more explicit instructions will be found in the text

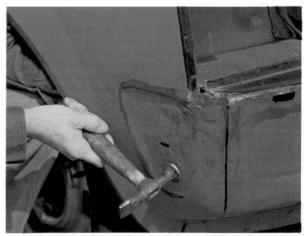

In the case of a dent the first job — after removing surrounding trim — is to hammer out the dent where access is possible. This will minimise filling. Here, the large dent having been hammered out, the damaged area is being made slightly concave

Now all paint must be removed from the damaged area, by rubbing with coarse abrasive paper. Alternatively, a wire brush or abrasive pad can be used in a power drill. Where the repair area meets good paintwork, the edge of the paintwork should be 'feathered', using a finer grade of abrasive paper

In the case of a hole caused by rusting, all damaged sheet-metal should be cut away before proceeding to this stage. Here, the damaged area is being treated with rust remover and inhibitor before being filled

Mix the body filler according to its manufacturer's instructions. In the case of corrosion damage, it will be necessary to block off any large holes before filling — this can be done with aluminium or plastic mesh, or aluminium tape. Make sure the area is absolutely clean before ...

... applying the filler. Filler should be applied with a flexible applicator, as shown, for best results; the wooden spatula being used for confined areas. Apply thin layers of filler at 20-minute intervals, until the surface of the filler is slightly proud of the surrounding bodywork

Initial shaping can be done with a Surform plane or Dreadnought file. Then, using progressively finer grades of wet-and-dry paper, wrapped around a sanding block, and copious amounts of clean water, rub down the filler until really smooth and flat. Again, feather the edges of adjoining paintwork

The whole repair area can now be sprayed or brush-painted with primer. If spraying, ensure adjoining areas are protected from over-spray. Note that at least one inch of the surrounding sound paintwork should be coated with primer. Primer has a 'thick' consistency, so will find small imperfections

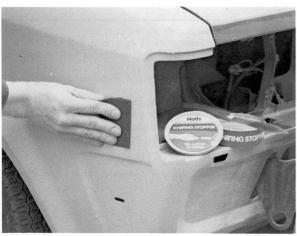

Again, using plenty of water, rub down the primer with a fine grade wet-and-dry paper (400 grade is probably best) until it is really smooth and well blended into the surrounding paintwork. Any remaining imperfections can now be filled by carefully applied knifing stopper paste

When the stopper has hardened, rub down the repair area again before applying the final coat of primer. Before rubbing down this last coat of primer, ensure the repair area is blemish-free – use more stopper if necessary. To ensure that the surface of the primer is really smooth use some finishing compound

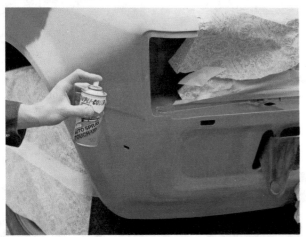

The top coat can now be applied. When working out of doors, pick a dry, warm and wind-free day. Ensure surrounding areas are protected from over-spray. Agitate the aerosol thoroughly, then spray the centre of the repair area, working outwards with a circular motion. Apply the paint as several thin coats

After a period of about two weeks, which the paint needs to harden fully, the surface of the repaired area can be 'cut' with a mild cutting compound prior to wax polishing. When carrying out bodywork repairs, remember that the quality of the finished job is proportional to the time and effort expended

6.5 Rear bumper screw

Rear

4   Unscrew the mounting screws which hold the ends of the bumpers to the front wings.
5   Using a Torx bit, remove the screws which hold the bumper to the body (photo).
6   Remove the bumper.
7   Refitting is a reversal of removal.

7   Radiator grille – removal and refitting

1   Push out the centre pins from the top three plastic retaining clips (photo).

2   Pull the grille upwards to release the lower spigots from their grommets (photo).
3   Refitting is a reversal of removal.

8   Bonnet – removal and refitting

1   With the help of an assistant, open the bonnet and support it. Disconnect the support strut (photo).
2   Mark the position of the hinges using a pencil or masking tape (photo).
3   Unscrew and remove the hinge bolts and lift the bonnet from the car.
4   Refit by reversing the removal operations, but do not fully tighten the hinge bolts until the bonnet has been gently closed and the gap on both sides of the bonnet checked for equal size and parallelism. Adjust if necessary by moving the bonnet within the limits of the elongated hinge bolt holes.
5   Adjust the bonnet lock and striker as described in the following Section.

9   Bonnet lock and remote control – removal, refitting and adjustment

1   Open the bonnet and fit the support strut.
2   Remove the radiator grille as described in Section 7.
3   Unbolt the bonnet lock from the cross rail or disconnect the control cable from the lock (photo).
4   Unclip the lock control cable from its engine compartment attachments.
5   Working inside the car, disconnect the control knob from below the facia and withdraw the cable (photo).
6   Fit the new cable by reversing the removal operations. Connect the inner cable to the lock after first having eliminated all slackness from the cable.
7   If the lock was removed, bolt it to the top rail.
8   Lower the bonnet gently and check that the striker spigots enters

7.1 Radiator grille upper clip

7.2 Radiator grille lower spigot

8.1 Bonnet support strut pivot

8.2 Bonnet hinge

9.3 Bonnet lock

9.5 Bonnet release control

9.9 Bonnet closure bump stop and wing retaining bolt

the lock centrally. If it does not, release the striker bolts and adjust its position.

9   The bonnet should close smoothly and positively when dropped from a distance of 305.0 mm (12 in) from the closed position. Do not press the lid to close it. Where necessary, release the striker locknut and turn the striker spigot in or out to adjust the pressure of closure. At the same time, screw the two bonnet rubber bump stops in or out as a compensating measure to prevent any vibration or rattle when the bonnet is closed (photo).

10   Always keep the striker spigot well greased.

10 Front wing – removal and refitting

1   Remove the front indicator lamp.
2   Unscrew the bumper and mounting screw.
3   Unscrew the flange connecting bolts from inside the front of the wing.
4   Open the front door wide and remove the wing bolts from the body A pillar (photo).
5   With the bonnet propped open, unscrew and remove the row of wing top fixing bolts.
6   Remove the wing. The mastic bead between the mating flanges may require cutting in order to free the wing.
7   Before fitting the new wing, apply a good thick bead of mastic to the flanges and then bolt it into position.
8   Apply protective coating to the underside of the wing and refinish the outside to match the body colour.

11 Door – removal and refitting

1   The door hinges are welded to the body pillar and bolted to the door (photo).
2   Remove the plastic caps from the hinge pivot pins.
3   Drive out the roll pins from the door check straps.
4   Support the door in the fully open position by placing blocks, or a jack and a pad of rag, under its lower edge.
5   Drive out the hinge pivot pins and remove the door.
6   Refit by reversing the removal operations.
7   Where necessary, the striker on the body pillar may be adjusted to provide smooth positive clearance (photo).

12 Door trim panel – removal and refitting

1   Open the door and extract the three screws from the armrest/door pull. Remove the armrest (photos).

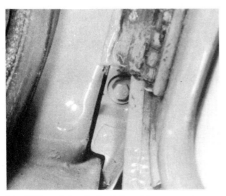

10.4 Wing fixing bolt at door hinge opening

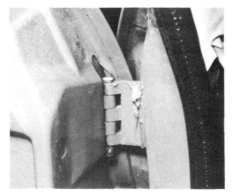

11.1 Door upper hinge

11.7 Door striker retained with Torx screws

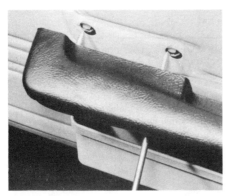

12.1A Armrest and screws

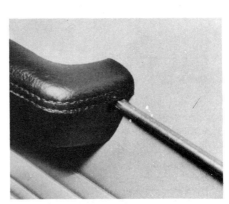

12.1B Armrest end screw

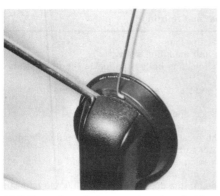

12.2 Extracting window regulator handle clip

12.3 Removing door trim panel

12.4 Window regulator handle and clip ready for fitting

2   Press back the mounting plinth at the rear of the window regulator handle and pull out the handle retaining spring clip using a piece of wire with a hook at its end. Remove the handle (photo).
3   Insert the fingers between the trim panel and door and jerk the panel clips out of their holes in the door (photo).
4   Refit by reversing the removal operations but assemble the clip to the winder handle before fitting and drive the handle onto its splined shaft by striking it with the hand. Make sure that with the window closed, the winder handle is fitted as shown in Fig. 12.1 (photo).

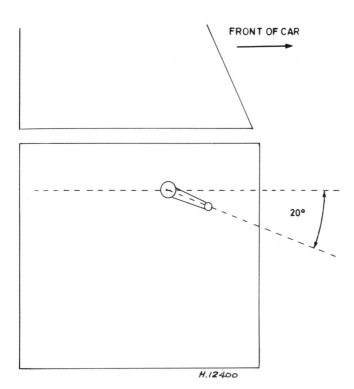

FRONT OF CAR

20°

H.12400

Fig. 12.1 Window regulator handle position with glass fully up
(Sec 12)

13 Door – dismantling and reassembly

1   Remove the trim panel as described in the preceding Section (photo).
2   Remove the waterproof patches from the openings in the door.
3   The window regulator may be removed from the door cavity after unscrewing its fixing bolts and sliding the regulator arms out of the glass channel. Support the glass during this operation.
4   The door glass may be withdrawn upwards by tilting it, provided the glass inner and outer weatherseals have first been removed by pulling them out of their fixing clips.
5   The door latch is secured to the door edge by Torx type screws. It may be removed after disconnecting the link rods from it (photos).
6   The door exterior handle is held by nuts reached from inside the door cavity and the cylinder lock is secured by a spring clip.
7   Reassembly is a reversal of dismantling.

14 Quarter trim panel – removal and refitting

1   Remove the rear seat by pulling it upwards out of its retaining clips.
2   Remove the self-tapping screw from the trim panel.
3   Insert the fingers between the trim panel and the body and jerk the plastic retaining clips out of their locating holes (photo).
4   Unbolt the cover plate to expose the seat belt inertia reel. Prise up the lip of the glass weatherseal to remove the plate and reel (photos).
5   Refit by reversing the removal operations.

15 Tailgate – removal and refitting

1   Open the tailgate.
2   With an assistant supporting the tailgate, disconnect the strut (photo).
3   Prise out the two small blanking plates from the rear edge of the headlining to expose the nuts which hold the tailgate hinges to the body (photo). The hinges are welded to the tailgate.
4   Remove the nuts and lift the tailgate from the car.
5   Refit by reversing the removal operations, but do not fully tighten the hinge nuts until the tailgate has been carefully closed and the gap at each side of it checked for equal width.
6   Adjust the striker and buffers if necessary to ensure smooth positive closure.

16 Windscreen, tailgate, quarter-light glass – removal and refitting

1   If you are unlucky enough to have a windscreen shatter or crack or should you wish to renew your windscreen, fitting a replacement is one of the jobs which the average owner is advised to leave to a professional. For the owner who wishes to attempt the job himself the following instructions are given.
2   Cover the bonnet and front bodywork with a blanket to prevent damage and block the space between the top of the facia and the windscreen with rags to prevent chips entering the defrosting ducts. Remove the windscreen wiper blades and arms as described in Chapter 10.
3   If the screen is still in one piece or of laminated type, put on a pair of lightweight shoes and get into a front seat. With a pad of soft,

13.1 Door with trim panel removed

13.5A Door latch

13.5B Lock/latch control rods

14.3 Quarter trim panel removed

14.4A Seat belt reel cover panel bolt

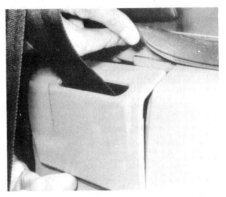

14.4B Removing seat belt reel cover panel

15.2 Tailgate strut attachment

15.3 Tailgate hinge bolts

folded cloth between the soles of your shoes and the windscreen glass, put both feet on one corner of the screen and push firmly.

4   When the seal has freed itself from the body flange in that area work round the windscreen, leaving the bottom edge engaged. From outside the car remove the windscreen and seal together.

5   If the screen was of toughened type (the tailgate and quarter-light are always of this type) clean up all glass fragments especially from the groove in the weatherseal.

6   If the screen had been leaking or if the seal is old, cracked or damaged, a new seal should be used on fitting the new screen.

7   Fit the rubber seal to the new screen, making sure that it is well bedded down. Clean the body flange on the car ready for refitting the screen.

8   A length of smooth strong cord, about $\frac{1}{8}$ in (3 mm) thick is now required, long enough to wrap round the seal and overlap by at least a foot (300 mm). Fit the cord into the groove in the seal into which the body flange fits. Lubricate the body flange and its groove in the seal

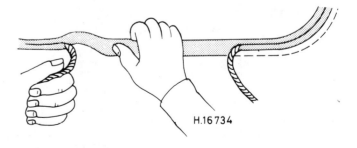

H.16 734

Fig. 12.2 Using cord to fit windscreen seal lip (Sec 16)

with, preferably, a rubber lubricant or a mixture of soap and water, don't use lubricating oil or grease which could affect the seal rubber.

9   With the help of an assistant, fit the lower edge of the glass and seal assembly onto the body flange and push it down so that it seats well home. Make sure that the glass is central and fit a bottom corner of the seal onto the body flange. Make sure that the ends of the cord are inside the car and, with an assistant pressing down firmly on the outside of the screen, pull on one end of the string to lift the seal progressively onto the body flange. Work round the screen until the seal is completely bedded on the body flange.

10   If required a layer of sealant should be applied between the seal and the body flange, inside and outside the car. Clean off any surplus before it hardens.

17 Front seat – removal and refitting

1   The front seat slide rails are fixed to the floor by socket-headed screws (photo).
2   Push the seat fully forward to reach the rear screws and fully rearwards to reach the front ones.

18 Rear seat – removal and refitting

1   Disconnect the rear parcels shelf lift cords.
2   Push the shelf upwards and remove it from its clips.
3   Release the seat locking levers on top of the strut turrets and push the seat back forwards and downwards (photo).
4   Hold the seat assembly at an angle of 45° to the floor and pull it from its securing clips (photo).
5   Refit by reversing the removal procedure.

19 Centre console – removal and refitting

1   From the rear end of the console, extract the two fixing screws (photo).

17.1 Front seat slide rail and screw

2   At the front end of the console loosen, but do not remove, the fixing screw.
3   Slide the console rearwards to release it from the head of the front screw and then remove it (photo).

20 Facia panel – removal and refitting

1   Remove the steering column upper shrouds (Chapter 8).
2   Remove the instrument panel as described in Chapter 10.
3   Working under the facia panel unscrew and remove the nut from each end bracket, also the one at the centre (photos).

18.3 Rear seat lock lever and suspension strut mounting nuts

18.4 Rear seat mounting clips

19.1 Centre console fixing screws

19.3 Centre console removed

20.3A Facia panel end nuts

20.3B Facia mounting bracket at side

20.3C Facia mounting bracket at centre

20.4 Facia mounting spigot grommet

20.5 Facia rear side showing air duct

4   Push the front edge of the facia panel upwards at the same time pulling it towards you until the spigots at the front of the panel are disengaged (photo).
5   Disconnect the wiring plugs and earth wires and remove the panel (photo).
6   Refitting is a reversal of removal.

21 Front parcels shelf – removal and refitting

Driver's side
1   Unscrew the self-tapping screws and slide the shelf rearwards off its locating spigot.

Passenger side
2   The shelf on this side is secured by nuts.

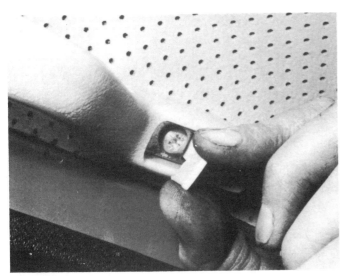

22.1 Grab handle screw

22 Grab handles – removal and refitting

1   Prise up the cover plates for access to the screws (photo).
2   Remove the screws and the grab handles.
3   Refitting is a reversal of removal.

23 Seat belts – maintenance, removal and refitting

1   Regularly check the seat belts for fraying or damage.
2   If the belts require cleaning use only warm water and detergent.
3   Never attempt to alter the seat bolt anchorages and if the belts are

removed always make sure that the original fitted sequence of anchor bolt components is maintained when refitting.
4   The front seat belt lower attachment is by means of a bar on which the belt loop can slide in order to facilitate entry to the rear passenger compartment (photo).
5   The belt reel is mounted behind the rear quarter trim panel as described in Section 14 (photo).

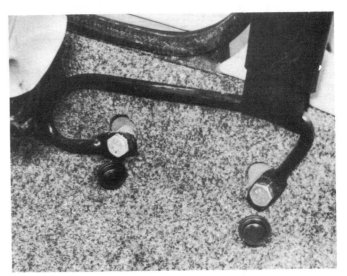

23.4 Seat belt lower attachment

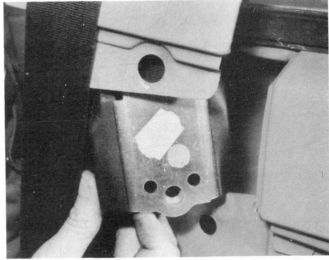

23.5 Removing seat belt reel from behind quarter panel cover plate

6   Tapped holes are provided in the luggage area for fitting rear seat belts if desired.

24 Rear view mirrors – removal and refitting

Interior mirror
1   This is mounted in the conventional way, to the roof panel above the windscreen using two self-tapping screws.

Exterior mirror
2   This is mounted on the door panel. Access to its fixing screws is obtained after removing the door trim panel (Section 12).

25 Hood (Cabriolet) – removal and refitting

1   Refer to Fig. 12.3 and prise off the hinge covers (A).
2   Refer to Fig. 12.4 and remove the rear parcels shelf and trim panels (C and D).

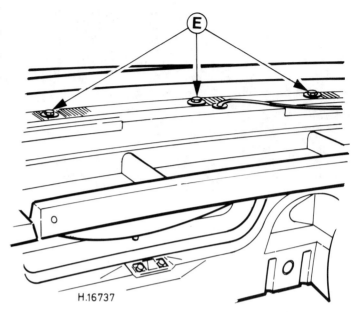

Fig. 12.5 Rear screen member screws (E) (Sec 25)

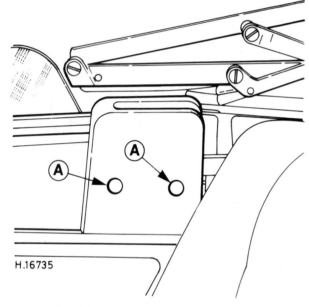

Fig. 12.3 Hood hinge bolt covers (A) (Sec 25)

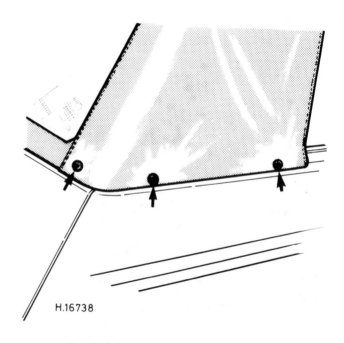

Fig. 12.6 Hood side section screws (Sec 25)

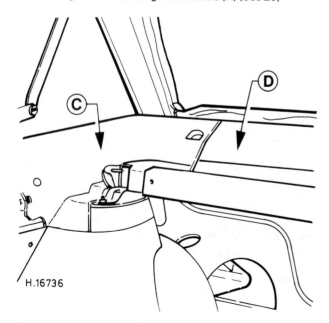

Fig. 12.4 Rear parcel shelf trim panels (C and D) (Sec 25)

3   Extract the screws (E) Fig. 12.5 which retain the rear screen member.
4   Open the rear screen and fold it down onto the rear parcels shelf.
5   Release the hood and then open it.
6   Extract the hood screws arrowed in Fig. 12.6.
7   Unscrew and remove the hinge bolts (F) Fig. 12.7.
8   Remove the hood and frame. The help of an assistant will be required.
9   When refitting, do not tighten the hinge bolts until the hood has been closed and locked.

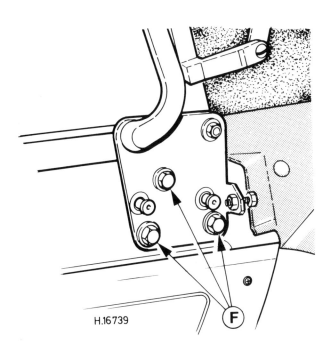

Fig. 12.7 Hood hinge bolts (F) (Sec 25)

26 Hood screen (Cabriolet) – renewal

1   Release the hood latches and remove the rear stretcher covers.
2   Remove the seven nuts (A) Fig. 12.8 which hold the hood to the rear stretcher.
3   Remove the plastic trim panels from the rear parcels shelf.
4   Extract the screws from the hood side sections.
5   Free the hood fabric from the quarter pillar frame and lift the side sections upwards.
6   Remove the hood tensioner bolts (E) Fig. 12.9.

7   Free the hood fabric rear section.
8   Extract the eight rivets (F) which hold the screen to the rear stretcher, Fig. 12.10.
9   Extract the screws from the rear screen member and withdraw the screen.
10 Fitting the new screen is a reversal of removal.

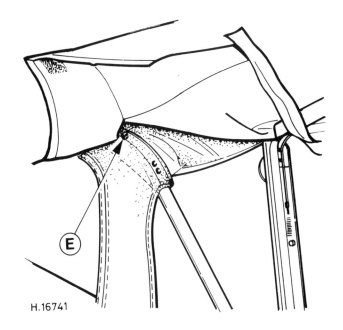

Fig. 12.9 Hood tensioner bolt (E) (Sec 26)

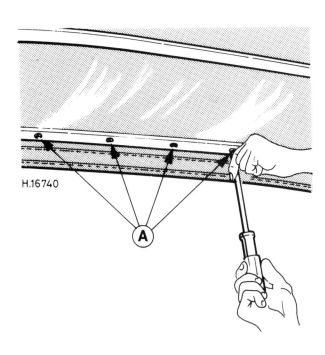

Fig. 12.8 Hood to rear stretcher screws (A) (Sec 26)

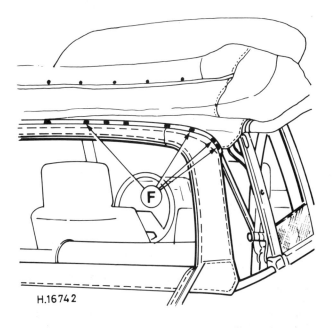

Fig. 12.10 Rear screen to stretcher rivets (F) (Sec 26)

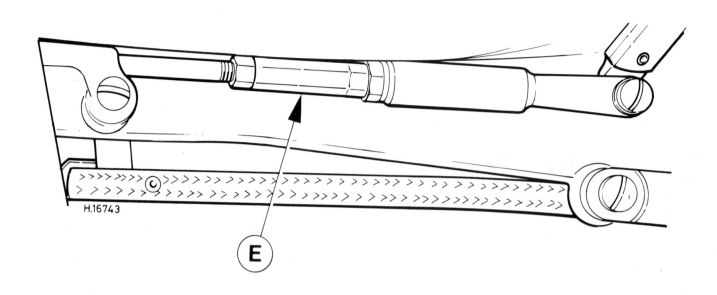

Fig. 12.11 Hood side tensioner pillar nut (E) (Sec 27)

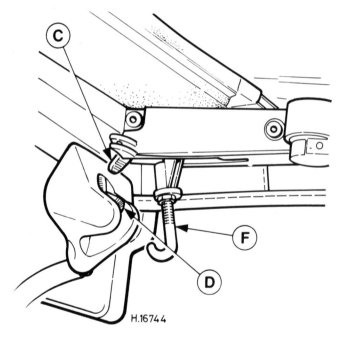

Fig. 12.12 Hood fixing parts (Sec 27)

C	Spigot	D	Striker plate	F	Hook

27 Hood (Cabriolet) – adjustment

1   This is not a routine operation, but will normally only be required if components have been renewed or the hood no longer closes smoothly and positively.

Centralising
2   This is carried out by releasing the locknuts and turning the pillar nut (E) Fig. 12.11.

Latch spigot adjustments
3   Turn both the pillar nuts (E) until the latch spigots (C) Fig 12.12 are aligned with the centres of the striker plates (D).

Latch handle adjustment
4   Release the hinge securing bolts.
5   Adjust the projection of the hooks (F) until the tension of the handles is satisfactory.
6   Tighten the hinge bolts and refit their covers.

Chapter 13 Supplement:
Revisions and information on later models

Contents

2 Specifications

Fuel system
Calibrations and settings
Solex 32 PBISA-12 fitted to 954 cc XV8 engine

Choke	25
Main jet	115/125
Air correction jet	135/175
Idle jet	39/49
Accelerator pump jet	30/40
Fuel enrichment	35/75
Float weight	5.7g
Fuel inlet needle valve	1.6 mm
Idle speed (rev/min)	600/700
CO percentage in exhaust gas	1.0 to 2.0

Ignition system
Spark plugs (1985 models)
All engines except XY8

Peugeot	CC 10
Bosch	H 7 DC
Champion	S 281 YC
XY8 engine	
Peugeot	CC 8
Bosch	H 6 DC
Champion	S 279 YC

1 Introduction

Since its introduction in 1982, most modifications to the Samba have been of a minor nature with the exception of the facia and instrument panels which have been re-designed.

It is suggested that reference be made to this Supplement before the main Chapters of the manual; thus ensuring that any relevant information can be collated into the procedures originally described in Chapters 1 to 12.

Vehicle identification

Model	Engine capacity	Engine type number	Code
LE/LS	954 cc	108.3	XV5
LE/LS (Sept 83 on)/Style	954 cc	108.C	XV8
LS (Oct 84 on)/GL/Trio/Roller	1124 cc	109.3	XW7
GLS/Cabriolet	1360 cc	150.3	XY6B
S/Rallye/Cabriolet (1985 on)	1360 cc	150.B	XY8

Routine maintenance intervals

In order to remain competitive in the area of vehicle maintenance costs, Peugeot Talbot have amended the main service intervals for later models in the following way.

1984 models
10 000 miles (16 000 km) extended to 15 000 miles (24 000 km)
1985 models
5000 miles (8000 km) extended to 6000 miles (9600 km)
15 000 miles (24 000 km) reduced to 12 000 miles (19 200 km)
The oil filter to be renewed at every other oil change only.

To the home mechanic, where servicing costs are not of paramount importance, it is recommended that the servicing intervals originally specified in *Routine Maintenance* at the beginning of this manual are adhered to. This will ensure that the vehicle is maintained in the best possible condition in the interests of safety and economy.

3   Engine

Engine strengthening spacer
1   On 1984 and later models with 1360 cc engines, the left-hand underwing mounting member is fitted with a strengthening spacer.
2   The spacer (Part number 00007147-21) may be fitted to earlier models (Fig. 13.1).

Engine specifications (Rallye)
3   For all practical purposes, the specifications, overhaul and tuning procedures given in this manual for S (XY8 engine) models apply equally to Rallye models.

4   Cooling and heating system

Modified heater hose connections
1   As from February 1983, the heater hose connections to the cylinder head have been rearranged as shown in Fig. 13.2.
2   Old and new types of cylinder head are interchangeable, provided the appropriate type of connector is substituted for the one already in position on the cylinder head obtained as a replacement.

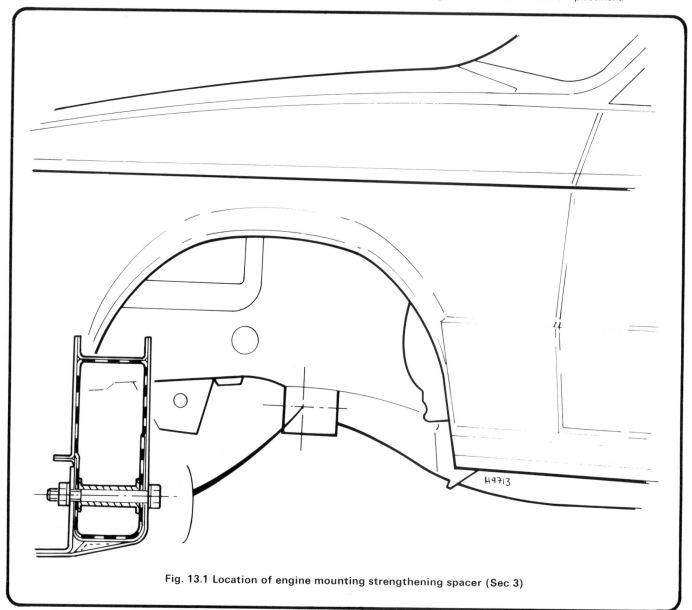

Fig. 13.1 Location of engine mounting strengthening spacer (Sec 3)

Heater control panel (1984 on)
3 The heater control panel is retained by Torx type screws on later models.

5 Fuel system

Carburettor modifications
1360 cc engine fitted with twin Solex 35 PBISA-8
1 Commencing with 1984 models, the idle cut-off solenoid is no longer fitted to the carburettor and also the fuel inlet needle valve size is reduced from 1.5 to 1.2 mm.
2 The idling speed for this particular engine is between 850 and 900 rev/min.
954 cc engine (XV8) fitted with Solex 32 PBISA-12 carburettor
3 From 1984 on, the Solex 32 PBISA-12 is fitted to the 954 cc engine (XV8) and supersedes the 32 PBISA-11 fitted previously. Refer to the Specifications at the beginning of this Supplement for calibrations and settings.

6 Ignition system

Ignition fault (1984 models)
1 On models equipped with a Ducellier ignition control unit it is possible for an engine misfire to occur accompanied by intermittent oscillations of the tachometer needle.
2 The problem is caused by the coil high tension lead being too close to the distributor low tension lead or the electronic control unit.
3 Re-route the high tension lead away from the items mentioned to cure the fault.

Spark plugs
4 The engines of 1985 models are fitted with copper-cored spark plugs. Refer to the Specifications for relevant types. These plugs may be used on earlier models to improve performance.

7 Transmission

Reverse gear selector
1 As from February 1983, selection of reverse gear has been modified by the incorporation of a synchroniser on the reverse gear and a sliding gear.

2 The sliding gear is located by a pin through the idle shaft.
3 The length of the reverse idle shaft has been extended to 112.0 mm (4.4 in), and the casing has also been modified.

8 Driveshafts, hubs, wheels and tyres

Wheels and tyres – general care and maintenance
Wheels and tyres should give no real problems in use provided that a close eye is kept on them with regard to excessive wear or damage. To this end, the following points should be noted.
Ensure that tyre pressures are checked regularly and maintained correctly. Checking should be carried out with the tyres cold and not immediately after the vehicle has been in use. If the pressures are checked with the tyres hot, an apparently high reading will be obtained owing to heat expansion. Under no circumstances should an attempt be made to reduce the pressures to the quoted cold reading in this instance, or effective underinflation will result.
Underinflation will cause overheating of the tyre owing to excessive flexing of the casing, and the tread will not sit correctly on the road surface. This will cause a consequent loss of adhesion and excessive wear, not to mention the danger of sudden tyre failure due to heat build-up.
Overinflation will cause rapid wear of the centre part of the tyre tread coupled with reduced adhesion, harsher ride, and the danger of shock damage occurring in the tyre casing.
Regularly check the tyres for damage in the form of cuts or bulges, especially in the sidewalls. Remove any nails or stones embedded in the tread before they penetrate the tyre to cause deflation. If removal of a nail *does* reveal that the tyre has been punctured, refit the nail so that its point of penetration is marked. Then immediately change the wheel and have the tyre repaired by a tyre dealer. Do *not* drive on a tyre in such a condition. In many cases a puncture can be simply repaired by the use of an inner tube of the correct size and type. If in any doubt as to the possible consequences of any damage found, consult your local tyre dealer for advice.
Periodically remove the wheels and clean any dirt or mud from the inside and outside surfaces. Examine the wheel rims for signs of rusting, corrosion or other damage. Light alloy wheels are easily damaged by 'kerbing' whilst parking, and similarly steel wheels may become dented or buckled. Renewal of the wheel is very often the only course of remedial action possible.
The balance of each wheel and tyre assembly should be maintained to avoid excessive wear, not only to the tyres but also to the steering and suspension components. Wheel imbalance is normally signified by

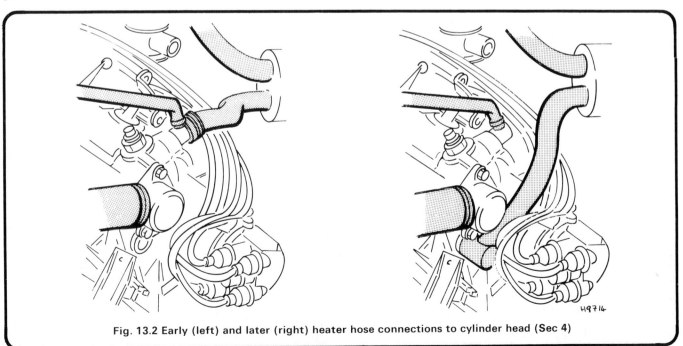
Fig. 13.2 Early (left) and later (right) heater hose connections to cylinder head (Sec 4)

vibration through the vehicle's bodyshell, although in many cases it is particularly noticeable through the steering wheel. Conversely, it should be noted that wear or damage in suspension or steering components may cause excessive tyre wear. Out-of-round or out-of-true tyres, damaged wheels and wheel bearing wear/maladjustment also fall into this category. Balancing will not usually cure vibration caused by such wear.

Wheel balancing may be carried out with the wheel either on or off the vehicle. If balanced on the vehicle, ensure that the wheel-to-hub relationship is marked in some way prior to subsequent wheel removal so that it may be refitted in its original position.

General tyre wear is influenced to a large degree by driving style – harsh braking and acceleration or fast cornering will all produce more rapid tyre wear. Interchanging of tyres may result in more even wear, but this should only be carried out where there is no mix of tyre types on the vehicle. However, it is worth bearing in mind that if this is completely effective, the added expense of replacing a complete set of tyres simultaneously is incurred, which may prove financially restrictive for many owners.

Front tyres may wear unevenly as a result of wheel misalignment. The front wheels should always be correctly aligned according to the settings specified by the vehicle manufacturer.

Legal restrictions apply to the mixing of tyre types on a vehicle. Basically this means that a vehicle must not have tyres of differing construction on the same axle. Although it is not recommended to mix tyre types between front and rear axles, the only legally permissible combination is crossply at the front and radial at the rear. When mixing radial ply tyres, textile braced radials must always go on the front axle, with steel braced radials at the rear. An obvious disadvantage of such mixing is the necessity to carry two spare tyres to avoid contravening the law in the event of a puncture.

In the UK, the Motor Vehicles Construction and Use Regulations apply to many aspects of tyre fitting and usage. It is suggested that a copy of these regulations is obtained from your local police if in doubt as to the current legal requirements with regard to tyre condition, minimum tread depth, etc.

Tyre and wheel option – GLS models

Alloy wheels of 14 inch diameter are available as an option for fitment to the GLS model and require a tyre size of 165/65 HR 14. The recommended tyre pressures are given in the Specifications at the beginning of Chapter 7.

---

9 Electrical system

Radio aerial
1 The 1984 Cabriolet model has the radio aerial incorporated in the windscreen glass.
2 In consequence of the new aerial location, additional interference suppression has been fitted as follows:

Ignition coil – 2.2 microfarad condenser
Coil to tachometer – filter
Windscreen wiper motor supply filter
Wiper motor braid to earth
Bonnet earthed to body

Engine/transmission oil level sensor
3 As from 1985 models, a Jaeger type of oil level sensor is fitted.
4 The device comprises a sensor in the oil sump, an electronic control unit located under the facia panel on the driver's side and a warning lamp (combined with low coolant level) on the instrument panel.
5 The sensor comprises a high resistance wire which, when electrical current is passing through it, has a different conductivity rating when exposed to air than when immersed in a liquid. This variation in resistance is measured by the electronic control unit and illuminates a warning lamp if the resistance is such that the sensor is not immersed.
6 In order to obtain an accurate indication of the oil level, observe the following procedure carefully.
7 Have the car standing on a level surface with the engine off and not having been run for at least ten minutes.
8 Turn the ignition key to the AC position when the oil warning lamp should light.
9 If, after a period of two seconds, the warning lamp goes out, then the oil level is correct; if the lamp flashes then the oil level is low.

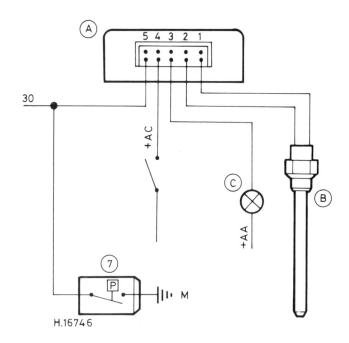

Fig. 13.3 Engine/transmission oil level sensor wiring diagram (Sec 9)

A   *Electronic control unit*
B   *Sensor*
C   *Warning lamp*
AA *Accessory supply*
AC *Ignition controlled positive supply*
7   *Oil pressure switch*
M   *Earth (through oil pressure switch)*

Heated tailgate and rear wash/wipe
10 As from 1985 models, power to these items is transmitted by a conventional wiring harness. The contact block used on earlier models is no longer fitted.

Electrically-operated windows
11 These are fitted as standard equipment on Cabriolet models.
12 The operating switches are located on each side of the radio control panel.
13 Access to the glass regulating motors can be obtained after removal of the door trim panel as described in Chapter 12, Section 12.

Instrument panel (1984 on) removal and refitting
14 Disconnect the battery.
15 Preferably, remove the steering wheel (Chapter 8), although this is not essential (photos).
16 Remove the parcels shelf from the driver's side. This is held by screws, nuts and a plastic plug (photo).
17 Extract the screws and remove the lower section of the steering column shroud (photo).
18 Remove the four steering column mounting bracket nuts (photos).
19 Lower the steering column and remove the upper shroud section (photo).
20 Extract the instrument panel hood screws. One is located above the choke control knob, one above the cigar lighter, one under the instrument upper bezel, two under the radio panel upper bezel and one behind the lower right-hand edge of the facia panel (photos).
21 Lift off the instrument panel (binnacle) hood (photo).
22 Extract the instrument panel mounting screws (photo).
23 Withdraw the instrument panel forward until the speedometer cable and wiring multiplugs can be disconnected (photos).
24 Refitting is a reversal of removal.

Radio and control panel (1984 on) – removal and refitting
25 Removal of the radio can be carried out by pulling off the control

9.15A Removing steering wheel crash pad

9.15B Steering wheel retaining nut and washer

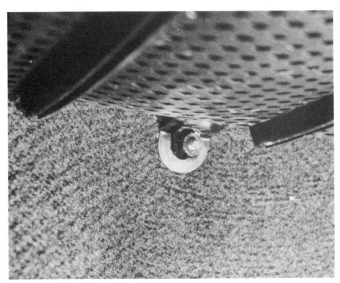

9.16 Parcel shelf end retaining nut

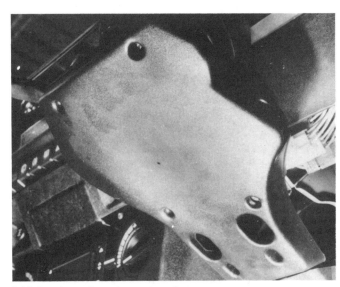

9.17 Steering column lower shroud

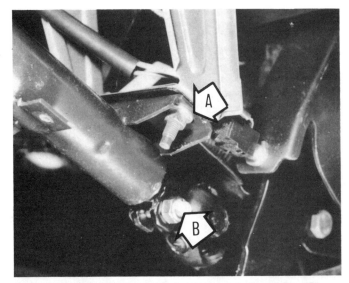

9.18A Steering column lower bracket (A) and shaft coupling (B)

9.18B Steering column upper bracket nut (arrowed)

9.19 Removing steering column upper shroud

9.20A Extracting instrument panel upper bezel screw

9.20B Extracting radio upper bezel screw

9.21 Removing instrument panel hood

9.22 Extracting instrument panel screw

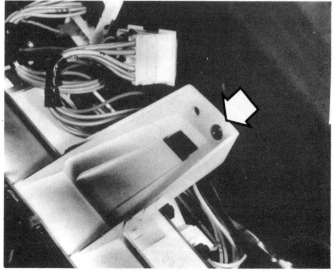

9.23A Instrument panel upper mounting bracket and screw
(arrowed)

9.23B Removing instrument panel

9.27A Extracting radio/push-button switch panel screw

9.27B Removing rear wash/wipe switch

9.27C Extracting screw behind wash/wipe switch (arrowed)

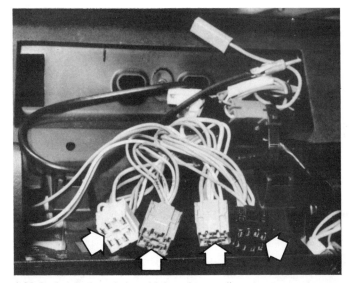

9.28 Push-button switch multiplugs (arrowed)

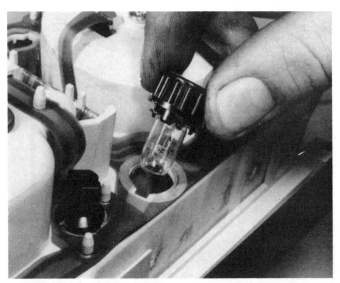

9.31 Removing instrument panel bulb and holder

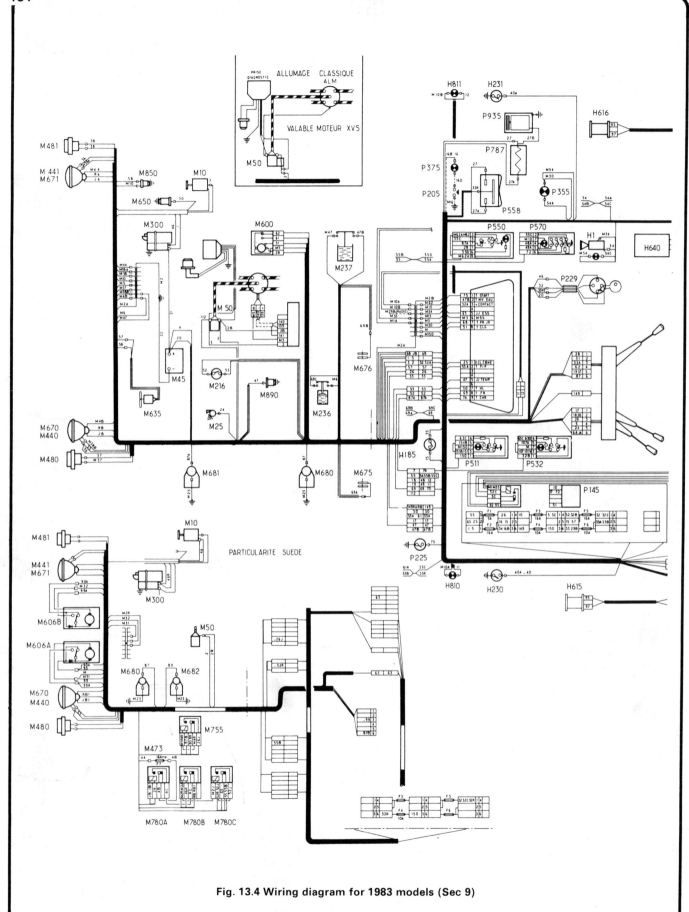

Fig. 13.4 Wiring diagram for 1983 models (Sec 9)

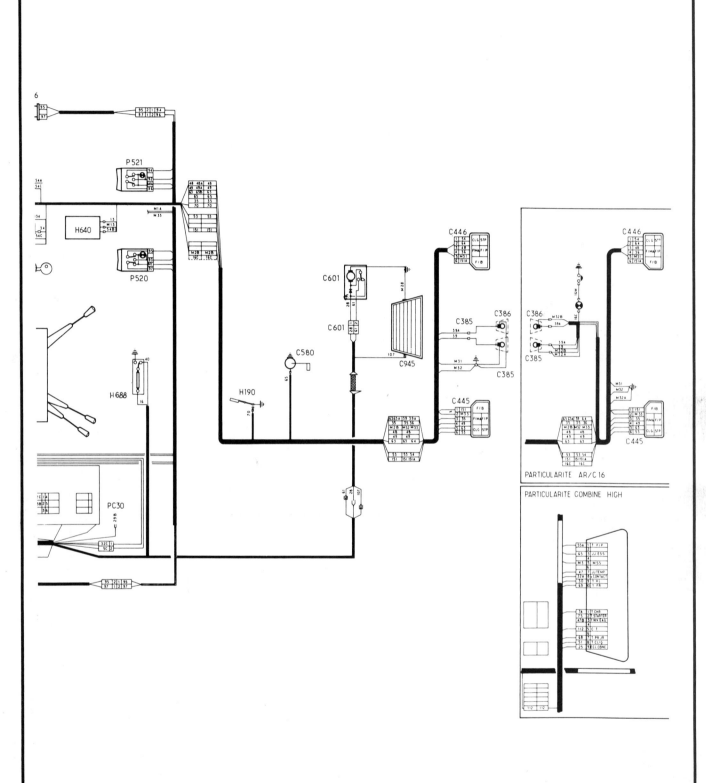

Fig. 13.4 Wiring diagram for 1983 models (Sec 9) (continued)

Key to wiring diagram for 1983 models (Sec 9)

M1	Battery		H10	Heater blower switch
M2	Alternator		H11	Heater blower motor
M3	Starter motor		H13	Clock illumination
M4	Ignition coil		H14	Heater controls illumination
M5	Ignition control unit		H17	Rear fog lamp switch
M6	Distributor		H18	Direction indicator switch
M7	Reverse lamp switch		H19	Interior lamp
M8	Cooling fan thermal switch		H20	Courtesy lamp switch
M9	Radiator cooling fan		H21	Clock
M10	Coolant temperature switch		H22	Cigar lighter
M11	Oil pressure switch		H23	Flasher unit
M12	Coolant level switch		H25	Steering column switch (lighting/horn)
M13	Brake fluid level switch		H26	Hazard warning switch
M14	Windscreen washer pump		H27	Heater blower resistor
M15	Windscreen wiper motor		H28	Handbrake warning switch
M16	Tailgate washer pump		H29	Tailgate wash/wipe switch
M17	Direction indicator (LH)		H30	Heated tailgate relay
M18	Headlamp (RH)		H31	Electric window switch (RH)
M20	Headlamp (LH)		H32	Electric window motor (RH)
M21	Direction indicator (RH)		H33	Electric window switch (LH)
M22	Side repeater lamp (LH)		H34	Electric window motor (LH)
M23	Side repeater lamp (RH)		H35	Choke warning lamp
H1	Ignition/starter switch		C1	Rear lamp cluster (LH)
H2	Stop lamp switch		C2	Rear lamp cluster (RH)
H3	Heated tailgate switch		C3	Heated tailgate element
H8	Radio power supply		C4	Fuel sender unit
H9	Steering column switch (wash/wipe)		C5	Tailgate wiper motor

Key to wiring diagram for **1984 and later models (Sec 9)**

M10	Alternator		P225	Choke control switch
M25	Horn		P229	Ignition/starting switch
M45	Battery		P355	Heater controls illumination
M50	Ignition coil		P375	Glove box illumination
M216	Reverse lamps switch		P511	Rear fog lamps switch
M236	Brake fluid level switch		P520	LH electric window switch
M237	Coolant level switch		P521	RH electric window switch
M300	Starter motor		P532	Heated rear window switch
M440	Sidelamp (LH)		P550	Tailgate wash/wipe switch
M441	Sidelamp (RH)		P558	Heater blower motor switch
M473	Headlamp wiper fuse		P570	Hazard warning switch
M480	Direction indicator (LH)		P787	Heater motor resistor
M481	Direction indicator (RH)		P935	Heater blower motor
M600	Windscreen wiper motor		PC30	Radio supply
M606A	Headlamp wiper (LH)		H1	Cigar lighter
M606B	Headlamp wiper (RH)		H185	Stop lamps switch
M635	Engine cooling fan motor		H190	Handbrake 'on' switch
M650	Oil pressure sender unit		H230	LH courtesy switch
M670	Headlamp (LH)		H231	RH courtesy switch
M671	Headlamp (RH)		H615	LH electric window motor
M675	Front LH brake wear indicator		H616	RH electric window motor
M676	Front RH brake wear indicator		H640	Clock
M680	Windscreen washer pump		H688	Interior lamp
M681	Tailgate wash/wipe pump		H810	LH indicator repeater
M682	Headlamp wash/wipe pump		H811	RH indicator repeater
M755	Headlamp wiper relay		C385	Rear number plate illumination
M780A	Running lights relay		C386	Rear number plate illumination
M780B	Running lights relay		C445	LH rear lamp cluster
M780C	Running lights relay		C446	RH rear lamp cluster
M850	Cooling fan temperature switch		C580	Fuel tank gauge unit
M890	Coolant temperature sender unit		C601	Tailgate wiper motor
P145	Direction indicators flasher unit		C945	Heated rear window element
P205	Glove box lamp switch			

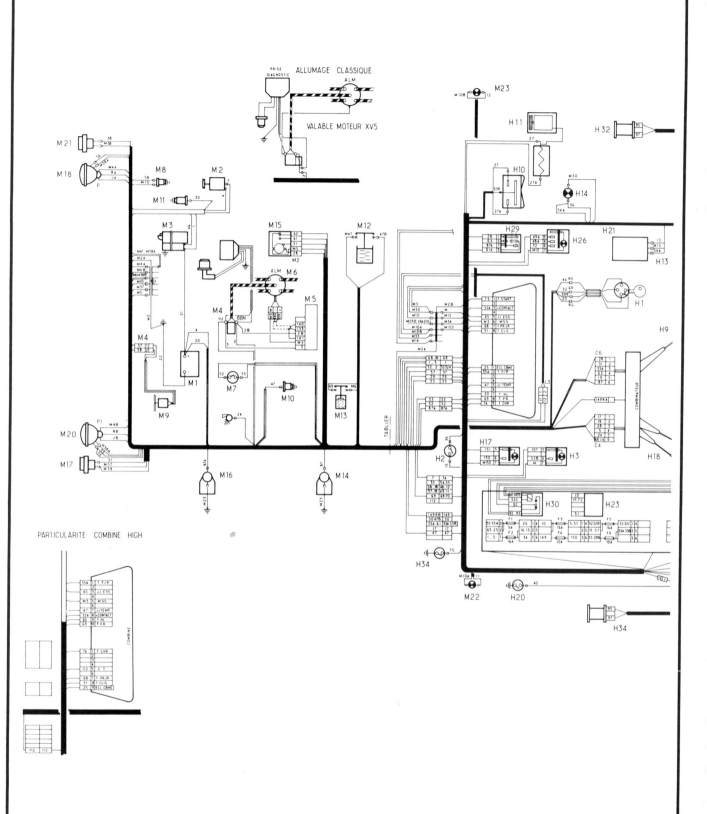

Fig. 13.5 Wiring diagram for 1984 and later models (Sec 9)

189

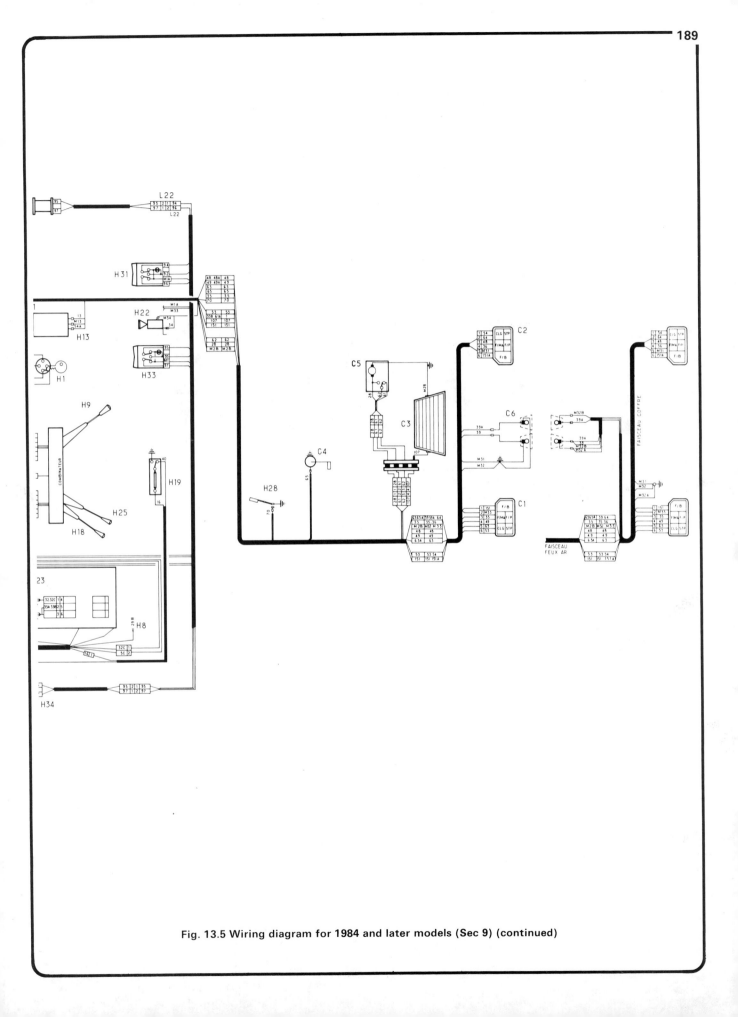

Fig. 13.5 Wiring diagram for 1984 and later models (Sec 9) (continued)

knobs, unscrewing the bezel nuts and removing the radio escutcheon panel. Insert a small screwdriver into the slots at each side of the radio tuning panel, compress the locking springs and withdraw the radio. Disconnect the aerial, power supply and speaker wires.

26 To remove the radio/push-button switch panel, first take off the instrument panel hood as described in paragraph 20.

27 Extract the radio/push-button switch panel fixing screws, noting that one screw is located under the rear wash/wipe switch. The switch will have to be removed for access to the screw (photos).

28 Withdraw the panel and disconnect the multiplugs noting that each plug has a colour-coded dot on its matching switch (photo).

29 Refitting is a reversal of removal.

Instrument panel bulbs (1984 on) renewal

30 Withdraw the instrument panel as described in the preceding paragraphs until the bulb holders can be reached by sliding a hand behind the panel. Ease the speedometer cable through the bulkhead grommet during the withdrawal of the panel.

31 Twist the holder from its seat and renew the wedge type bulb (photo).

10 Bodywork

Facia panel (1984 on) removal and refitting

1 Remove the instrument panel as described in Section 9 of this Supplement.

2 Remove the two sections of the front parcels shelf.

3 Working underneath the facia panel, remove the two mounting bolts from each end (photo).

4 Remove the mounting nut from each side of the heater control panel (photo).

5 Disconnect the choke control cable (Chapter 3) and the leads from the cigar lighter.

6 Withdraw the facia panel when the front locating spigots are out of their grommets just below the windscreen glass (photo).

7 Disconnect the heater ducts as the facia panel is withdrawn.

8 Refitting is a reversal of removal.

10.3 Facia end mounting bracket and bolt (arrowed)

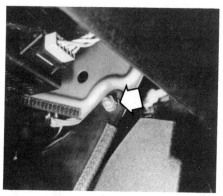

10.4 Facia centre mounting bracket and bolt (arrowed)

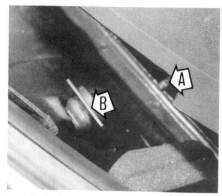

10.6 Facia forward edge spigot (A) and grommet (B)

Conversion factors

Length (distance)
Inches (in)	X	25.4	= Millimetres (mm)	X 0.0394	= Inches (in)
Feet (ft)	X	0.305	= Metres (m)	X 3.281	= Feet (ft)
Miles	X	1.609	= Kilometres (km)	X 0.621	= Miles

Volume (capacity)
Cubic inches (cu in; in^3)	X	16.387	= Cubic centimetres (cc; cm^3)	X 0.061	= Cubic inches (cu in; in^3)
Imperial pints (Imp pt)	X	0.568	= Litres (l)	X 1.76	= Imperial pints (Imp pt)
Imperial quarts (Imp qt)	X	1.137	= Litres (l)	X 0.88	= Imperial quarts (Imp qt)
Imperial quarts (Imp qt)	X	1.201	= US quarts (US qt)	X 0.833	= Imperial quarts (Imp qt)
US quarts (US qt)	X	0.946	= Litres (l)	X 1.057	= US quarts (US qt)
Imperial gallons (Imp gal)	X	4.546	= Litres (l)	X 0.22	= Imperial gallons (Imp gal)
Imperial gallons (Imp gal)	X	1.201	= US gallons (US gal)	X 0.833	= Imperial gallons (Imp gal)
US gallons (US gal)	X	3.785	= Litres (l)	X 0.264	= US gallons (US gal)

Mass (weight)
Ounces (oz)	X	28.35	= Grams (g)	X 0.035	= Ounces (oz)
Pounds (lb)	X	0.454	= Kilograms (kg)	X 2.205	= Pounds (lb)

Force
Ounces-force (ozf; oz)	X	0.278	= Newtons (N)	X 3.6	= Ounces-force (ozf; oz)
Pounds-force (lbf; lb)	X	4.448	= Newtons (N)	X 0.225	= Pounds-force (lbf; lb)
Newtons (N)	X	0.1	= Kilograms-force (kgf; kg)	X 9.81	= Newtons (N)

Pressure
Pounds-force per square inch (psi; lbf/in^2; lb/in^2)	X	0.070	= Kilograms-force per square centimetre (kgf/cm^2; kg/cm^2)	X 14.223	= Pounds-force per square inch (psi; lbf/in^2; lb/in^2)
Pounds-force per square inch (psi; lbf/in^2; lb/in^2)	X	0.068	= Atmospheres (atm)	X 14.696	= Pounds-force per square inch (psi; lbf/in^2; lb/in^2)
Pounds-force per square inch (psi; lbf/in^2; lb/in^2)	X	0.069	= Bars	X 14.5	= Pounds-force per square inch (psi; lbf/in^2; lb/in^2)
Pounds-force per square inch (psi; lbf/in^2; lb/in^2)	X	6.895	= Kilopascals (kPa)	X 0.145	= Pounds-force per square inch (psi; lbf/in^2; lb/in^2)
Kilopascals (kPa)	X	0.01	= Kilograms-force per square centimetre (kgf/cm^2; kg/cm^2)	X 98.1	= Kilopascals (kPa)

Torque (moment of force)
Pounds-force inches (lbf in; lb in)	X	1.152	= Kilograms-force centimetre (kgf cm; kg cm)	X 0.868	= Pounds-force inches (lbf in; lb in)
Pounds-force inches (lbf in; lb in)	X	0.113	= Newton metres (Nm)	X 8.85	= Pounds-force inches (lbf in; lb in)
Pounds-force inches (lbf in; lb in)	X	0.083	= Pounds-force feet (lbf ft; lb ft)	X 12	= Pounds-force inches (lbf in; lb in)
Pounds-force feet (lbf ft; lb ft)	X	0.138	= Kilograms-force metres (kgf m; kg m)	X 7.233	= Pounds-force feet (lbf ft; lb ft)
Pounds-force feet (lbf ft; lb ft)	X	1.356	= Newton metres (Nm)	X 0.738	= Pounds-force feet (lbf ft; lb ft)
Newton metres (Nm)	X	0.102	= Kilograms-force metres (kgf m; kg m)	X 9.804	= Newton metres (Nm)

Power
Horsepower (hp)	X	745.7	= Watts (W)	X 0.0013	= Horsepower (hp)

Velocity (speed)
Miles per hour (miles/hr; mph)	X	1.609	= Kilometres per hour (km/hr; kph)	X 0.621	= Miles per hour (miles/hr; mph)

Fuel consumption*
Miles per gallon, Imperial (mpg)	X	0.354	= Kilometres per litre (km/l)	X 2.825	= Miles per gallon, Imperial (mpg)
Miles per gallon, US (mpg)	X	0.425	= Kilometres per litre (km/l)	X 2.352	= Miles per gallon, US (mpg)

Temperature
Degrees Fahrenheit = (°C x 1.8) + 32   Degrees Celsius (Degrees Centigrade; °C) = (°F - 32) x 0.56

*It is common practice to convert from miles per gallon (mpg) to litres/100 kilometres (l/100km),
where mpg (Imperial) x l/100 km = 282 and mpg (US) x l/100 km = 235

Index

Printed by
J H Haynes & Co Ltd
Sparkford Nr Yeovil
Somerset BA22 7JJ England